1 & 2
CHRONICLES

Brazos Theological Commentary on the Bible

1 & 2
CHRONICLES

PETER J. LEITHART

BrazosPress
a division of Baker Publishing Group
Grand Rapids, Michigan

Published by Brazos Press
a division of Baker Publishing Group
PO Box 6287, Grand Rapids, MI 49516-6287
www.brazospress.com

Paperback edition published 2024
ISBN 978-1-5409-6766-4

The Library of Congress has cataloged the hardcover edition as follows:
Names: Leithart, Peter J., author.
Title: 1 & 2 Chronicles / Peter J. Leithart.
Other titles: First and Second Chronicles
Description: Grand Rapids : Brazos Press, a division of Baker Publishing Group, 2019. | Series: Brazos theological commentary on the Bible | Includes bibliographical references and index.
Identifiers: LCCN 2018056286 | ISBN 9781587433405 (cloth)
Subjects: LCSH: Bible. Chronicles—Commentaries.
Classification: LCC BS1345.53 .L45 2019 | DDC 222/.607—dc23
LC record available at https://lccn.loc.gov/2018056286

To my granddaughter Frankie:

May you sing forever in the choir of God

CONTENTS

SERIES PREFACE

Near the beginning of his treatise against gnostic interpretations of the Bible, *Against Heresies*, Irenaeus observes that scripture is like a great mosaic depicting a handsome king. It is as if we were owners of a villa in Gaul who had ordered a mosaic from Rome. It arrives, and the beautifully colored tiles need to be taken out of their packaging and put into proper order according to the plan of the artist. The difficulty, of course, is that scripture provides us with the individual pieces, but the order and sequence of various elements are not obvious. The Bible does not come with instructions that would allow interpreters to simply place verses, episodes, images, and parables in order as a worker might follow a schematic drawing in assembling the pieces to depict the handsome king. The mosaic must be puzzled out. This is precisely the work of scriptural interpretation.

Origen has his own image to express the difficulty of working out the proper approach to reading the Bible. When preparing to offer a commentary on the Psalms, he tells of a tradition handed down to him by his Hebrew teacher:

> The Hebrew said that the whole divinely inspired scripture may be likened, because of its obscurity, to many locked rooms in our house. By each room is placed a key, but not the one that corresponds to it, so that the keys are scattered about beside the rooms, none of them matching the room by which it is placed. It is a difficult task to find the keys and match them to the rooms that they can open. We therefore know the scriptures that are obscure only by taking the points of departure

for understanding them from another place because they have their interpretive principle scattered among them.[1]

As is the case for Irenaeus, scriptural interpretation is not purely local. The key in Genesis may best fit the door of Isaiah, which in turn opens up the meaning of Matthew. The mosaic must be put together with an eye toward the overall plan.

Irenaeus, Origen, and the great cloud of premodern biblical interpreters assumed that puzzling out the mosaic of scripture must be a communal project. The Bible is vast, heterogeneous, full of confusing passages and obscure words, and difficult to understand. Only a fool would imagine that he or she could work out solutions alone. The way forward must rely upon a tradition of reading that Irenaeus reports has been passed on as the rule or canon of truth that functions as a confession of faith. "Anyone," he says, "who keeps unchangeable in himself the rule of truth received through baptism will recognize the names and sayings and parables of the scriptures."[2] Modern scholars debate the content of the rule on which Irenaeus relies and commends, not the least because the terms and formulations Irenaeus himself uses shift and slide. Nonetheless, Irenaeus assumes that there is a body of apostolic doctrine sustained by a tradition of teaching in the church. This doctrine provides the clarifying principles that guide exegetical judgment toward a coherent overall reading of scripture as a unified witness. Doctrine, then, is the schematic drawing that will allow the reader to organize the vast heterogeneity of the words, images, and stories of the Bible into a readable, coherent whole. It is the rule that guides us toward the proper matching of keys to doors.

If self-consciousness about the role of history in shaping human consciousness makes modern historical-critical study critical, then what makes modern study of the Bible modern is the consensus that classical Christian doctrine distorts interpretive understanding. Benjamin Jowett, the influential nineteenth-century English classical scholar, is representative. In his programmatic essay "On the Interpretation of Scripture," he exhorts the biblical reader to disengage from doctrine and break its hold over the interpretive imagination. "The simple words of that book," writes Jowett of the modern reader, "he tries to preserve absolutely pure from the refinements or distinctions of later times." The modern interpreter wishes to "clear away the remains of dogmas, systems, controversies, which are

---

1. Fragment from the preface to *Commentary on Psalms 1–25*, preserved in the *Philokalia*, trans. Joseph W. Trigg (London: Routledge, 1998), 70–71.
2. *Against Heresies* 9.4.

encrusted upon" the words of scripture. The disciplines of close philological analysis "would enable us to separate the elements of doctrine and tradition with which the meaning of scripture is encumbered in our own day."[3] The lens of understanding must be wiped clear of the hazy and distorting film of doctrine.

Postmodernity, in turn, has encouraged us to criticize the critics. Jowett imagined that when he wiped away doctrine, he would encounter the biblical text in its purity and uncover what he called "the original spirit and intention of the authors."[4] We are not now so sanguine, and the postmodern mind thinks interpretive frameworks inevitable. Nonetheless, we tend to remain modern in at least one sense. We read Athanasius and think of him stage-managing the diversity of scripture to support his positions against the Arians. We read Bernard of Clairvaux and assume that his monastic ideals structure his reading of the Song of Songs. In the wake of the Reformation, we can see how the doctrinal divisions of the time shaped biblical interpretation. Luther famously described the Epistle of James as a "strawy letter," for, as he said, "it has nothing of the nature of the Gospel about it."[5] In these and many other instances, often written in the heat of ecclesiastical controversy or out of the passion of ascetic commitment, we tend to think Jowett correct: doctrine is a distorting film on the lens of understanding.

However, is what we commonly think actually the case? Are readers naturally perceptive? Do we have an unblemished, reliable aptitude for the divine? Have we no need for disciplines of vision? Do our attention and judgment need to be trained, especially as we seek to read scripture as the living word of God? According to Augustine, we all struggle to journey toward God, who is our rest and peace. Yet our vision is darkened and the fetters of worldly habit corrupt our judgment. We need training and instruction in order to cleanse our minds so that we might find our way toward God.[6] To this end, "the whole temporal dispensation was made by divine Providence for our salvation."[7] The covenant with Israel, the coming of Christ, the gathering of the nations into the church—all these things are gathered up into the rule of faith, and they guide the vision and form of the soul toward the end of fellowship with God. In Augustine's view, the reading of scripture both contributes to and benefits from this divine pedagogy. With countless variations in both exegetical conclusions and theological frameworks, the same pedagogy

---

3. Benjamin Jowett, "On the Interpretation of Scripture," in *Essays and Reviews* (London: Parker, 1860), 338–39.

4. Jowett, "On the Interpretation of Scripture," 340.

5. *Luther's Works*, vol. 35, ed. E. Theodore Bachmann (Philadelphia: Fortress, 1959), 362.

6. *On Christian Doctrine* 1.10.

7. *On Christian Doctrine* 1.35.

of a doctrinally ruled reading of scripture characterizes the broad sweep of the Christian tradition from Gregory the Great through Bernard and Bonaventure, continuing across Reformation differences in both John Calvin and Cornelius Lapide, Patrick Henry and Bishop Bossuet, and on to more recent figures such as Karl Barth and Hans Urs von Balthasar.

Is doctrine, then, not a moldering scrim of antique prejudice obscuring the Bible, but instead a clarifying agent, an enduring tradition of theological judgments that amplifies the living voice of scripture? And what of the scholarly dispassion advocated by Jowett? Is a noncommitted reading—an interpretation unprejudiced—the way toward objectivity, or does it simply invite the languid intellectual apathy that stands aside to make room for the false truism and easy answers of the age?

This series of biblical commentaries was born out of the conviction that dogma clarifies rather than obscures. The Brazos Theological Commentary on the Bible advances upon the assumption that the Nicene tradition, in all its diversity and controversy, provides the proper basis for the interpretation of the Bible as Christian scripture. God the Father Almighty, who sends his only begotten Son to die for us and for our salvation and who raises the crucified Son in the power of the Holy Spirit so that the baptized may be joined in one body—faith in *this* God with *this* vocation of love for the world is the lens through which to view the heterogeneity and particularity of the biblical texts. Doctrine, then, is not a moldering scrim of antique prejudice obscuring the meaning of the Bible. It is a crucial aspect of the divine pedagogy, a clarifying agent for our minds fogged by self-deceptions, a challenge to our languid intellectual apathy that will too often rest in false truisms and the easy spiritual nostrums of the present age rather than search more deeply and widely for the dispersed keys to the many doors of scripture.

For this reason, the commentators in this series have not been chosen because of their historical or philological expertise. In the main, they are not biblical scholars in the conventional, modern sense of the term. Instead, the commentators were chosen because of their knowledge of and expertise in using the Christian doctrinal tradition. They are qualified by virtue of the doctrinal formation of their mental habits, for it is the conceit of this series of biblical commentaries that theological training in the Nicene tradition prepares one for biblical interpretation, and thus it is to theologians and not biblical scholars that we have turned. "War is too important," it has been said, "to leave to the generals."

We do hope, however, that readers do not draw the wrong impression. The Nicene tradition does not provide a set formula for the solution of exegetical problems. The great tradition of Christian doctrine was not transcribed, bound in folio, and issued in an official, critical edition. We have the Niceno-Constantinopolitan Creed, used for centuries in many traditions of Christian worship. We have ancient baptismal affirmations of faith. The Chalcedonian definition and the creeds and canons of other church councils have their places in official church documents. Yet the rule of faith cannot be limited to a specific set of words, sentences, and creeds. It is instead a pervasive habit of thought, the animating culture of the church in its intellectual aspect. As Augustine observed, commenting on Jer. 31:33, "The creed is learned by listening; it is written, not on stone tablets nor on any material, but on the heart."[8] This is why Irenaeus is able to appeal to the rule of faith more than a century before the first ecumenical council, and this is why we need not itemize the contents of the Nicene tradition in order to appeal to its potency and role in the work of interpretation.

Because doctrine is intrinsically fluid on the margins and most powerful as a habit of mind rather than a list of propositions, this commentary series cannot settle difficult questions of method and content at the outset. The editors of the series impose no particular method of doctrinal interpretation. We cannot say in advance how doctrine helps the Christian reader assemble the mosaic of scripture. We have no clear answer to the question of whether exegesis guided by doctrine is antithetical to or compatible with the now-old modern methods of historical-critical inquiry. Truth—historical, mathematical, or doctrinal—knows no contradiction. But method is a discipline of vision and judgment, and we cannot know in advance what aspects of historical-critical inquiry are functions of modernism that shape the soul to be at odds with Christian discipline. Still further, the editors do not hold the commentators to any particular hermeneutical theory that specifies how to define the plain sense of scripture—or the role this plain sense should play in interpretation. Here the commentary series is tentative and exploratory.

Can we proceed in any other way? European and North American intellectual culture has been de-Christianized. The effect has not been a cessation of Christian activity. Theological work continues. Sermons are preached. Biblical scholars produce monographs. Church leaders have meetings. But each dimension of a formerly unified Christian practice now tends to function independently. It is as if a weakened army has been fragmented, and various corps have retreated to isolated fortresses in order to survive. Theology has lost its competence in exegesis.

8. *Sermon* 212.2.

Scripture scholars function with minimal theological training. Each decade finds new theories of preaching to cover the nakedness of seminary training that provides theology without exegesis and exegesis without theology.

Not the least of the causes of the fragmentation of Christian intellectual practice has been the divisions of the church. Since the Reformation, the role of the rule of faith in interpretation has been obscured by polemics and counterpolemics about *sola scriptura* and the necessity of a magisterial teaching authority. The Brazos Theological Commentary on the Bible series is deliberately ecumenical in scope because the editors are convinced that early church fathers were correct: church doctrine does not compete with scripture in a limited economy of epistemic authority. We wish to encourage unashamedly dogmatic interpretation of scripture, confident that the concrete consequences of such a reading will cast far more light on the great divisive questions of the Reformation than either reengaging in old theological polemics or chasing the fantasy of a pure exegesis that will somehow adjudicate between competing theological positions. You shall know the truth of doctrine by its interpretive fruits, and therefore in hopes of contributing to the unity of the church, we have deliberately chosen a wide range of theologians whose commitment to doctrine will allow readers to see real interpretive consequences rather than the shadowboxing of theological concepts.

The Brazos Theological Commentary on the Bible endorses a textual ecumenism that parallels our diversity of ecclesial backgrounds. We do not impose the thankfully modest inclusive-language agenda of the New Revised Standard Version, nor do we insist upon the glories of the Authorized Version, nor do we require our commentators to create a new translation. In our communal worship, in our private devotions, and in our theological scholarship, we use a range of scriptural translations. Precisely as scripture—a living, functioning text in the present life of faith—the Bible is not semantically fixed. Only a modernist, literalist hermeneutic could imagine that this modest fluidity is a liability. Philological precision and stability is a consequence of, not a basis for, exegesis. Judgments about the meaning of a text fix its literal sense, not the other way around. As a result, readers should expect an eclectic use of biblical translations, both across the different volumes of the series and within individual commentaries.

We cannot speak for contemporary biblical scholars, but as theologians we know that we have long been trained to defend our fortresses of theological concepts and formulations. And we have forgotten the skills of interpretation. Like stroke victims, we must rehabilitate our exegetical imaginations, and there are likely to be different strategies of recovery. Readers should expect this reconstructive—

not reactionary—series to provide them with experiments in postcritical doctrinal interpretation, not commentaries written according to the settled principles of a well-functioning tradition. Some commentators will follow classical typological and allegorical readings from the premodern tradition; others will draw on contemporary historical study. Some will comment verse by verse; others will highlight passages, even single words that trigger theological analysis of scripture. No reading strategies are proscribed, no interpretive methods foresworn. The central premise in this commentary series is that doctrine provides structure and cogency to scriptural interpretation. We trust in this premise with the hope that the Nicene tradition can guide us, however imperfectly, diversely, and haltingly, toward a reading of scripture in which the right keys open the right doors.

R. R. Reno

ACKNOWLEDGMENTS

I agreed to write this commentary during a long evening walk through Midtown Manhattan. Chad Raith had been working on Chronicles and was looking to unload it. I jumped at the opportunity, seeing a chance to complete a hat trick on the Old Testament's 1–2s. This volume joins my commentaries on 1 & 2 Samuel (*A Son to Me*, Canon Press) and *1 & 2 Kings* (Brazos Press).

Thanks to Chad for the gift, as well as to Rusty Reno and the rest of the series editors, and to Dave Nelson and the efficient team at Brazos for the privilege of reappearing in this series.

Thanks also to the elders and members of Trinity Presbyterian Church in Birmingham, where I taught a Sunday school class on 1 & 2 Chronicles over an excruciatingly extended period of time. I preached on Chronicles several times at Christ Church in Branch Cove, Alabama, and once at Christ Church in Santa Clarita, California. Those sermons helped me to solidify my reading of those chapters, and I hope they were edifying to those congregations.

This book is dedicated to Frances ("Frankie") Gray Leithart, fourth child of my oldest son, Woelke, and his wife, Megan. Frankie was born in the midst of a scramble, shortly before her family moved from Yazoo City, Mississippi, to Savannah, Georgia. She was only nine days old when I first met her, at a Books-A-Million in Meridian, Mississippi. Given her parentage and siblings, I expect it will not be the last bookstore she visits. Frankie is now settled into her new home, has begun to crawl, and, with her full head of hair, looks twice her six months. She can't talk yet, but already her infant voice stills the enemy and avenger (Ps. 8). I dedicate this book to her with the prayer that she will remain forever what she is now, a member of God's choir, filled with the Spirit of song to offer her breath in sacrifice and to raise her voice to raze cities and scatter armies.

Epiphany 2019
Beth-Elim
Gardendale, Alabama

ABBREVIATIONS

General

$\rightarrow$ indicates a cross-reference to within this commentary on passages in 1–2 Chronicles

Old Testament

Gen.	Genesis	Song	Song of Songs
Exod.	Exodus	Isa.	Isaiah
Lev.	Leviticus	Jer.	Jeremiah
Num.	Numbers	Lam.	Lamentations
Deut.	Deuteronomy	Ezek.	Ezekiel
Josh.	Joshua	Dan.	Daniel
Judg.	Judges	Hosea	Hosea
Ruth	Ruth	Joel	Joel
1–2 Sam.	1–2 Samuel	Amos	Amos
1–2 Kgs.	1–2 Kings	Obad.	Obadiah
1–2 Chr.	1–2 Chronicles	Jon.	Jonah
Ezra	Ezra	Mic.	Micah
Neh.	Nehemiah	Nah.	Nahum
Esther	Esther	Hab.	Habakkuk
Job	Job	Zeph.	Zephaniah
Ps. (Pss.)	Psalm (Psalms)	Hag.	Haggai
Prov.	Proverbs	Zech.	Zechariah
Eccles.	Ecclesiastes	Mal.	Malachi

New Testament

Matt.	Matthew	1–2 Thess.	1–2 Thessalonians
Mark	Mark	1–2 Tim.	1–2 Timothy
Luke	Luke	Titus	Titus
John	John	Philem.	Philemon
Acts	Acts	Heb.	Hebrews
Rom.	Romans	James	James
1–2 Cor.	1–2 Corinthians	1–2 Pet.	1–2 Peter
Gal.	Galatians	1–3 John	1–3 John
Eph.	Ephesians	Jude	Jude
Phil.	Philippians	Rev.	Revelation
Col.	Colossians		

INTRODUCTION

The bulk of 1–2 Chronicles covers the same period of history covered by 1–2 Samuel and 1–2 Kings, from the reign of Saul to the exile and restoration. Chronicles, though, covers the period in a significantly different manner. The book opens with nine detailed chapters of genealogy, beginning with Adam. Saul's reign, which occupies two-thirds of 1 Samuel, is reduced to a single chapter, a record of Saul's death (1 Chr. 10). David's boyhood heroism and life as a refugee from Saul are deleted, as are the scandalous goings-on of David's court—his adultery, murder, and the household mayhem that follows. Instead, the Chronicler focuses on David's role in preparing for the construction of the temple.

In 1 Kings, Adonijah contests the transfer of the kingdom to Solomon; in 1 Chronicles, the kingdom passes smoothly from David to his son. After the kingdom is split during the reign of Rehoboam, the Chronicler keeps his eyes fixed on the southern kingdom. The northern kingdom appears only when it is in conflict or alliance with Judah. The Chronicler condenses the account of the divided kingdom in 1–2 Kings and entirely ignores the lives of Elijah and Elisha. Yet this is no *Reader's Digest* version. Chronicles is as long as Kings, since the Chronicler adds episodes in the lives of numerous kings. Only from the Chronicler do we know of Joash's late-life apostasy (2 Chr. 24), or Uzziah's proud attempt to offer incense in the temple (2 Chr. 26), or Manasseh's repentance (2 Chr. 33).

The Chronicler makes passing references to the prophecy of Ahijah the Shilonite regarding Jeroboam's future (→ 2 Chr. 10–11; cf. 1 Kgs. 11) and alludes only glancingly to Jeroboam's golden calves. Prominent in 1 Kings, Ahab is a bit player in Chronicles, little more than Jehoshaphat's tempter, and we never learn anything about Jezebel. Writing after Samuel and Kings are already available, the Chronicler expects his readers to know the rest of the story.

The shape of the Chronicler's history is determined by two factors: the southern kingdom's relationship with the northern kingdom of Israel on the one hand, and the increasingly stark distinction of upright and evil kings on the other. The two threads of narrative overlap and come to a climax when the northern kingdom falls, which occurs during the reigns of Ahaz and Hezekiah of Judah. Let me sketch the course of these two narrative threads in more detail.

The Chronicler's attitude toward the north is complex. He never acknowledges the legitimacy of the northern kingdom as a polity and vehemently rejects it as an alternative liturgical community. His position is stated clearly in the speech of Abijah before his battle with Jeroboam ($\rightarrow$ 2 Chr. 13): Jeroboam's kingdom originated in rebellion, and Yahweh's promise rests with the Davidic dynasty alone. Some of the sharpest ironies of the Chronicler's narrative arise from the failure of Davidic kings to act on the theological promise that "all Israel" should by right submit to the Davidic dynasty. At the same time, the Chronicler regards the northern tribes as part of all Israel, and Judah is incomplete without the other tribes. His history presses toward a reconciliation of the tribes, which can only take place when all Israel worships Yahweh alone at the chosen house in the chosen city of Jerusalem under the hand of the chosen king.

That is the ideal, realized most fully in the reigns of David and Solomon ($\rightarrow$ 1 Chr. 11–2 Chr. 9), and the Chronicler devotes enormous, loving attention to presenting this model of Israel and its calling. The ideal is realized in partial ways in the reigns of Asa, Hezekiah, and Josiah. After the division of the kingdom, though, the history of Judah is largely a history of its fraught relationship with its brothers to the north. There are several stages to this history:

1. Judah is dominant over Israel (Abijah; $\rightarrow$ 2 Chr. 13).
2. Judah allies with Gentiles against Israel (Asa; $\rightarrow$ 2 Chr. 14–16).
3. Judah allies with Israel (Jehoshaphat; $\rightarrow$ 2 Chr. 17–20).
4. Israelite gods and ways dominate Judah (Jehoram to Athaliah; $\rightarrow$ 2 Chr. 21–24).
5. Israel is militarily dominant over Judah (Amaziah; $\rightarrow$ 2 Chr. 25).
6. Israel proves more faithful to Torah than Judah (Ahaz; $\rightarrow$ 2 Chr. 28).

After Ahaz, the northern kingdom ends. The last time we glimpse Israel, they are releasing Judahite slaves and restoring plunder to them. Israel, in short, leaves the stage looking like an exodus people.

The end of the northern polity opens the possibility for a reunion of the divided kingdom on *Davidic* terms. Hezekiah celebrates a Passover that includes people from the north ($\rightarrow$ 2 Chr. 30), and Josiah's reforms extend into the territory once ruled by northern kings ($\rightarrow$ 2 Chr. 34–35). These are tantalizingly hopeful moments, but Judah is, like Israel, finally driven from the land. The reason for that has to do in part with Judah's habit of imitating northern ways. But it also has to do with an internal dynamic that produces kings who do evil in Yahweh's sight.

The Chronicler is an exceedingly generous judge of royal virtue. Nearly every king of Judah leaves a mixed record behind. Good King Asa breaks faith by hiring Arameans to attack Israel; Jehoshaphat establishes circuit schools and courts, but he also allies with Ahab and Ahab's son; Joash restores the temple but abandons the Lord after his mentor Jehoiada dies; Uzziah's prosperity makes him proud, and he tries to offer incense in the temple; Hezekiah, too, becomes proud; and Josiah refuses to listen to Yahweh's word delivered through Neco, king of Egypt. Yet all of these are judged "good" or "upright" in the eyes of Yahweh. None is wholly evil.

Jehoshaphat's immediate descendants (Jehoram, Ahaziah) are evil, but the Chronicler, without excusing them, shifts blame to the house of Ahab. Jehoram walks in the way of the kings of Israel, "for Ahab's daughter was his wife" (2 Chr. 21:6), and Ahaziah continues in the way of Ahab because "his mother was his counselor to do wickedly" (22:3). Both texts refer to the same woman, Athaliah, who becomes queen after her son dies at the hands of Jehu. Only with Ahaz do we come to a Davidic king who defiantly walks in the ways of the kings of Israel, with none of the blame placed on counselors or family connections. He alone "did *not* do right in the eyes of Yahweh" (28:1 AT), and he alone among the Davidic kings makes "molten images for the Baals," becoming a direct promoter of Baal worship (28:2).

Up to the time of Ahaz, virtually all the kings have a mixed record, and those who do not are not entirely blamed for their wickedness. With the northern kingdom gone, Judah has no one to blame. Ahaz cannot shift responsibility to wife or counselors, and following his reign, the difference between good and evil kings becomes stark. Manasseh repents while in exile in Assyria (2 Chr. 33:12–13), but he spends much of his reign doing evil and promoting Canaanite abominations (33:2). His son Amon follows his example, and later kings are worse than

3

Manasseh, refusing to humble themselves before the word of the Lord's prophets, even when Babylonians invade and deport the people (36:12).

Another form of regression is evident. The cycles of good and evil kings become shorter, the persistence of idolatry longer. Between the heights of David and Solomon and the nadir of Athaliah are four kings of mixed faithfulness (Rehoboam, Abijah, Asa, Jehoshaphat) and two kings who follow the ways of Ahab (Jehoram, Ahaziah). Only three kings (Amaziah, Uzziah, Jotham) intervene between Joash and Ahaz. Ahaz is immediately followed by the righteous Hezekiah, but after Hezekiah come two generations of wickedness (Manasseh, Amon). Josiah recovers the law and purges idols, but his gains are lost immediately by his sons. Periods of relative faithfulness get shorter, periods of wickedness longer. Asa's reforms hold on for several generations; Hezekiah and Josiah cannot sustain their reforms into the reigns of their successors. Hezekiah and Josiah are not to blame for this. By the time they appear on the scene, idolatry has its own institutional inertia. Judah has developed its own *tradition* of wickedness. As thorough as their reforms are, they are not enough. Judah needs to be leveled and rebuilt.

These are among the narrative arcs of the history that the Chronicler records. But beneath the heard melodies are melodies unplayed, heard only by those with ears to hear. A virtual history intertwines with the history of Judah's Davidic kings. The clues come at the beginning and end of the book. Chronicles begins with the name Adam and ends with the decree of Cyrus. It is a hint that the Chronicler is retelling the entire history of the Old Testament in, with, and under the history of kings. The scheme is essentially this:

Chronicles	Israel's history
Genealogies, 1 Chr. 1–9	Genesis
Saul's death, 1 Chr. 10	Slavery in Egypt
David, 1 Chr. 10–29	Exodus and Sinai, to the land
Solomon, 2 Chr. 1–9	Joshua's conquest
Divided kingdom, 2 Chr. 10–35	Period of judges, ending with Saul
Decree of Cyrus, 2 Chr. 36	Establishment of monarchy

The scheme will be filled out as we move through the commentary, but let me provide some indicators here.

1. The Chronicler's genealogy resembles the book of Genesis generically. Genealogies are sprinkled throughout Genesis (Gen. 4–5; 10; 11:10–26, 25:12–18; 36). Genesis as a whole is structured by ten *toledoth* (generations) statements,

and the word reappears frequently in 1 Chronicles (1:29; 5:7; 7:2, 4, 9, etc.). Substantively, the genealogies of both Genesis and Chronicles begin with humanity as a whole (Gen. 1; 4–5; 10) and then narrow primarily to the ancestors and descendants of Israel. The early genealogies culminate in the priestly genealogy of Moses and Aaron (Exod. 6). The Chronicler's genealogy has a similar priestly focus: the tribe of Levi is structurally central in 1 Chr. 1–9.

2. The Chronicler's narrative proper begins with Saul's death in 1 Chr. 10. In the aftermath of the collapse of Saul's house, the Philistines retake portions of Israel's land, reversing the conquest. Given the genealogical link between Philistines and Egyptians, it is also a reverse exodus, as Israel is once again subjected to "Egyptian" dominance. In Exodus, Yahweh triumphs over the gods of Egypt; in 1 Chr. 10, Dagon celebrates the "good news" of Saul's defeat.

3. David is a Moses figure. He liberates Israel by defeating the Philistines. But he is a Moses figure primarily in being a founder of Israel's cult. He brings the ark of the covenant into Jerusalem and, like Moses, pitches a tent (1 Chr. 13–16). He organizes priests and Levites (→ 1 Chr. 23–27; cf. Exod. 27–28; Num. 1–9) and receives the *tabnit* (pattern) for a new sanctuary from Yahweh (→ 1 Chr. 28–29; cf. Exod. 25:9). His "ordinances" rank with the *torah* of Moses as authoritative guides for Israel's worship.

4. In the final chapters of 1 Chronicles, David assembles Israel to crown Solomon and to apportion assignments for the building and maintenance of the temple. David's speeches to his son resemble the speeches of Moses to Joshua: "Be strong and courageous" (→ 1 Chr. 28–29; Josh. 1:6). Solomon's temple-building fulfills the conquest of the land and requires similar courage and skill. Solomon conquers kings, not with the sword but with the force of Yahweh's wisdom in him. He carries out a program of "sapiential conquest."

5. After Joshua's death, Israel entered a time of flux and confusion. The history of the period is a cycle of idolatry, political oppression, repentance, and deliverance, which always slides into another round of idolatry. Peace and faithfulness give way to renewed idolatry. At that level of abstraction, the divided kingdom period is similar to that of the judges. Good kings reform, bad kings restore the idols; a good king reforms again, and another bad king turns to Baal. Beyond the general similarity of pattern, 2 Chronicles includes a number of specific links with Judges: Rehoboam becomes king at Shechem (→ 2 Chr. 10), the site of Abimelech's seizure of royal power (Judg. 9); Jehoram kills his brothers (→ 2 Chr. 21), as Abimelech killed his rivals; Asa, Jehoshaphat, Hezekiah, and Josiah cast down idols, including Baals, as Gideon did in earning the epithet "Jerubbaal" (Judg. 6);

the Chronicler borrows the language of Judg. 2 to describe the sins of Judah ("played the harlot," "forsook Yahweh," "provoked Yahweh to anger"); Hezekiah and Josiah are heroic reformers who, like Samuel the judge, have wicked sons.

6. The messy period of the divided kingdom effectively ends with the death of Josiah in a battle with Neco, king of Egypt (→ 2 Chr. 35). Josiah's death by arrows resembles the death of Saul, which brought an end to his dynasty. Several kings reign after Josiah (→ 2 Chr. 36), but Judah's history is essentially over.

7. If the pattern proves true, then the king who follows the Saul-like Josiah should be a new David. But here is the surprising punch line of the Chronicler's history: After Josiah, Judah *does* get a liberating king who initiates and sponsors the rebuilding of Yahweh's house. But he is not a descendant of David. Cyrus, the king of Persia, inherits the Davidic task.

Though the history of the monarchy is a variation on themes from the book of Judges, the Chronicler does not outline a cyclical view of history. The rise of Babylon and Persia is a new establishment of kingship for Israel, but it is not identical to the establishment of the Davidic line. Cyrus is an anointed Gentile, a servant of Yahweh, who takes up the Davidic task but is not himself a Davidic king. First and Second Chronicles provides a narrative history of the transition that the prophets describe in other terms, a transition from a world order centered on the Davidic monarchy and Solomon's temple to a world order dominated by Gentile emperors who are called by Yahweh to care for Israel. Chronicles provides the back history of the formation of the *oikoumenē* that provides the stage for ancient history between the fall of Jerusalem and the coming of the Christ.

For my purposes, the most important theological insights have to do with ecclesiology, though I recognize that this may be more a symptom of my own obsessions than the Chronicler's. In any case, the Chronicler's vision of the people of Yahweh is challenging, especially for Protestants in the genus *evangelicum*. Few books of the Bible stress the organizational features of the people of God more than the Chronicler does. First Chronicles includes several chapters of Levitical duty rosters. The Chronicler describes the gathering, storage, accounting, and distribution of temple gifts in great, not to say excruciating, detail. For the Chronicler, the people of God is not some formless community but a nation and people with an institutional structure. Every revival in Judah's history is a revival of priestly organization, contributions to the temple, and careful oversight of the temple and palace treasuries. Church bureaucracies can become as clogged as federal agencies, but there can be no strong or vibrant church without them.

In keeping with this affirmation of the public, institutional character of the church, the Chronicler regularly depicts Israel in assembly. Nearly every major event of David's life takes place when he is presiding as head of a great assembly (*qahal*)—his coronation, the ascent of the ark to Jerusalem, and the preparations for the temple. Solomon gathers Israel to Jerusalem for the temple dedication, and every rededication is marked by a reassembly of the people. It is in assembly that Israel experiences the favor of Yahweh and the joy that comes with it. It is in assembly that Israel fights its battles and resists invaders.

One final note about the Chronicler's contribution to ecclesiology: 1–2 Chronicles is one of the Bible's great texts about music. The Psalms give us words to sing (perhaps also designating instruments and melodies). Chronicles tells us who sings when, and why. Music-making is a priestly activity. Song rises to God like the smoke of a sacrifice, and Chronicles describes music as a form of "guarding" (1 Chr. 25:8; the Hebrew *mishmeret*, or "duties," is from *shamar*, "guard") and Levitical "bearing" (1 Chr. 15:22, 27; for more, see Leithart 2003: 65). Kings make music too. To sing, we rule our bodies and breath. To make musical instruments, we cut and trim trees, pull guts into strings, mine and shape metals, train our fingers to pluck. Music turns creation into culture and cult. Music makes us warriors by enlivening our spirit. Soldiers march to battle in rhythm. The pounding beat and soaring chords of warm-up music fill athletes with the spirit of the game. Martyrs go to the arena singing psalms and hymns. Singing is, finally, a form of prophecy (→ 1 Chr. 25:1). Chronicles is a manual for church reformers, as well as for church musicians.

This commentary is not comprehensive in any way. It does not examine every verse in 1–2 Chronicles. I do not give much attention to the synoptic problem of coordinating Kings and Chronicles, or to the historical problems that Chronicles raises. There is no survey of the literature on Chronicles. I have consulted some of the major recent commentaries, articles, and monographs, as well as a handful of older works, but do not interact much with their arguments.[1] Instead, this commentary is an attempt to discern the shape of the book, to follow thematic threads as they begin, develop, diverge, and come to rest. I pay attention to literary structures and stylistic features and attempt to tease out theological conclusions from both the events recorded and the pattern of the Chronicler's record. It is an effort to make Chronicles preachable.

---

1. Far and away the most illuminating work is that of Johnstone (1998a; 1998b), whose fingerprints are everywhere here.

1

ISRAEL'S GENESIS

1 Chronicles 1–9

Chronicles begins with a nine-chapter section of genealogies. It is a challenging text for modern readers, perhaps also for ancient ones. Lists and brief genealogies are scattered throughout Chronicles (e.g., 1 Chr. 11:26–47; 12:1–14, 23–37; 15:4–11; 23:1–24; 24:7–31; 25:1–31; 26:1–11; 27:1–34; 2 Chr. 17:10–19; 29:12–14). It is something of an obsession for the Chronicler. The lists demonstrate the fruitfulness of Israel and Israel's kings. The lists are also a literary embodiment of another of the Chronicler's obsessions, the "assembly" (*qahal*) of Israel. David's reign seems to consist of nothing but public assemblies—for coronation, to carry the ark into Jerusalem, to exhort Solomon to build the temple, to assign duties to priests and Levites, to crown Solomon (twice!). Solomon presides over assemblies, as do Asa, Jehoshaphat, Joash, Hezekiah, and Josiah. At the outset of his book of assemblies, the Chronicler assembles an intergenerational "all Israel" on the page.[1]

---

1. Umberto Eco, author of *The Infinity of Lists*, says, "The list is the origin of culture. It's part of the history of art and literature. What does culture want? To make infinity comprehensible. It also wants to create order—not always, but often. And how, as a human being, does one face infinity? How does one attempt to grasp the incomprehensible? Through lists, through catalogs, through collections in museums and through encyclopedias and dictionaries. There is an allure to enumerating how many women Don Giovanni slept with: It was 2,063, at least according to Mozart's librettist, Lorenzo da Ponte. We also have completely practical lists—the shopping list, the will, the menu—that are also cultural achievements in their own right." "We Like Lists Because We Don't Want to Die," interview by Susanne Beyer and Lothar

The Chronicler assembles Israel and names names. Israel is not a faceless mob. Neither are David's assembly of mighty men and warriors, the assembly of priests and Levites and elders, or the gatekeepers and singers assigned to the temple. Individuals are named; they earn a spot in the credits; their names appear on the acknowledgments page. The Chronicler's genealogy is a literary portrayal of the one-body, many-limbs design of Israel. Even as they gather as one man to carry out a single intention, individual Israelites have a name, heritage, and specific vocation and task.

Genealogies can function "tribally." For tribal cultures, change is the enemy. Genealogies inevitably record change, but they may record change that holds the present hostage to the past, sons in thrall to fathers. Someone in the present has status—as king, priest, citizen—because of his genealogical connection with the founder, through a trail of descent, fathers begetting and sons begotten.

Biblical genealogies have a different orientation. To be sure, priests have status only because they are genetically linked with Aaron, then Zadok. For the writer of Hebrews, this is a sign of the preliminary character of the old covenant, its "fleshliness" (Heb. 7). As status legitimation, the Chronicler's genealogies diverge from earlier biblical genealogies. Genesis records genealogies from Adam through the sons of Jacob, but the priestly genealogy of Exod. 6 brings those lists to a climax. Genesis-Exodus traces descent from Adam through Aaron, thus underscoring the legitimacy of Aaron's priesthood. The Chronicler's genealogy includes "all Israel." Levites are at the center of his concern (see below), but every son and tribe is given an elevated status. Simply by tracing the genealogy of every tribe, the Chronicler shows that Israel is "a kingdom of priests and a holy nation" (Exod. 19:6). Holy places are measured; holy things are counted and weighed; a holy people is delimited through its heritage and ancestry.

Though biblical genealogies identify humanity's or Israel's roots, they are fundamentally about looking forward. The key term in the genealogies of Genesis is "generations" (*toledoth*). The *toledoth* of Adam (Gen. 5:1) does not trace Adam's roots but Adam's fruit, what he begets. In Chronicles, too, *toledoth* describes chiefs and heads according to generations, that is, according to what they produce. Biblical genealogies lean eschatologically, not protologically.

One hint of this future-orientation is the repeated phrase "heads of the father's households" (e.g., 1 Chr. 5:15) or, more startlingly, "heads of the fathers" (e.g., 8:6 AT). In the Chronicler's view, a son does not merely become head of his

Gorris, *Spiegel*, November 11, 2009, http://www.spiegel.de/international/zeitgeist/spiegel-interview-with-umberto-eco-we-like-lists-because-we-don-t-want-to-die-a-659577.html.

father's house after his father has died. Sons are described as heads of the fathers themselves. In a number of texts, the phrase appears in conjunction with *toledoth* (7:2, 9; 8:28; 9:9, 34). As head of the father's house, the son is *source* rather than product, root rather than fruit. Sons become heads of fathers not because of their fathers but because of what they themselves beget. Sons become heads of fathers by themselves becoming fathers.

In normal reckoning, fathers are, of course, prior to sons, but the phrase hints at the son's priority to (or equality with) the one who begets him. The sons are not merely extensions of their fathers; they are "heads" of fathers, crowning their fathers with glory as mighty men of valor. Sons secure their fathers' paternal name: without begotten sons, fathers would not be begetters; sons make fathers fathers. This can be stated christologically: biblical genealogies trace a line of descent from the first Adam to the last Adam. Genealogies end with Matthew and Luke. Fleshly qualification for priesthood (or kingship, or covenant membership) gives way to the indestructible power of the risen Priest-King after the order of Melchizedek (Heb. 7). Abram's standing is finally founded not on his ancestry but on his descent, in being forefather of the ultimate Seed, Jesus. Jesus the son of Abram is "head of the father." Insofar as the genealogies are oriented toward the Messiah, they are oriented to the future rather than the past, and it is the future that secures the past rather than vice versa. More speculatively, the point can be stated trinitarianly: The Father is only Father by eternal generation of the Son. Without the Son, the Father is barren and unfruitful, without *toledoth*. The Father is "head" of the Son (1 Cor. 11:3), yet the Son is, in the Chronicler's sense, "head" of his Father, the filial source of the Father's paternity.

A similar point can be made from another direction. Genealogies trace the persistence of a family, clan, or nation through time. It is not enough to dig to the roots because a root without a trunk, branches, and leaves is no family tree. To be an origin, the origin must be supplemented. The Chronicler's genealogy demonstrates that Abram is a fountain, since he has descendants all the way to the Chronicler's own time. This becomes especially important at the end of the genealogy, when the Chronicler continues tracing the genealogy after it appears to come to an end in exile (→ 1 Chr. 9:1–2). Even when the descendants of Abraham have lost everything—land, temple, capital, king—they persist. Institutional continuity depends on procreation; unless people have children, there is no one to replace dying kings, priests, prophets, officials, elders, gatekeepers, or singers. When institutions collapse, procreation simply is the persistence of a community. When the inertia of court, capital, and temple stalls, Israel continues because it continues to bear children. This is the logic behind Jeremiah's exhortation to exiles: seek the peace of the city, settle, reproduce, because that is the only way for a nation to rise again from the grave of exile (Jer. 29).

Some portions of the genealogies consist of name lists without any indication of the relation between them (1 Chr. 1:1–4, 24–27). At times the lists are lists of sons (1:5–7); at other times the emphasis is on "begetters," fathers (1:10–16). Mothers (1:32; 2:3, 26; 3:1–5; 4:9) and wives (1:50; 2:18, 24, 26, 29, etc.) are occasionally named, as are sisters (1:39; 2:16; 3:9, 19; 4:3, 19; 7:15, 19, 30, 32). In addition, the lists are punctuated by narrative vignettes (1:10; 2:3–4; 4:9–10; 5:1–2, 18–22) and recurring patterns that introduce fundamental themes that run through 1–2 Chronicles. All this suggests that the purpose of the genealogies is not simply to list parents and children but to identify the "things begotten" by Israelites. Ultimately, what Israel begets is its history in all its fullness.

According to Dorsey (2004: 145–58), the genealogies are arranged chiastically (cf. Williamson 1982: 46; Boda 2010: 27–28; Merrill 2015: 83; Sparks 2008: 29 and passim):

A Before tribes (1:1–54)
  B Royal tribe: Judah (2:1–4:23)
    C Peripheral tribes: Simeon, Reuben, Gad, Manasseh (4:24–5:26)
     D Levites (6:1–81)
    C′ Peripheral tribes: Issachar, Benjamin, Naphtali, Manasseh, Ephraim, Asher (7:1–40)
  B′ Royal tribe: Benjamin (8:1–40)
A′ New Israel after exile (9:1–34)

With Levites at the center, the structure indicates one purpose of the genealogy: to authorize the temple personnel to carry out their role in the chosen house (Sparks 2008: 32).

First Chronicles 1 presents a "barren" humanity (the term is from Sparks 2008: 325–31). The world before Israel is bereft of worship, joy, song, and the house of God's name—all the things that, from the Chronicler's perspective, Israel will introduce into the human race. Israel serves the nations not by political means but through Levites, who stand at the center of the genealogy of Israel. We can be more specific. The center of the center of the genealogy is a list of Levitical musicians and singers appointed by David (6:31–48, embedded between genealogies of the three clans of Levites [6:16–30] and priests [6:49–53]). To be a priestly nation is, by the Chronicler's lights, to be a choral nation. Israel fulfills its role among the nations through a continuous liturgy of praise. With the reference to Adam (1:1) in mind, we may draw a wider anthropological inference: God created Adam (not merely Israel) to produce a race of singers. Israel exhibits the destiny of humanity: to be brought into God's choir to sing in God's heavenly city (cf. Leithart 2018).

Musicians are at the center. At the edges of the genealogy are kings. Israel's genealogy proper begins with a lengthy genealogy of Judah (1 Chr. 2:3–4:23) and ends with the genealogy of the original royal tribe, Benjamin (8:1–40). As William Johnstone (1998a: 14–17 passim) puts it, Israel's kings play a "sacramental" role. As Yahweh's sons (17:13), they sit on Yahweh's throne (28:5) and lead the Lord's "hosts" into battle (5:18). The Davidic kings are effective signs of Yahweh's reign over the nations. Good kings accurately signify; bad kings do not.

David accomplishes this sacramental role in part by bringing surrounding territories into submission to Israel (1 Chr. 18–20), extending Israel's boundaries to those promised to Abraham (Gen. 15:18), from the river (Euphrates) to the brook of Egypt. The more fundamental task of the king is portrayed in the shape of the genealogy: the king guards the boundaries of Israel to protect Israel's central activity, which is worship. Good kings build and maintain temples, supply material for worship, and organize priests and Levites (1 Chr. 29:30; 2 Chr. 9:23). Bad kings neglect the Lord's house, its worship, and the Levitical priests. A literary "all Israel" is assembled on the opening of Chronicles, since the whole nation is implicated in this priestly mission to the nations (1 Chr. 9:1; 11:1; on the use of "all Israel" in Chronicles, see Sparks 2008: 269–89). Embraced by kings who serve the King, Israel participates through the Levites in the Lord's gathering of all nations into his liturgical community. The Chronicler is drawing pictures with lists (cf. Boda 2010: 98).[2]

Before Israel (1 Chronicles 1)

John's "in the beginning" (John 1:1) signals that his Gospel records a "new Genesis" for the world, as does Mark's more subtle "the beginning of the gospel" (Mark

2. The Chronicler highlights the king's role through the use of the key word "seek" (*darash, baqash*). David serves as the model king who seeks Yahweh (1 Chr. 13:3; 15:13; 28:8–9), while Saul is the negative type, a king who failed to seek God (10:13). Worship is one of the chief ways of seeking God (1 Chr. 22:19; 2 Chr. 11:16; 14:1–4; 30:18–19), and kings seek Yahweh through preparations for worship, such as transporting the ark into Jerusalem (1 Chr. 15:13). Yahweh rewards those who seek him (2 Chr. 14:1–7; 15:2–7; 17:3–4; 18:4–7) and disciplines unfaithful kings who do not seek him (1 Chr. 10:13–14; 2 Chr. 12:14; 16:12). Even good kings can fail by not seeking Yahweh according to his laws, statutes, and ordinances (1 Chr. 15:13). Worship is regulated; the path toward Yahweh is pre-*scribed* in the scriptures.

1:1). The Chronicler also begins with an allusion back to the first chapters of scripture: the name Adam (1 Chr. 1:1). It is an initial clue that the history of the monarchy recapitulates the history of humanity and of Israel between Adam and David. First Chronicles begins with Adam, and 2 Chronicles ends with Cyrus. Israel and its history are not isolated but entwined with the nations. Nor is Israel originary. Unlike ancient Egyptian or Babylonian cosmogonies, Israel's does not claim that Israel is the primordial human race. Israel is instead *selected* from within a wider humanity. Israel's place in the world depends on God's loving choice, not natural origin (Hahn 2012: 20; Boda 2010: 30).

This is not to say that the Chronicler diminishes Israel's stature among the nations. On the contrary, Israel is the leading player on the stage of ancient history. This is indicated by the way the Chronicler's patterned genealogy locates Abram within the history of the human race. The genealogy of pre-Israelite humanity is framed by ten-generation lists of names. The Chronicler rapidly lists the generations from Adam to Noah (1:1–4) and closes his universal genealogy with a ten-generation list connecting Noah to Abraham (1:24–27).[3]

The initial list ends with the names of Noah's sons in the traditional order of Shem, Ham, Japheth (1:4). Like Israel later, Noah is chosen from among the nations, and his son Shem is also a chosen one (Pratt 2006: 63). The more detailed genealogies that follow are arranged in the opposite order: Japheth, Ham, Shem. Thus,

A Ten generations, Adam to Noah (1:1–4)
  B Shem (1:4)
    C Ham (1:4)
      D Japheth (1:4)
      D' Japheth (1:5–7)
    C' Ham (1:8–16)
  B' Shem (1:17–23)
A' Ten generations, Noah to Abram (1:24–27)

Abram is the climax of primordial human history, the last of a three-man line of human founders. Adam is father of the human race, Noah of the postdiluvian

3. According to Deut. 23, illegitimate children are excluded from the community of Israel until the tenth generation. Because Judah fathers two illegitimate sons, the royal tribe attains royalty only with David, ten generations from Judah. That principle may also be operative in the early part of the Chronicler's genealogy: the lines of Adam and Noah are tainted, and so there is a ten-generation gap before a legitimate seed appears.

human race, Abram of the new humanity that is Israel. Yahweh's call of Abram is as decisive a genesis of human history as the creation of Adam and the preservation of Noah.

Royal Tribe (1 Chronicles 2:1–4:23)

First Chronicles 2 begins with a list of the sons of Israel, organized not in birth order but by mother:

A   Six sons of Leah (Reuben, Simeon, Levi, Judah, Issachar, Zebulun)
  B   One son of Bihah, Rachel's maid (Dan)
    C   Two sons of Rachel (Joseph, Benjamin)
  B'   One son of Bilhah, Rachel's maid (Naphtali)
A'   Two sons of Zilpah, Leah's maid (Gad, Asher)

Dan and Zebulun appear on this list, but they are not given genealogies (Pratt 2006: 66). Instead, both Ephraim and Manasseh, sons of the "firstborn" Joseph, are given double lists. A genealogy organized by the names of Jacob's sons keeps us in the "Genesis" context established by the name Adam. Though the genealogy covers the whole history of Israel, from Jacob to exile and return, the Chronicler presents it as a recapitulation of the book of Genesis, anticipating the quasi-Egyptian slavery that followed the death of Saul (→ 1 Chr. 10).

Israel's genealogies begin with Judah, the fourth-born son of Jacob (1 Chr. 2:1–2). The three older sons of Jacob—Reuben, Simeon, and Levi—are disqualified from their birth status by their sins. Reuben takes his father's concubine (1 Chr. 5:1–2; Gen. 35:22), and Simeon and Levi massacre the freshly circumcised residents of the city of Shechem (Gen. 34:1–31). The Chronicler acknowledges the complexity of preeminence in Israel (1 Chr. 5:1–2), with Reuben, Judah, and Joseph each possessing primacy of a different sort.

The longest of the genealogies (see statistics in Merrill 2015: 103–4), that of Judah, occupies three chapters, with emphasis placed on the descendants of Perez, the "breakthrough" baby, a replacement firstborn born to Judah (himself a replacement firstborn) and his daughter-in-law Tamar (cf. Williamson 1982: 49; Boda 2010: 44–45; Sparks 2008: 229):

A   Judah's sons with Bath-shua, including Shelah (2:3)
  B   Judah's sons with Tamar (2:4)

C Descendants of Perez (2:5–4:20)
A′ Descendants of Shelah (4:21–23)

The long central section is subdivided into three. The sons of Perez are named (Hezron and Hamul, 2:5), then the sons of Hezron (2:9), before the Chronicler takes off with a lengthy and complex treatment of Perez's descendants through Hezron and Hamul (2:10–4:20).

Numerical patterns reinforce the Chronicler's themes. David is ten generations from Judah, through Judah's son Ram (cf. Ruth 4:18–22). That lines him up with Noah, tenth from Adam (1 Chr. 1:1–4), and Abraham, tenth from Noah (1:24–27). Like Noah and Abraham, David is the founder of a new world order and a new humanity. Solomon is also associated with the number ten: he is tenth in the list of David's sons (3:1–9), midpoint in a list of nineteen sons.[4] The tenth generation is the generation of new birth. The new-creation significance of David's reign is underscored by sevens. David's father, Jesse, is the seventh from Ram (2:10–12), and David is the seventh of Jesse's sons (2:13–15). These numerological hints are filled out in the brief narrative vignettes that punctuate the genealogy, which foreshadow the later narrative of Chronicles (Boda 2010: 30; see further below).

David appears within a history that is already under way. David's birthplace, Bethlehem (cf. 2:51, 54; 4:4), eventually took on the name City of David, but the city was not founded by David or even by David's ancestors. Hur, from the Judahite line of Caleb, founded the city (2:18–20). As with Israel, so with David: Yahweh's choice, not one's origin, determines destiny. The fact that the genealogy embeds David's line within a larger genealogy is consistent with the Chronicler's presentation of David. He is never a lone hero or isolated king, but is always surrounded by a company. The genealogy lists his brothers and sisters (2:9–17), and he relies on mighty men (11:10–47; 12:1–40) and captains (13:1) for victory, protection, and advice. No role is more typical of the Chronicler's David than that of the convener of a *qahal*, the assembly of all Israel. The Chronicler does not tell us of David's man-on-man fight with Goliath, though he does record the giant-killing heroics of David's *gibborim* (20:4–8).

Nor is David alone in being associated with rebirth and new creation. The brief stories told in Judah's genealogy are all stories of death and resurrection. We presume that all of the men and women listed in 1 Chr. 1 lived and died, but death is first mentioned in the list of Edomite kings (1:43–51; *vaiyamot*, used

4. Solomon is also a twelve: counting inclusively, he is the twelfth from Abram (Hahn 2012: 36).

eight times; cf. Hahn 2012: 21). Death intrudes again early in the genealogy of Judah, Israel's royal tribe. Sons of Judah die because of their wickedness (2:1–4). Yahweh himself is involved in their deaths. This is the first time the Chronicler uses the name Yahweh and the first reference to God by any name in Chronicles. To this point, it would have been perfectly possible to read the genealogy secularly, as a purely immanent descent of the human race from Adam. When Yahweh does appear, he comes not as Creator but as *Killer*, Judge, and Executioner. God is a killer of kings, a theme to which the Chronicler returns (1 Chr. 10:14; 2 Chr. 36:17–18). The fragility of the king and the king's accountability to Yahweh are critical elements of the Chronicler's political theology. Kings are not invulnerable incarnations of divine power. Kings are of flesh, fleshly.

Though Judah's genealogy begins with death, it is largely an account of rescue from death. The genealogy begins with Judah's three sons by Bath-shua: Er, Onan, and Shelah. Er was so wicked that Yahweh put him to death (1 Chr. 2:3). None of the other sons appear to have children; we know from Genesis that God put Onan to death too (Gen. 38), and Shelah's line is (canonically if not historically) aborted. Judah gets a new lease on life through Tamar, his Gentile daughter-in-law, who bears the twins Perez and Zerah. The abortive line of Judah is renewed through a Gentile. Tamar is, like Bathsheba (Bath-shua), a scandalous woman incorporated into the genealogy of Davidic kings (Boda 2010: 53).

Then it happens again. Zerah's sons are listed, then disappear (1 Chr. 2:6–8)—another abortive line. His descendants end with Achan/Achar, "the troubler of Israel, who violates the ban" (2:7) and is stoned. Zerah, whose name means "rising" and puns on the word for "seed," is *not* fruitful. Another false start; another blind alley for Judah. But Perez, the one who breaks through, has two sons, Hezron and Hamul. The Chronicler's genealogy focuses on the former, whose three sons are Jerahmeel, Ram, and Chelubai (2:9), and the extended genealogy moves from the descendants of Ram to "Caleb" (presumably the Chelubai of 2:9) to Jerahmeel and back:

A   Ram's descendants to ten generations (2:10–17)
  B   Caleb's children (2:18–20)
    C   Herzon's second family (2:21–24)
      D   Jerahmeel (2:25–33)
    C′   Jerahmeel's line continues through his Egyptian slave (2:34–41)
  B′   Caleb's descendants (2:42–55)
A′   David (descendant of Ram) (3:1–9)

The C/C' sections both describe second families. Hezron has three sons, then reappears in the list of his own descendants, as if he were part of the following generation, within a list of sons born to a second wife he married in old age (2:21). Jerahmeel's line through Onam stalls three times over. One line goes from Onam through Shammai to Nadab to Seled, who "died without sons" (2:30). Another line from Onam goes through Jada to Jether, who "died without sons" (2:32). Sheshan (2:34) also has no sons, but his line is restarted through his daughter, whom he gives to an Egyptian slave, Jarha (2:34). It is another sign of the death and resurrection of Judah, and the renewal is again linked with the incorporation of Gentiles.

Judah comes to the throne after a history of repeated brushes with death. From the beginning, the line of David is a line of "risen" kings. David, the *seventh* son of Jesse and the king of the *tenth* generation, comes from a tribe of resurrected ancestors.[5] Davidic kings do not escape mortality, but they are promised an eternal kingdom, a kingdom that will forever rise again from the grave because it began as a kingdom from the grave. In several cases, Judah is revived by Gentiles, by the mutual reincorporation of the chosen nation with the rest of humanity. As soon as the Chronicler begins to speak of the Davidic dynasty, he is anticipating the end, where the final "Davidic" king is a Gentile (→ 2 Chr. 36:22–23).

Judah's resiliency is all the more remarkable because members of this tribe are guilty of the evil that dooms other dynasties, the evil that the Chronicler describes as *ma'al* (see Boda 2010: 108; Milgrom 1976: 21; Johnstone 1998c: 116–20; Japhet 1993: 229–30; Hahn 2012: 36, 46). The genealogy of Judah is interrupted by a reference to the *ma'al* of Achan, the troubler of Israel who seized Yahweh's plunder and brought disaster on the nation (2:3). The Chronicler claims that the Transjordanian tribes likewise committed *ma'al* (5:25), and in the Chronicler's account, Saul dies and his dynasty ends because of the *ma'al* that he *ma'al*-ed against the Lord (Johnstone 1998a: 95; → 1 Chr. 10:13–14).[6]

The sin of the Judahite Achan is a paradigmatic case: he violates the ban of holy war (*herem*), seizes the holy plunder of Jericho as his own, and commits

5. Boda (2010: 52) points out that the Chronicler leaves out one of Jesse's sons to place David in the seventh position.

6. According to Johnstone (1998c: 96), after 1 Chr. 10 "there is a long gap, but there are a further 12 occurrences [of the word] in 2 Chronicles." The gap corresponds to the reigns of David and Solomon, which the Chronicler presents as a rare un-*ma'al* period of Israel's history. The earlier tendency resumes with the reign of Solomon's son Rehoboam, continues through Uzziah, Ahaz, and Manasseh, and finally spreads to the entire nation under King Zedekiah (97). Ultimately, this history of *ma'al* ends in exile (1 Chr. 9:2). As Johnstone puts it, "The Chronicler's message is clear: his explanation for why Israel is 'in exile' is that from beginning to end of its occupation of the land ... Israel has been guilty of *ma'al* and paid the penalty for it" (97).

trespass and sacrilege. As Johnstone (1998c) puts it, the concept of *ma'al* is double-sided: "*ma'al* is not only to deprive God of that which is rightfully his; it is also to misapply what has thus been wrongfully gained to one's own profit" (97). It can be an individual or national trespass. As a nation, Israel owes God "exclusive obedience and utter reliance" and exhibits *ma'al* when it turns "to other gods," thereby "defrauding God and misapplying that which is holy" (97–98). The results can be catastrophic: Saul dies, Uzziah becomes leprous, the people are sent into exile, the land is devastated—"in a word, forfeiture of status, life or land" (98).

Alongside Israel's history of *ma'al*, Chronicles describes the atonement that undoes trespass and restores Israel's fortunes. Hezekiah's ceremony of rededication and covenant making, which includes king, priests, prophets, and people "harmoniously integrated with one another in a national act of atonement," is an act of un-*ma'al*-ing (Johnstone 1998c: 99). In the end, Israel's *ma'al* accumulates so that atonement can only come through the death of exile (→2 Chr. 36:14). The notice of Achan's sin initiates this long narrative thread, making clear that David's dynasty is rescued not because it avoids the taint of *ma'al* but by a gracious atonement that undoes the sacrileges of David's descendants.

The brief vignette concerning Jabez (4:9–10) provides an additional perspective on the persistence of the Davidic dynasty (on the chiastic shape of the story, see Sparks 2008: 241). Jabez's name reflects the pain (*'ozeb*) his mother experienced at his birth. Etiological etymologies typically link the name with a circumstance in a causal way. Dan is "Dan" because by his birth God "judges" (*dan*) Rachel favorably. By contrast, Jabez's name does not directly name his origin but reverses that origin (Japhet 1993: 109) and sets up the reversal of his biography: the son born in pain is surprisingly "more honorable than his brothers" (4:9) and has a prosperous life. He escapes the "fate" of his name because there is a power beyond the power of origin, a power to which Jabez can and does appeal. Jabez prays, and the Lord overcomes the destiny of his name. Having been "called" (*qara*) Jabez, his only hope is to "call" (*qara*) on the God of Israel (Japhet 1993: 110).

"In pain" alludes to Gen. 3:16: "In pain you will bring forth children" (Japhet 1993: 109). Jabez is a child of Eve, a child of curse; the name he inherits from his mother names the curse of his origin. There is nothing but pain in his ancestry, but God makes a new future, answering Jabez's prayer for blessing, for an enlarged border, for God's hand to be with him, and for deliverance from the pain of his birth, the pain of primordial curse. The God who addressed Abram is addressable; the God who chose Abram for a "supernatural" destiny hears the prayers of those who seek deliverance from "nature."

In the context of Chronicles, Jabez provides a small glimpse of the fulfillment of Yahweh's commitment to bring Israel from the "pain" of its exilic new birth into an enlarged space, blessed and guided by the hand of God. More specifically, Jabez ben Judah stands for the hope that the seed of David, despite being guilty of *ma'al*, can call on the Lord and be delivered into a large place of blessing (cf. Exod. 34:24; Deut. 19:8; Hahn 2012: 41). Prayer will be one of the keys to the Chronicler's political theology. The vignette about Jabez, coming close to the end of the genealogy of Judah, is a fitting capstone to a genealogy that began with a reminder of the *ma'al* of Achan (Sparks 2008: 242). The shape of Judah's genealogy will be the shape of the kingdom's history: from sacrilege to prayer, from death to open borders and new life. And in the larger canonical context, Jabez stands for Adamic humanity, born of pain but destined by the merciful power of God to become a new humanity in the last Adam. Jabez's prayer bridges origin and eschaton.

Transjordanian Tribes (1 Chronicles 4:24–5:26)

After chapter 4, the Chronicler turns attention to the Transjordanian tribes of Reuben, Gad, and Manasseh. Chapter 5's structure is essentially chiastic:

A   Reuben's genealogy (5:1–10)
   B   Gad's genealogy (5:11–17)
      C   War of Reuben, Gad, and Manasseh against the Hagrites
         (5:18–22)
   B′   Manasseh's genealogy (5:23–24)
A′   Exile of Reuben, Gad, and Manasseh (5:25–26)

The A, C, and A′ sections all refer to Reuben, but the B sections do not. In both A and A′, the Chronicler refers to the conquest of the Transjordan tribes by the Assyrians under Tiglath-pileser (or Pul), punishment for the whoredom of Israel (Merrill 2015: 121). The central section describing the war against the descendants of Hagar (cf. Ps. 83) in the days of Saul is anticipated with a brief mention (5:10). Initially, it seems that Reuben is the only tribe to fight the Hagrites, but after Gad is introduced, we learn that Gad joined Reuben in the war (Japhet 1993: 131–32, 135–40). Even *before* Manasseh has been introduced, he is fighting alongside Reuben and Gad.[7] Thus,

---

7. This is one of the early examples of the Chronicler's stylistic habit of mentioning incidents and people, and citing words he has not recorded. In 2 Chr. 36, for instance, he mentions the fulfillment of Jeremiah's prophecy of exile even though he has never cited the prophecy itself.

---

a   Reubenites fight Hagrites (5:10)
   b   Genealogy of Gad (5:11–17)
a′ Reuben, Gad, and Manasseh versus the Hagrites (first reference to Manasseh) (5:18–22)
   b′ Genealogy of Manasseh (5:23–24)

Reuben fights, then Gad is introduced; Reuben, Gad, and Manasseh fight, then Manasseh is introduced.

The structure highlights the theological thrust of the genealogy and the tragedy of the history of the firstborn. In the opening verses, the Chronicler provides a brief summary of Reuben's fall from preeminence among his brothers, as recorded in Genesis. Because Reuben "defiled his father's bed" (5:1; cf. Gen. 35:22), he loses the birthright, the double portion that is instead given to Joseph (whose two sons each receive a tribal inheritance). Yet Joseph is not preeminent in power; Judah becomes strong and takes the lead, though the birthright remains with Joseph (an allusion back to the events of Gen. 37–50). As Japhet puts it, there are three degrees of preeminence: "the biological firstborn, the legally nominated elder, and the one who wielded actual authority" (1993: 133). Again we note that the Chronicler does not treat origin as destiny; one's history, guided by Yahweh's interventions, determines the future as much as one's starting point. At the end of the passage, Reuben is again deprived of inheritance since, along with Gad and Manasseh, the Reubenites "played the harlot after the gods of the peoples of the land" (5:25). Actual sexual transgression is matched by spiritual adultery. The first deprives Reuben of his inheritance; the latter leads to the tribe's complete (permanent?) expulsion from the land.

At the center of the chapter is a "might have been" scenario, a story of heroic faithfulness by the very tribes that later turned from Yahweh to follow the gods of the nations. The Transjordan tribes win a battle because they, like Jabez, "cried out to God" and "trusted in Him," so that "He answered their prayers" (5:20). In a stunning formulation, we learn that "many fell slain" because the "war was of God" (5:22); a high body count is a sign of Yahweh's engagement in war. The episode is a small-scale conquest, a tiny book of Joshua, a story of divine aid in battle followed by settlement. The sequel is also the story of all Israel, of unfaithfulness in the land and eventual expulsion. For the Chronicler, the promise of divine help remains in force: if those who return will cry out to Yahweh, he will help them once again. The question will linger: *Will* they cry out?

The overall movement of the chapter is not encouraging. First Chronicles 5 begins with a reminder of Reuben's "defilement" (*khalal*) of his father's bed, and it ends with a statement of the reasons for the northern kingdom's exile: "They acted treacherously [*ma'al*] against the God of their fathers, and played the harlot [*zanah*] after the gods of the peoples" (5:25; cf. 2 Chr. 21:11, 13). Jabez was rescued from the fate of his origin through prayer, but the Transjordanian tribes turn to other gods and so their end repeats their beginning. Prayer rescues Jabez from the identical repetition reflected in the history of the Transjordan tribes that follow Jabez's biography. Yet the mere fact that these tribes are included in the "all Israel" of the Chronicler's genealogy is hopeful. Even after their unfaithfulness, they are not forgotten. The tribes that break from the house of David share in the renewal of the people of God (Hahn 2012: 33; Pratt 2006: 75).

Levi (1 Chronicles 6)

No sooner has the Chronicler mentioned exile than he begins the genealogy of the tribe that is responsible for the acts of atonement that prevent and overcome exile (Sparks 2008: 180–81). As noted above, the Levites stand at the center of the Chronicler's genealogy, a literary symbol of their central significance in Israel's life and history. The genealogy of Levi is organized as a modified chiasm:

A   Genealogy of Aaron (6:1–15)
   B   Genealogy of Levite clans (6:16–30)
      C   Levitical singers (6:31–47)
   B¹   Brother Levites at tent (6:48)
A¹   Work of Aaron and sons (6:49–53)
A²   Priestly cities (6:54–60)
   B²   Levitical cities (6:61–81)

In general, the genealogy divides into two sections (cf. charts in Williamson 1982: 69; Pratt 2006: 55–57; Japhet 1993: 149): the genealogies of the priests and Levites (6:1–53), followed by a list of cities assigned to priests and Levites (6:54–81).[8] The first section is also organized chiastically (see the slightly different analysis in Boda 2010: 73):

8. Sparks (2008: 92–93) is correct to note that the Chronicler distinguishes Levites from priests and treats both as distinct from the people. He observes that "Levite" sometimes designates a tribe and sometimes names a set of functions distinct from those of priests (song, gatekeeping; 2008: 102). This is an important caution against exaggerated claims about the Chronicler's understanding of the Levites, but it remains the case that the Levites take on an elevated role in Chronicles and that other tribes, simply by being included within the genealogy, are treated as a part of a "kingdom of priests."

A Genealogy of the priests (6:1–15)
   B Genealogy of Levitical clans (6:16–30)
      C Levitical singers (6:31–47)
   B' Levites given to serve tabernacle (6:48)
A' Duties of the priests (6:49–53)

First Chronicles 6:48 is an outlier. Possibly it links back to 6:31–32, forming a frame around the genealogies of Levitical singers. Verses 31–32 and 48 share several terms: "service," "tabernacle," and "house." Yet it seems best to link 6:48 with the generic genealogy of 6:16–30. The Levites listed in 6:16–30 perform what 6:48 calls (oddly) the "service of the tabernacle of the house of God." The singers listed in the intervening section perform a different ministry in a different place; they are appointed for the service of song before the ark (6:31) at the tent of David rather than the tabernacle of Moses. The structure of the genealogy of Levi, like the structure of the genealogy as a whole, points to the centrality of the cult (Sparks 2008: 42–45).

That skeletal outline smooths over the density of the text's texture. First, the chapter begins with a list of the three sons of Levi in the order Gershon, Kohath, and Merari (6:1). After recording the descendants of Aaron (who is from Kohath through Amram, 6:2–3), 6:16 repeats 6:1: "The sons of Levi were Gershom, Kohath and Merari" (the alternate spelling Gershon/Gershom is in the Masoretic Text). So the genealogy of the priests is framed by the list of Levi's sons, or 6:16 marks a resumption of the genealogy begun in 6:1.

Second, the most extended genealogy of the three sons of Levi (6:16–30) unfolds in three cycles of three:

1. Three sons: Gershom, Kohath, Merari (6:16)
2. Sons of Gershom, Kohath, Merari (6:17–19)
3. Descendants of Gershom (seven generations), Kohath (ten generations), Merari (seven generations) (6:20–30)

That triple pattern returns at the end of the chapter. After listing the cities given to the Aaronic priests from the tribal areas of Judah and Benjamin (6:54–60), the Chronicler lists the cities of the other Levitical clans in two cycles of three:

1. Number of cities given to Kohath (ten), Gershom (thirteen), Merari (twelve) (6:61–65)
2. List of cities given to Kohath, Gershom, Merari (6:66–81)

Note that the order of the sons has changed: Kohath has taken first position in the inheritance. That revised order is first introduced at the center of the genealogy, with the list of Levitical singers and musicians. Heman the Kohathite is listed first (6:33–38), with Asaph of Gershom at his right hand (6:39–43) and Ethan of Merari on his left (6:44–47). Intriguingly, that change in the order of the clans is accompanied by a reversal in the direction of the genealogy itself. Instead of tracing the descendants from Levi to Heman, Asaph, and Ethan, the Chronicler moves from the three chief singers backward to Israel (in the case of Heman) or Levi (for the other two). At the very center of the Chronicler's genealogy, time backs up (cf. the "backward" genealogy of Jesus in Luke 3). At that point, the end reaches back to determine the beginning. It is yet another sign of the forward-reaching character of biblical genealogy, its emphasis on fruits as well as roots.

First Chronicles 6:16–30 is straightforward in general but tangled in details. The overall pattern is clear. The three sons of Levi are named: Gershom, Kohath, and Merari (6:16). The sons of each are listed in a numerically symmetrical pattern: two sons of Gershom, five of Kohath, two of Merari (6:17–19). Then a summary statement announces that "these are the families of the Levites according to their fathers" (6:19b AT). From there the genealogy provides an intergenerational list, again organized in the triad of three sons and in the same order. The general structure of 6:20–30 is also clear and again is numerically symmetrical:

A Seven generations of Gershom (6:20–21)
  B Generations of Kohath (6:22–28)
A′ Seven generations of Merari (6:29–30)

If we include Gershom and Merari in their genealogies, then the lists stretch to eight generations. Overall, we have three genealogical cycles, each expanding on the former, each organized around the three sons of Levi: first the sons themselves; then their sons; then their descendants to seven or more generations.

The tangle comes at the center of the genealogy in the list of generations from Kohath, the longest and most complex of the lists. It begins with a straightforward list of ten generations from Kohath (eleven if inclusive). First Chronicles 6:25 focuses on Elkanah, who is the fourth generation from Kohath, and names two sons (Amasai and Ahimoth), neither of whom is named as a son of Elkanah in 6:23. Then 6:26 begins yet another list of Elkanah's descendants, listing five generations of descendants that ends with another Elkanah (6:27). From 6:23 to

6:27, the name Elkanah appears five times. (The name appears three more times in 6:34–36, which gives a different genealogy from Kohath.)

First Chronicles 6:29 suddenly introduces Samuel, unmentioned to this point. His sons are Joel and Abijah, who are listed as the sons of the prophet Samuel in 1 Sam. 8:2. The Chronicler's Samuel is *the* Samuel, and one of the Elkanahs is his father (cf. 1 Sam. 1). That is one reason for focusing on Elkanah, and the other is the centrality of this clan of Levites in the formation of the Levitical choir whose genealogy occupies 6:31–48. The tangle of Elkanahs may be resolved as follows:

A   Two sons of Elkanah (6:25)
    B   Five generations of Elkanah (6:26–27)
A′ Two sons of Samuel (6:28)

That numerically matches the lists of the sons of Levi at the beginning of the section (two-five-two; 6:17–19) and may suggest that the clan of Elkanah is a clan of "Levites within Levi," even a clan of super-Levites. Each of the sons of Levi is mentioned three times in this section of genealogy, but the name Elkanah is mentioned *five* times (not always the same man). The Hebrew *'elqanah* means "God possesses" or "God buys" or "God makes." Elkanah is a perfect name for a Levite, the tribe purchased by God by exodus and the tribe that is God's special possession among the special possession that is Israel. He is the Levitest of Levites.

We will see later (→ 1 Chr. 23–27) that David dramatically rearranges the priests and Levitical clans and the regulations of worship that accompany them. Where there is a change of priesthood, there is also a change in law. To be sure, the priests continue to "turn to smoke" and have unique access to Yahweh in his sanctuary, but the Levites take on new, elevated responsibilities for the service (*'abodah*) of the house of God. The Chronicler signals that heightened role by giving extra attention to a subordinate clan like that of Elkanah.

Following the genealogy of Levi, the Chronicler lists Levitical cities and cities of refuge that assigned to the priests and the priestly tribe (6:54–81) their "dwellings according to their fenced/walled areas in their borders" (6:54 AT). As far as the distribution of land is concerned, the Chronicler is most interested in the holy cities assigned to the holy tribe. The description of the distribution of cities is, like the genealogy of Levi, broken up by clan and arranged symmetrically:

A   Priests' cities of refuge in Judah and Benjamin (6:54b–60)
    B   Kohathite cities in Manasseh (6:61)

      C Gershomite cities in Issachar, Asher, Naphtali, and Manasseh (6:62)

      D Merarite cities in Reuben, Gad, and Zebulun (6:63)

    A' Cities given by the sons of Israel in Judah, Benjamin, and Simeon (6:64–65)

      B' Kohathite cities in Ephraim and Manasseh (6:66–70)

        C' Gershomite cities in Manasseh, Issachar, Asher, and Naphtali (6:71–76)

          D' Merarite cities in Zebulun, the Transjordan (Reuben and Gad) (6:77–81)

B–D makes general statements about the tribal territories where each clan of Levi settled, while B'–D' contains lists of cities. The reference to Ephraim in 6:66 bisects the entire list. The priests are assigned cities in Judah, and the rest of the Levites receive cities in the territory that will become the northern kingdom, often identified with the dominant tribe Ephraim.

In the wilderness camp, the clans of Levi formed a cordon around the tabernacle, each clan assigned to one side of the tent. Priests were to the east, Kohathites to the south, Gershomites to the west, and Merarites to the north. The city lists are organized geographically, but they do not follow the arrangement of the wilderness camp. Instead, the arrangement moves roughly from south to north, the priests at the southern edge in Benjamin and Judah and the Gershomites and Merarites in the north, which is the opposite of the arrangement of the visionary tribal territories in Ezek. 48. Though not identical in details, the geographical arrangement points to the vocation of the tribe of Levi as guardians of the land of Yahweh in the same way as they are caretakers of his house.

Benjamin (1 Chronicles 7–9)

First Chronicles 7–9 records genealogies for a number of tribes, but the Chronicler gives most attention to the tribe of Benjamin. Fittingly, the genealogy that begins with Judah, the royal tribe, ends with the original royal tribe, Benjamin. Benjamin's genealogy exhibits a number of parallels with the history of Judah, not only in its structural placement but also in the details of the tribe's history. First Chronicles 8:8 records, without explanation, that Shaharaim "sent away" his wives Hushim and Baara to go to Moab, where he becomes father of seven presumably mixed-race sons: Jobab, Zibia, Mesha, Malcam, Jeuz, Sachia, and

Mirmah (8:9–10). Like the Davidic line, the tribe of Benjamin embodies a union of Israel and Gentiles. Shaharaim's descendants by his wife Hushim "put to flight the inhabitants of Gath" (8:13), one of the chief Philistine cities and hometown of Goliath. Five clans of Benjamin reside in Jerusalem (8:12–28, 32; cf. 9:3, 34, 38), making it as much a Benjamite city as a Judahite city.

Benjamin is given three distinct genealogies (7:6–12; 8:1–40; 9:35–44). Johnstone explains that the repeated portion "concerns, on the one hand, the population of Jerusalem, and, on the other, the family of Saul." Both are Benjamite: Jerusalem is a Benjamite city (cf. Josh. 18:11–28) and Saul a Benjamite king. The two lists—of the inhabitants of Jerusalem and of the family of Saul—fit into the general Benjamite genealogy of chapter 8 (Johnstone 1998c: 112–13). Yet "both receive a supra-Benjamite significance. In the immediately ensuing chapter (1 Chr. 10), in which the Chronicler begins his historical narrative proper, tracing the theme of guilt and atonement, it is Saul, the Benjamite, who provides the Chronicler with his first example of *ma'al*." Yet this first breakdown is associated with Jerusalem, "the place where the new centralized atonement cult will be introduced." This is the message: "Where Israel falls into guilt, there God provides the means of atonement. The reason that Benjamin appears last in the tribal genealogies is, therefore, not merely that Benjamin, as one of the last survivors, constitutes an enclosing bracket around the more vulnerable northern tribes; rather, it is that Benjamin provides the Chronicler with the double link of both guilt and atonement forward into this account of Israel's history" (Johnstone 1998c: 113).

This explains, too, the climax of the genealogy with the gatekeepers of the temple treasury: "*Ma'al*, in the legislation of Leviticus 5.15–26, concerns precisely the violation of the holy things, the supreme, tangible token of Israel's rendering of its duty towards God as the giver of the land and the possibilities of life within it. It is to the storehouses of the Temple that such holy things were brought to the Levites to confirm that Israel's duty towards God had been completely fulfilled" (Johnstone 1998c: 113–14). In short, the genealogy ends with a description of an ideal Israel—the Lord's holy things brought into his house, guarded by gatekeepers who prevent *ma'al* and who maintain the holiness of the temple by keeping their "trust" (Japhet 1993: 204). Once again, we can see why the Chronicler places the Levites at the center of his list of names and tribes, highlighting their role in providing atonement for those who prove unfaithful to Yahweh (Sparks 2008: 45–51).

The Chronicler has recorded the genealogy of the human race from Adam, focusing on the descendants of Abraham through Jacob. Summing it all up, he says, "So all Israel was enrolled by genealogies; and behold, they are written in the Book of the Kings of Israel" (9:1a). It is the first time the Chronicler uses the important phrase "all Israel," and it appears to indicate that the genealogy is finished. He provides genealogies for virtually all the tribes and covers the whole time period from the twelve sons of Israel to the exile, and in some cases beyond. It seems a *tragic* ending. "Judah was carried away into exile in Babylon for their unfaithfulness" (9:1b). Judah was "stripped" (*galah*) to Babylon, stripped of land, temple, king, and priest. After this long history, a history of exodus, conquest, and kings, Judah is no longer. What more is there to say?

But the genealogies are *not* over, and Chronicles still has a long way to go. After 9:1, 9:2 follows, then 9:3 and 9:4 and on to the end of the chapter and then new chapters. The apparent ending is not a final ending. The end of the genealogies, like the ending of 1–2 Chronicles as a whole, is an end but not *the* end. Like all the endings in the Bible, this end leads to a new beginning.

The list that begins in 9:2 is headed by the phrase "the first dwellers." "First" is *ri'shon*, from the same root as *re'shit* in the first phrase of Genesis. After the end that is exile, God speaks again "in the beginning."[9] The end of the section confirms a creation motif: after listing returned exiles from various tribes, especially among priests and Levites, the passage closes with the claim that "some of the brothers of the sons of the Kohathites were over the showbread to prepare it every Sabbath" (9:32 AT). The continuation of the genealogy begins with "beginning" and ends with a reference to "Sabbath." First Chronicles 9 rewrites Gen. 1:1–2:4. At the end of a genealogy that begins with "Adam," the Chronicler takes us back to the beginning. The Chronicler describes a new arrangement of creation following the de-creation of exile.

Return from exile is also a new exodus. Judah is carried away, but then they return to possess and dwell in the land (*yashav*, "dwell," is used twenty-five times in the genealogy; Japhet 1993: 208). The Chronicler even provides a mini book of Numbers, enumerating the returned exiles from Judah (9:6) and Benjamin (9:9), and among the priests (9:13) and gatekeepers (9:22). The gatekeepers are portrayed as if Israel were still in the wilderness. Though they are assigned to guard the rebuilt temple, the sanctuary is described as the "camp of the sons of Levi" (9:18) and the "camp of Yahweh" (9:19).[10] The word for "camp" (*makhaneh*) is

---

9. See Boda (2010: 99), McConville (1984: 9–10), and the note on the phrase "in the beginning" in Merrill (2015: 92). Japhet (1993: 207–8) disputes the conclusion that chapter 9 lists returning exiles.
10. I have sometimes altered the New American Standard Bible translation by replacing "the LORD" with "Yahweh."

typically used for a military camp (1 Chr. 11:15, 18; 12:22; 14:15–16; 2 Chr. 14:13; 18:33; 22:1; 32:21). The gatekeepers guard a liturgical space, which is also a military camp—Yahweh's headquarters for liturgical battle. The description of the priests as *gibbore khel* (9:13) reinforces their role in Israel's civil defense. All the other uses of the phrase in 1 Chr. 1–9 (ten uses) refer to warriors, "mighty men of valor." And that is the same connotation when the phrase is used of the Levites and gatekeepers. The temple is called a "tent" (9:19) and "the house of the tent" (9:23). The gatekeepers are stationed at the four corners of the sanctuary—east, west, north, south—to prevent incursions from every direction (9:24), with the chief of the gatekeepers, Shallum, stationed at the east gate, previously reserved for priests (9:17–18). The postexilic city replicates Israel's wilderness camp, in which Israel is arranged in concentric rings around the tabernacle.

The two story lines—creation and exodus—belong together. Creation is the original exodus, bringing the world from nothing, from the formless void, to an ordered, teeming cosmos—and the first exodus recreates Israel and the world. New exodus means new creation, as new creation is always the result of an exodus from an old world into a new.

The company of returned exiles includes four categories of people to spread to the four corners of the land: Israel, priests, Levites, and temple servants (9:2). As the Chronicler expands the list, he mentions seven categories: some from the tribes of Manasseh and Ephraim, from Judah and Benjamin, also priests, Levites, and gatekeepers. Surprisingly, the longest part of this new-creation account is devoted to the temple gatekeepers. This, too, fits the submerged Genesis framework. In Gen. 2:15–16, Yahweh places Adam in the garden and commissions him as a servant and guard (*shamar*) of Eden. The Levitical gatekeepers are new Adams, guarding the garden that is the temple. Gatekeepers are just what Israel needs to survive and flourish after the exile, since they were sent into exile for failures of gatekeeping.[11]

Gatekeepers keep bad things away from Yahweh's house to preserve the good things taking place within. The Levitical gatekeepers were "over the chambers" (9:26), perhaps chambers of feasting for common Israelites. Levitical gatekeepers

---

11. Centuries before, when a plague broke out against Israel in the wilderness because of its idolatry and fornication, Phinehas arrested the plague by impaling a fornicating couple in their tent (Num. 25). Phinehas is the archetypal gatekeeper, full of the jealousy and zeal of Yahweh, always ready to prevent Israel from defiling the Lord's sanctuary. The Chronicler tells us that Yahweh was with Phinehas (9:20), that Yahweh stood with him at the gates of Yahweh's own house, and that Yahweh is both resident and guardian of his palace. Yahweh is the glory within the tent, and gatekeepers are the fire of jealousy that surrounds it.

were in charge of the flour, wine, oil, and incense of the sanctuary (9:28–32). The sanctuary is a place of festivity, but Israel can rejoice in that feast only if the Levitical guardians are zealous and faithful in their work. If they slack, defilements undermine the joy of God's house.

In the new covenant, God establishes a new temple in the world, a temple made of people, not stones. This temple is the church, and it is a temple for the same reasons that the ancient temples were temples: because it is the place of God's dwelling. Every Christian is individually a gatekeeper of his own body, a temple of the Spirit. Parents are gatekeepers of children, church members of one another, and pastors of the entire body. This surveillance does not appeal to us. We like to be left alone nursing our autonomy. But the logic of 1 Chr. 9 applies to the church: by guarding one another, we prevent bitterness and sin from taking root. We guard one another from the sacrilege that can lead to desolation and disaster. We *are* our brothers' keepers, each a gatekeeper of this holy house.

We guard one another so that our Eucharist will be a feast of joy rather than a deadly poison. We guard one another to preserve the peace and joy we have in the Spirit. We guard our families to preserve the festivity of a dinner table or a Christmas celebration. We guard our hearts to protect the joy of the Lord that is our strength. "Communion" is life in common, life together. We can share in good things—ultimately, in the greatest good thing, communion in the Spirit, who is the Lord and Giver of life—only as we show the zeal of Phinehas.

First Chronicles 1–9 is infused with the genealogical spirit of the book of Genesis, the book of origins that records Yahweh's election of Abram to a history that surpasses his origin. In the overall design of Chronicles, the genealogy prepares us for the beginning of the Chronicler's narrative, a story of defeat and enslavement haunted by the memory of Israel's sojourn in Egypt.

2

BACK TO EGYPT

1 Chronicles 10

If 1 Chronicles were a movie, it would begin with two hours and forty-five minutes of credits: name after name scrolling across the screen, most of them (as far as modern readers are concerned) obscurities and nonentities and unknowns, forgotten fathers and sons and mighty men—all the bit players in the cast, the assistant assistant assistant to the assistant, key grips, best boys. When the action finally gets under way, it begins with an extraordinary bang, a chaotic scramble of troops, the end of a battle whose beginning we never see. We are *in medias res*: the Philistines are already winning, Israel already fleeing and falling on Mount Gilboa.

Why start the story here?

The Chronicler begins his genealogy at the beginning, with the name of Adam; and the history of Judah, which is the focal point of his chronicle, is a story of Yahweh's formation of a new humanity chosen and formed from within the old. Like Genesis, the narrative of Chronicles begins with the formless void, the *tohu wabohu* (Gen. 1:2) of a fallen dynasty. From there, 1 Chronicles will follow the sequence of the creation week, then opening a new week with the eighth-day Sabbath rest of Solomon's reign:

Day 1: The Spirit knits together David's helpers (1 Chr. 11–12).

Day 2: David brings the ark into the tent-firmament (1 Chr. 13–15).

Day 3: David sends the people home from the ark installation with bread and raisins, replicating the grains and fruits of day three (1 Chr. 16:1–3).

Day 4: David appoints singers, like the stars that sang at creation (1 Chr. 16).

Day 5: Yahweh promises David a seed, a swarm of descendants (1 Chr. 17).

Day 6: David fights as the new Adam to extend just dominion over the world (1 Chr. 18–20).

Day 7: David falls and makes atonement, and prepares for building a new temple (1 Chr. 21–29).

Day 8: Solomon brings the Lord's throne into its permanent Sabbath rest (2 Chr. 1–9).

The death of Saul also fits the Chronicler's "recapitulative" record of the history of the monarchy. As noted above (→ introduction), he tells the story of the monarchy as a reenactment of the history of humanity from Adam through Israel's judges. The genealogies of 1 Chr. 1–9 are reminiscent of genealogies in Genesis, spiced with narrative material drawn from Genesis. As chapter 10 begins, we are moving from Genesis to Exodus: after Saul's death, Philistines, cousins to Mizraim/Egypt (Gen. 10:13–14; 1 Chr. 1:11–12), capture portions of Israel. 'Tis like another Egyptian sojourn, leaving Israel to wait for a new Moses.

Structure

The genealogies include the ancestry and descent of Saul, but that positive portrayal is undermined by the episode that follows (Pratt 2006: 104–5). The Chronicler's account of the death of Saul (1 Chr. 10) is organized in three paragraphs: first, the battle of Mount Gilboa; then, the Philistines' seizure of Saul's body until its rescue by men from Jabesh-gilead; finally, an editorial evaluation of Saul.

The first of these falls out in a fairly neat chiasm:

A Philistines fight Israel (10:1)
  B Philistines strike Saul's sons (10:2)
    C Saul's death (10:3–5)
  B' Death of Saul and his sons (10:6)
A' Philistines capture cities of Israel and settle in them (10:7)

The central section alternates from Saul to his armor-bearer and back:

A Saul is wounded by Philistine archers (10:3)
    B Saul asks armor-bearer to kill him (10:4a)
        C Armor-bearer refuses (10:4b)
    B′ Saul kills himself (10:4c)
        C′ Armor-bearer kills himself (10:5)

Saul wants his armor-bearer to kill him to keep him from being killed by "uncircumcised" Philistines. The passage turns on a contrast between arrows and swords. Arrows are weapons of the uncircumcised, and the sword is the weapon of the circumcised. Saul dies by the latter, anticipating the deaths of Ahab ($\rightarrow$ 2 Chr. 18) and Josiah ($\rightarrow$ 2 Chr. 35).

First Chronicles 10:8 forms an *inclusio* with 10:1–2. It mentions Mount Gilboa and uses the verb "fall" (*naphal*). But the verse is also a hinge that introduces the next sequence of action. First Chronicles 10:8–12 is organized in a parallel structure that calls attention to the contrast between the Philistines and the men of Jabesh:

A Philistines find Saul and sons (10:8)
    B Philistines strip, decapitate, and take Saul's body (10:9)
        C Philistines put Saul's armor and head in house of Dagon (10:10)
A′ Men of Jabesh hear about Philistine treatment of Saul (10:11)
    B′ Men of Jabesh take the bodies of Saul and his sons (10:12a)
        C′ Men of Jabesh bring the bodies to bury them in Jabesh (10:12b)

Philistines abuse Saul's body; the men of Jabesh treat it with dignity. Philistines send out Saul's body on parade to proclaim the good news of Dagon; the men of Jabesh mourn.

The final paragraph of the chapter is a modified chiasm:

A Saul died (10:13a)
    B for the trespass he trespassed (*ma'al*-ed a *ma'al*) (10:13b)
        C because of the word of Yahweh he did not keep (10:13c)
    B′ because he inquired of a medium (10:13d)
        C′ and did not inquire of Yahweh (10:14a).
A′ So Yahweh killed him (10:14b).

The structure links Saul's trespass with his consultation with the witch of Endor (1 Sam. 28) and connects his failure to keep the word of Yahweh with his failure to inquire of Yahweh. The text moves from the passive "Saul died" to the more active, and threatening, "He [Yahweh] killed him." (Note: Saul falls on his sword, but Yahweh kills him; the sword is Yahweh's weapon against Saul.) The three uses of Yahweh's name (the only uses in the chapter) move toward a crescendo: Saul trespasses against Yahweh; he does *not* keep Yahweh's word and does *not* seek Yahweh. So Yahweh makes sure Saul himself is not. Yahweh's first acts in Chronicles are to see and kill (→ 1 Chr. 2:3). Edom's kings die (→ 1 Chr. 1:43–54), but Yahweh personally executes judgments against the kings of his people.

These concluding verses throw light back on the entire chapter. Even in the midst of battle, even when fleeing and wounded, Saul can seek help from Yahweh (→ 1 Chr. 5:18–22). Instead, he seeks the help of his armor-bearer. Saul provides a negative example of the Chronicler's chief principle of warfare: if you seek Yahweh, he will be found; if you forsake him, he will reject you (1 Chr. 28:9).

The King Is Dead

With Saul on the battlefield, the Philistines have a target—Saul and his three sons (cf. the Arameans and the king of Israel, → 2 Chr. 18). They take down Saul's sons. Three of the cornerstones of the house of Saul fall on the mountain, and only the chief cornerstone, the king himself, is left standing, alone with his armor-bearer. *Barely* standing—he is wounded by archers, shooting from a distance. The king from Benjamin, a tribe of archers and slingers (1 Chr. 12:2), is downed by his tribe's own specialty weapon. It is as if some invisible, ironic hand has directed an arrow to this specific destination.[1]

Wounded, Saul does not want to end up mocked, abused, and perhaps tortured before the assembled Philistine nobles, a toy to be sported with. No "eyeless in Gaza" for him (as earlier for Samson, Judg. 16:21). But Saul cannot even get his armor-bearer to follow orders. When Saul asks his armor-bearer to thrust him through, the armor-bearer refuses and Saul has to finish the archer's job himself. Saul is a Goliath: a giant of a man, downed by missiles, finished off with a sword. Perhaps the Philistines are aware of the delicious irony of removing the head of Israel's giant, as David decapitated the hero of Gath (cf. Hahn 2012: 47; Japhet

---

1. Israel's army is scattering as soon as we enter the scene, and after we hear of Saul's death, the narrative resumes that scene of flight (10:7). But 10:7 is ambiguous. The men of Israel see that "they had fled." Perhaps that reaches back to 10:1, and the antecedent of the pronoun is "men of Israel." The most natural antecedent, though, is "Saul and his three sons." Before they die, they flee (Japhet 1993: 224). The cowardice of Saul and his sons leads to their defeat, and that cowardice is a failure of faith in Yahweh.

1993: 227). But Saul's end is more pathetic than Goliath's: Goliath at least had the dignity of being killed by an opponent.

The Chronicler summarizes the destruction of Saul's house in a powerful sentence: "Saul died with his three sons, and all his house died as one" (10:6 AT). Descendants of Saul survive the battle, but the royal *house* collapses. The Chronicler reinforces the death of Saul's house with a fourfold repetition of the verb "die" (*mot*). Saul was *dead* . . . he fell on his sword and *died* . . . Saul *died* with his three sons . . . all his house *died*. A fourfold death for the four corners of the royal house. A four-cornered world dies on the slopes of Mount Gilboa. Saul dies by arrows, and his house dies with him. Ahab and Josiah will also die by arrows, and their deaths will mark the death of their respective dynasties. Saul's house goes to the grave without hope of resurrection. The Saul-like death of Josiah forces the question: Will the same be true for David's house? Can these bones live?

Saul's suicide is an appropriate gesture: he is the troubler of his own house. We are not informed of this until the end of the narrative, when the Chronicler tells us that Saul died "for his trespass which he trespassed against Yahweh" (10:13 AT). First Samuel fills in the details. Saul does not guard the word of the Lord: he does not wait for Samuel before offering sacrifice (1 Sam. 13), he does not carry out the ban against the Amalekites (1 Sam. 15), and he seeks a medium instead of seeking the Lord. His sins brought his downfall. As we have seen, the Hebrew word *ma'al* is a key term in Chronicles (→ 1 Chr. 2:3), denoting an "act of unfaithfulness" or "sacrilege." It is the sin that leads to Saul's fall (he *ma'al*-ed a *ma'al*, 1 Chr. 10:13) and later to the exile of Judah, whose officials and priests *ma'al*-ed a *ma'al* (2 Chr. 36:14).[2]

2. Summarizing the work of Rudolph Mosis, Saul Zalewski (1989) argues that Saul foreshadows the various kings who do evil in the eyes of Yahweh. Like other commentators, Mosis emphasizes the importance of "transgression" (*ma'al*) and points to specific cases where the concept plays a key role in the fate of kings: "the story of the death of Saul (1 Chr. x 13), the description of the evil deeds of Ahaz (2 Chr. xxviii 19), and the description of the destruction of Jerusalem (2 Chr. xxxvi 14)." There is a particularly close relationship between Saul and Ahaz:

> Whereas Hezekiah is conceived of as a second David, Ahaz his father is conceived of as a second Saul. The disasters which came down upon the state in the time of Ahaz are narrated in 2 Chr. xxviii. The king of Aram (*v.* 5) and the Edomites (*v.* 17) had taken captives from Judah while the Philistines had invaded the cities of Judah, had taken many cities, and had settled in them (*v.* 18). This description of the deeds of the Philistines in the time of Ahaz reminds us especially of the situation described in the story of the death of Saul (1 Chr. x 7). . . .

> Ultimately, Saul's death foreshadows "the sins of Israel and its kings caused the destruction of the Land and the exile of the people to Babylon." (Zalewski 1989: 451)

If Saul foreshadows Ahaz, he is a negative foreshadowing of the righteous kings of Judah. Saul's failure to guard the Lord's word is one dimension of his *ma'al*, and Josiah's righteousness is evident in his insistence

In the aftermath of the death of Saul's house, time runs backward. The men of Israel who live in the valley beneath Mount Gilboa see the flight of Saul and his sons and the army scattering, and they know that they are unprotected. In fear, they flee their cities. When Israel entered the land, the Lord gave them cities they had not built, vineyards they had not planted, trees they had not pruned. The Lord chased away the Canaanites, so that a thousand fled before a single Israelite. Now the Israelites turn Canaanite, fleeing before an invading army, and the Philistines take the place of the conquering hosts of Yahweh. Philistines settle in cities they have not built and enjoy the fruit of vineyards they did not plant. By losing Gilboa, Israel loses access to the northern territories, the richest land (McConville 1984: 15). It is a conquest in reverse.

What follows is a reverse exodus. As noted above (→ introduction), Philistines are B-league Egyptians. Every time the Philistines invade and dominate, Israel suffers a mini-sojourn in Egypt. Here the inversion of exodus goes further. When Yahweh delivered Israel from Egypt, he shamed the gods of Egypt. Now the gods of Philistia shame Yahweh by shaming Yahweh's anointed. Saul spares himself some shame by killing himself, but corpses can still be desecrated. When the Philistines find his body and the bodies of his sons the day after the battle, they strip his armor, the glory of the warrior, and make it their own. David deposited Goliath's armor in the tabernacle, a confession that Yahweh defeated Goliath. Now the Philistines parade Saul's armor and head around Philistia, proclaiming the glad tidings of Israel's defeat.

In 1 Samuel 31, the men of Jabesh walk all night and boldly take Saul's body from the wall of a Philistine city. The Chronicler tells us only that the men of Jabesh take the bodies of Saul and his sons and give them a decent burial. We are not told where the men of Jabesh find the bodies, and from Chronicles it seems that they are still on the mountain where they fell. This reinforces the shame of Saul's house and enhances the Philistine victory: Dagon defeats Saul utterly, and apparently upsets Yahweh's plans by overthrowing Yahweh's anointed. This is Dagon's exceptional, excellent, very good day, and throughout Philistia the messengers announce the exceptional, excellent, very good news, the gospel of Dagon.

The good news of Dagon is short-lived. The collapse of Saul's house is not Dagon's doing in the first place. Behind Saul's suicide is that invisible hand that guided the arrows. God's decree is determinative (Japhet 1993: 229). The verb "die" is used seven times in the chapter, and the climactic use is in 10:14. It does

---

on following the word of Yahweh (2 Chr. 34:21). Josiah is the last to follow Yahweh's word, and Judah goes into exile because it rejects and mocks the prophets, the Lord's messengers (Zalewski 1989: 453).

not describe passive dying but is an active "causing to die," and the subject is not Saul but Yahweh. Saul's house dies because Yahweh kills him. David never raises his hand against the Lord's anointed, and neither does Saul's armor-bearer. But Yahweh does. When his people transgress, Yahweh takes out not only the king but the whole royal house, the very house he established.

Saul's armor is taken to Dagon's temple. We have glimpsed the interior of Dagon's house before. When the Philistines defeated Israel at the battle of Aphek during Samuel's youth, the Philistines took the ark of the covenant and placed it in the house of Dagon, a trophy proclaiming the good news of Dagon's victory over Yahweh (1 Sam. 4–6). It soon became clear that the Philistines had misconstrued the battle's outcome. Dagon fell before the ark, doing homage to Yahweh's throne, and he was broken by the fall. What looked like Yahweh's defeat was in fact his invasion (Hahn 2012: 47).

Samson has the same effect on Dagon's house (Judg. 16). Taken as a trophy of Philistine triumph, he becomes the agent of Philistia's defeat. Saul does not allow that possibility. An antichrist, he refuses to bear the shame (cf. Heb. 12:2). He does not believe that Yahweh can overthrow the Philistines through him, and he is right: he has committed a trespass, and Yahweh is no longer defending him. He no longer seeks the Lord, so the Lord will not be found. Saul's house collapses when all four cornerstones fall on one day of battle. Because Samson does *not* despise the shame, it is not Samson's house that collapses but Dagon's. The good news of Dagon resolves into a subtheme in the song of Yahweh's triumph.

A pastoral gloss: Dagon has had an extraordinary string of victories of late. Christians built the West, but now our capital cities are in the hands of idols and their worshipers. Worse, churches have become temples of idols. Fashionable church leaders cannot settle the complex question of the difference between male and female or the meaning of the word "marriage" or whether helpless unborn babies deserve our protection. We need not be Sauls. If the Philistines have taken our cities and our churches, we can still be agents of Yahweh's victory. If we end up in exile or worse, it is because Jesus is sending us into new territory. When God is with us, we are never captives. We are always invaders. Wherever he sends us, he sends us with better news than Dagon's, the good news of Dagon's ultimate defeat. The ark was not captured, and neither was Samson. Neither is the church. When Peter goes to prison, he considers it another mission field. When Paul is hauled before kings, he calls them to serve Jesus the High King. We are never captured. We are deployed.

Saul's history will become a cautionary tale of exile (Williamson 1982: 93). Grim as it seems, it also assures the Chronicler's original audience. Israel can hope for return, because their history *begins* in exile. Further, though Saul's house falls all at once, the nation lives (Japhet 1993: 225). Israel survives the death of a king and the end of a dynasty. It will survive its deportation to Babylon too.

The Chronicler's history begins with the apostasy of a king, but it does not end there. After Saul comes David, and after each of the other Saul-like kings there is always another David. After Ahaz, a Hezekiah; after Manasseh, Josiah; after Josiah's sons, Cyrus and Darius and other upstanding Persians who carry out the Davidic commission better than the descendants of David. When Israel descends into shame and slavery, they cry out to Yahweh for healing. When Israel is subjected to Philistines, they start looking for a deliverer, a new Moses who can reverse the reverse exodus and take them to the promised land.

3

ROYAL MOSES

1 Chronicles 11–16

Saul is dead, but neither Israel nor its monarchy dies. Yahweh remains king, and even before Saul dies, he is preparing a new prince whose house will outlast Saul's. Israel's exodus is thrown into reverse, as Philistines invade and conquer. But Yahweh has already called a Moses to bring his people out (on David as Moses, see Throntveit 2003; Japhet 1993: 297).

David's reign is organized chiastically (cf. Siedlecki 1999: 246):

A David made king (1 Chr. 11)
  B David's *gibborim* (1 Chr. 11–12)
    C Failed attempt to bring the ark (1 Chr. 13)
      D War with Philistines (1 Chr. 14)
        E David and the ark (1 Chr. 15–17)
      D' Wars, framed by Philistines (1 Chr. 18–20)
    C' Census (1 Chr. 21)
  B' David's preparation for the temple (1 Chr. 22–29)
A' Solomon made king (1 Chr. 29)

David's successful installation of the ark in Jerusalem occupies the center of the narrative. David is above all concerned to establish Yahweh's throne in Yahweh's chosen city. The B and C sections are less obviously parallel, but the structure is illuminating. C and C' link David's two failures: his failure to bring the ark into Jerusalem "according to the ordinance" and his foolish census. B and B′ are connected by concern for personnel, military on the one hand and priestly/ administrative on the other. The Chronicler sees more continuity than contrast between the two types of helpers. Mighty men fight in faith, carrying on a form of liturgical warfare, while priests and royal officials have to act with courage and strength to establish a good order of justice in Israel. Warriors, priests, and bureaucrats are all "mighty men of valor" upholding Yahweh's kingdom.

The account of David's reign in 1 Chronicles alternates between house-building and relations with other nations. Those relations take two forms: war and international repute. David builds his house and then fights Philistines, spreading fear throughout the region (1 Chr. 14). Then David brings the ark into Jerusalem, places it in a tent, and makes plans to build a house (1 Chr. 15–17; on the centrality of ark, see Hahn 2012: 54). Then David fights Philistines and Ammonites (1 Chr. 18–20) before settling in for the rest of Chronicles to arrange for the temple project.[1]

From Ziklag to Hebron (1 Chronicles 11–12)

First Chronicles 11–12 forms a unit, framed by references to David's coronation ceremony at Hebron:

> A Gathering at Hebron, conquest of Jerusalem (11:1–10)
> B David's followers while a fugitive (11:11–47)
> B′ David's host at Ziklag (12:1–22)
> A′ Coronation festival at Hebron (12:23–40)

First Chronicles 11:1–10 is itself framed by references to "all Israel" (11:1, 10), the "word of Yahweh" (11:3, 10), and anointing/making David king (11:3, 10). The B–B′ sequence includes a flashback to a time when David was a fugitive from Saul (B) and when he was exiled in Philistia (B′). At the beginning, he has only a few followers, but that number grows as leaders from Gad, Benjamin, Judah, and Manasseh defect from Saul to join David at Ziklag. Over the course of the two chapters, David's company increases from a handful (initially 3 + 30; then a list of

---

1. Chapter 20 is one of the battle sequences. Like 1 Chr. 11, it recounts the exploits of David's mighty men: Joab's conquest of the Ammonite city of Rabbah and the giant-killing prowess of Sibbecai and Elhanan and Jonathan (11:4–8). Each of them fights giants, carrying on the conquest that Joshua had started. Elhanan and Jonathan kill giants that resemble Goliath: Elhanan defeats Lahmi, Goliath's brother, and Jonathan kills a six-fingered, six-toed giant of Gath, Goliath's hometown.

47 names in 11:26–47) to a collection of tribes (12:1–22, organized geographically; Boda 2010: 122; Williamson 1982: 105; Pratt 2006: 112) to an all-Israel of tribes, numbering over 300,000 fighting men (12:23–37).[2] David never acts alone in Chronicles. He is king, but always king over a company.[3]

Though he never appears in the narrative in person, Saul hovers behind David's early reign (12:1–2, 14, 23, 29; cf. Japhet 1993: 259). The few men who join at the beginning take a great risk in defecting from Saul to David. No doubt they have mixed motives, including resentment at Saul, but Johnstone (1998a: 151–52) captures the Chronicler's thrust: "These *gibborim* . . . , individual warriors, are the first to recognize that the failing order of Saul is doomed and that only through David can the threat to Israel's existence from the Philistines be neutralized. . . . Their perceptiveness about the trend of events energizes their natural gifts and enables them to triumph against seemingly impossible odds." Warriors are canaries in the coal mine; they are the first to choke, and abandon Saul for David. Because they take that risk, they bolster David's power and open a path for the more timid to join later. Because of their radical discipleship, because they leave father and mother to cling to the king, they form the core of the future Israel, Yahweh's bride.

The list of Benjamites who come to David at Ziklag (1 Chr. 12:3–7) is punctuated by names of men identified by their hometown or clan (Japhet 1993: 261):

1. Ahiezer, Joash, sons of Shemaah the Gibeathite (three names)
2. Jeziel, Pelet, sons of Azmaveth, Beracah, Jehu the Anathothite (five names)
3. Ishmaiah the Gibeonite (one name)
4. Jeremiah, Jahaziel, Johanan, Jozabad the Gederathite (four names)
5. Eluzai, Jerimoth, Bealiah, Shamariah, Shephatiah the Haruphite (five names)
6. Elkanah, Isshiah, Azarel, Joezer, Jashobeam the Korahites (five names)
7. Joelah, Zebadiah, sons of Jeroham of Gedor (three names)

It does not seem that every man in each sublist comes from the same town. That is, in the first sublist we know that Shemaah comes from Gibeah (Saul's

---

2. The Chronicler's numbers are enormous. For solutions to this crux, see Boda 2010: 121–22.

3. Johnstone (1998a: 150) notes the Chronicler's extensive use of *khazaq*, "to make strong." Fifteen of the twenty-four uses in the Hebrew Bible occur in Chronicles, usually to mean "assume control, be confirmed, show resolve, grow in strength" and usually used of kings (2 Chr. 1:1; 12:13; etc.). In 11:10, a title verse that opens the roll of those who joined with David, the heads of the army "assume control" along with David. Kingship is a joint enterprise between David and the helpers suitable to him.

hometown), but we do not know where the others come from. Overall, though, the list is patterned by geographic references, and that patterning has numerological significance: six Benjamite towns are mentioned, and one clan (Korahites, a Levitical clan?), for a total of seven sublists. David inherits a seven-fullness from Saul's house, a new creation of defectors.

The total number of personal names is also significant. The numbers are $3 + 5 + 1 + 4 + 5 + 5 + 3 = 26$, and twenty-six is the gematria of YHWH. "Your God helps you," Amasai says (12:18), and he surely does, sending a YHWH-number of men from Benjamin over to David. The Chronicler enumerates the list of Gadite defectors: "Ezer was the first, Obadiah the second," and so on (12:9–13). There are eleven names, one short of the all-Israel twelve. I suspect we are invited to supply the obvious twelfth name: David. With David, Gad becomes an Israel. Israel is a fractal people: twelve tribes, each of which is a twelve. Notably, Gad is a twelve only when allied with David, as Israel can be a twelvefold kingdom only under the Lord's anointed. So too the church, where each congregation is fractally related to the whole, and where the church is whole only as a body united with its head.

Triumph over impossible odds—that is the theme of chapter 11's catalogue of adventures. The Chronicler has modified the account from Samuel in strange ways. The Chronicler speaks of "the three" but mentions only two, and there appear to be two sets of three (11:21; Boda [2010: 115] blames scribal error). Despite the complications, the result is a numerologically patterned account:

1. Jashobeam kills three hundred at once (11:11)
2. Eleazar and David defend a barley field (11:12–14)
3. Three fetch water from Bethlehem for David (11:15–19)
4. Abshai kills three hundred at once (11:20–21)
5a. Benaiah strikes two Moabite sons of Ariel (11:22a)
5b. Benaiah kills a lion in a pit (11:22b)
5c. Benaiah kills an Egyptian giant (11:23)

Five mighty men are named, and five is the number of military power—five fingers to grasp a sword, five in a rank, five heroes or groups of heroes. But these five perform *seven* mighty acts. They help David form and fill a small cosmos in Israel. The creation symbolism is reinforced when we note that three anonymous heroes do one of the famous deeds; there are four (four corners, four winds) named heroes and three unnamed, for a total of seven. We note other patterns:

2 named + 3 unnamed + 2 named; Jashobeam and Abshai perform the same feat. Thus, Jashobeam to named to unnamed, then Abshai to named, an A-B-C-A'-B' arrangement.

The specific exploits demonstrate the truth of the confession of 11:2: even while Saul is king, David is the one who leads Israel out to battle and back home to celebrate victory. Designated as future shepherd, he functions as present shepherd. While a fugitive, while in exile, he proves a better protector and provider than Saul. David and Eleazar defend a plot of barley against Philistines and thus stall a Philistine advance. Passover takes place at the barley harvest, so the "salvation" (11:14) they achieve is linked with the deliverance from Egypt. Barley is food for horses, donkeys, and the poor who are the pack humans of ancient Near Eastern society, but David and Eleazar do not think them expendable. They win a victory and so provide the food of salvation to the poor. David and Eleazar protect and provide; they are shepherds of Israel. With this Passover exploit, David is shown to be a new Moses.

Like Yahweh in the wilderness, David gives bread and water and thus serves as a figure of another Good Shepherd who offers bread and wine. Jesus, too, gathers a small band and shepherds Israel while persecuted by the established shepherds. Jesus's band, like David's, grows after Pentecost to become a great company, a new-Israel host of God, gathered from all tribes of the earth.

Three of the thirty break through a Philistine garrison at Bethlehem ("house of bread") to bring David water from the well at the gate. David refuses to drink this unsurpassable water. It is virtually the blood of men who risked their lives to get it, and David treats it like blood, pouring it out on the ground. David will not refresh himself by sending his men into death. Before he becomes king, he proves himself an ideal king. He will defend a barley field to feed his people; he will *not* exploit the bold prowess of his mighty men for personal pleasure. His men take risks, but he will not make them spear fodder (cf. Pratt 2006: 117).

Three of Benaiah's exploits are recounted (11:22–25). He defeats two lionlike Moabites (sons of Ariel = "sons of the lion of God") and a giant Egyptian, and so defends Israel from foreign invasions. Benaiah's victory over the Egyptian is reminiscent of David's over the Gittite Goliath; he takes out a giant with nothing more than a stick and kills him with his own spear, like a weaver's beam (11:23; cf. 1 Sam. 17:7). He also kills a lion in a pit on a snowy day (11:22; one of the most evocative lines in biblical history!). It is another David-like exploit; before David kills Goliath, he fights lions and bears. Benaiah is also a new Samson, killing a lion. Though he does not gather honey from the lion as Samson does (a symbol of the restoration of the land of honey by Samson's victory over the Philistines), Benaiah does open a well. Like a later Hero, he descends to a pit to fight a beast and to release living water for Israel. He is well named: Benaiah means "Yahweh has built" but sounds like "son of Yahweh." As one of David's heroes, Benaiah is a shepherd who protects and provides.

First Chronicles 11 ends with a long list of David's *gibborim*. It is, strikingly, an international force, including an Ammonite (11:39), a Hittite (11:41), and a Moabite (11:46). Israel invaded and conquered the land with a "mixed multitude" (Exod. 12:38), and David reconquers and extends Israel's territory with a similar force, an army where Israelites of every tribe are knit together with Gentiles into the host of God. David is the scion of a Jew-Gentile royal house (→ 1 Chr. 2:1–4:23), and his company reflects the racial diversity of his ancestry. He anticipates the end of 2 Chronicles, where a Gentile emperor takes up the Davidic task. And beyond, he embodies the union of Jew and Gentile that comes to its fullness in the body of his greater Son.[4]

Chronicles envisions Israel as a "host" (*tsaba*) led by David. When "all Israel" gathers, they are represented by elders and army captains, and even the Levitical singers are established by David and the commanders of the host (1 Chr. 25:1). To be an Israelite is to be enlisted in the host of the Davidic king, which is the host of Yahweh Sabaoth, Yahweh of Armies. King + Israel, as Johnstone puts it, is a "sacrament" of the Lord and his hosts ("like the army of God" in 12:22 is not "hyperbole," contra Pratt 2006: 121).

When Israel gathers at Hebron to make David king, they greet him with a declaration: "Behold, we are your bone and your flesh" (1 Chr. 11:1). It is a declaration of kinship, but also echoes Adam's declaration in Gen. 2 concerning

---

4. The description of the giant of Gath in chapter 20 hints at other dimensions of these heroic battles. He is said to be a "man of stature" (*'ish middah*), literally a "man of measure" (20:6–8). *Middah* is typically used in architectural texts, referring to the measurements of tabernacle (Exod. 28:2, 8–9; 36:15) or temple (1 Kgs. 6:15; 7:9, 11, 37; 2 Chr. 3:3) curtains, furnishings, and areas. Ezekiel uses the term twenty-five times in chapters 40–48, all referring to measurements of his visionary temple, and in Nehemiah the term refers to "measured sections" of the city wall. A man of measure is large, even monumental; he is a walking building, perhaps a walking sanctuary, the human house of an idol. By overthrowing a man of stature, Jonathan overthrows the Philistine gods. Measured things are holy, devoted to God; and a man of measure is unwillingly sanctified to glorify Yahweh's name. Men of measure are mountainous men, but they are ground to rubble before David's giant-killers. In several other places, *middah* refers to human beings. Isaiah 45:14 envisions a day when Sabean "men of stature" will come to bow to the God of Israel and to the Israelites themselves. They are great, monumental men, but they are also measured because they have been devoted to Yahweh's service. Aaron is described in similar terms in Ps. 133: unity of the brethren is like oil on Aaron's head that comes to the edge of his *middah*. The psalm compares the priest to Mount Hermon. The priest is himself a mountainous man, a monumental figure, a temple-in-person, measured because he is devoted to the Lord from head to hem.

the woman Yahweh builds for him (Hahn 2012: 48–49). Coronation is marriage ceremony, uniting David as the bridegroom to Israel the bride.

Put these together: Israel is host. Israel is bride. Therefore, Israel is a warrior bride. And so is the church. Baptism is incorporation into the body that is the bride, and for that very reason is an enlistment in the host of the greater David, deployed in a spiritual war.

There is an anomaly. In Gen. 2 Adam the bridegroom declares Eve "bone of my bone, and flesh of my flesh." In 1 Chr. 11 the people (presumably the bride) say the same to David (presumably the bridegroom). The inversion suggests that David the bridegroom takes the role of bride, while Israel the bride speaks like a bridegroom. That fits the monarchical theology of the Chronicler, which treats David as the "executive of God" while insisting that "the monarchy is but the instrument of the people's realization of their destiny" (Johnstone 1998a: 144). David's warriors "help" him, but David is also anointed as a "helper" suitable to Israel, an Eve to a new-Adamic humanity of Israel.

First Chronicles 12 is a flashback. The Chronicler has told the story of Saul's death at the battle of Mount Gilboa. He has described how "all Israel" gathered to David at Hebron to make him king over all Israel (11:1–3). At the beginning of chapter 12, we move back to a time when David is exiled in Philistia, living in the city of Ziklag, which Achish the king of Gath had given to him (12:1; cf. 1 Sam. 27:6). Saul tries to kill David twice, and with the help of Saul's son Jonathan, David eventually flees the land.

While in Ziklag, David is "restricted" because of Saul (12:1). The verb is significant. David is king-designate, and even during Saul's reign he acts as king (Japhet 1993: 260). As the tribes say when they meet David at Hebron, "even when Saul was king, you were the one who led out and brought in Israel; and Yahweh your God said to you, 'You shall shepherd My people Israel, and you shall be prince over My people Israel'" (11:2). For the moment, David is "restricted." David is king in all but title, but his going in and out is constrained. He is not able to shepherd because there is a false shepherd in his way.

Yahweh does not leave David in that restricted place. While David is in Philistia, the Lord sends help. The word "help" appears seven times in 12:1–22 (12:1, 17, 18 [2×], 19, 21, 22; Hahn 2012: 48; Japhet 1993: 260; McConville 1984: 27–28), and several of the men who come to David have the word "help" (ezer) as part of their name: Ahiezer ("my brother helps," 12:3), Joezer ("Yah helps," 12:6), and just plain Ezer ("help," 12:9). David goes into Philistia alone, but the Lord knows that it is not good for David to be alone. So he sends helpers suitable for David. God helps David, and that divine help takes the very human form of mighty men skilled with sling, bow, sword, and shield. God's help comes in the form of lion-faced Gadites, as swift as mountain gazelles (12:8). They are like composite cherubim, warriors like the warriors of Yahweh's army, with their four faces and wings. As a host of cherubim surround Yahweh, so a host of cherubic warriors surround David.

Gad settled in the Transjordan, and to join David at Ziklag they have to cross the river. First Chronicles 12:15 says that they cross the river at its height, when it is overflowing the banks. They replicate the miracle crossing of Israel during the time of Joshua, when all Israel entered the land through the Jordan when it was overflowing its banks (Josh. 3:15; 4:18; Japhet 1993: 262). As they cross, the "valleys" flee before them. Literally, this means that they make the *residents* of the valleys flee, the Jordan valley in particular. Like the armies of Israel under Joshua, they strike terror into the people of the land, here the people who remain allied with Saul. The Hebrew is more poetic: the Gadites make the valleys themselves flee. When Yahweh comes in his glory, valleys rise up and mountains melt, and cherubic Gadites are like the army of God. With warriors like the Gadites, David has a fair bid to reconquer the land, to lead Israel from slavery under Philistia-Egypt.

David needs help, and God provides help in the form of helpers. And so chapter 12 traces a progression: David is restricted because of Saul; David gets help; then David becomes king at Hebron. Ultimately, David brings Yahweh's throne into Jerusalem. This is how the kingdom comes: from constriction to Yahweh's rule through Yahweh's help. This process begins before David becomes king. While David is still in Ziklag, while Saul is still king, David's army already becomes a "sacrament" of the army of God (Johnstone 1998a: 164–65). He increases as Saul decreases, because Saul drives his best men into the arms of David. Even in the stronghold, even in exile, even when he is restricted, David rises while Saul descends.

The same dynamic is in play in the history of the prophets during the divided kingdom (1 Kgs. 17 to 2 Kgs. 10). Elijah goes alone into the wilderness, but the Lord sends help in the form of Elisha. Over the lifetime of these two prophets, the Lord forms a company of prophets who are prepared to reconquer the land. David's history foreshadows the same process in the life of Jesus. Jesus offends the Jewish leaders, and they want to kill him. He withdraws from Israel, and mighty men gather to him—mighty men like Peter and Andrew and James and John, men of prowess and wisdom who understand the times and defect from the mainstream of Israel to cling to Jesus the Bridegroom. A renewed Israel emerges from within Israel, led by the anointed Jesus, who is king even though he does not bear the title of king. Even for Jesus, it is not good for a king to be alone. The same process is repeated throughout the history of the church. Faithful Christians have often found themselves excluded from the centers of power, forced into exile, often by other Christians. But when the Lord sends a remnant into exile, he does not leave them alone. He sends help, and eventually he fulfills his promise to place David on the throne.

The Chronicler gives particular attention to David's reception of men from Judah and Benjamin (1 Chr. 12:16–18). He greets Saul's kinsmen with understandable suspicion, asking whether they have come in peace or to betray him. Clothed by the Spirit, Amasai assures David of their intentions. The first two verses, 12:17–18, run in neat parallel:

A *David* said:
　B If you come in *peace*
　　C to *help*, my heart will be one with you.
　　　D If you come to betray, *God* judge between us.

Amasai responds:

A′ We are yours, *David*.
　B′ *Peace, peace, peace*
　　C′ to him who *helps*.
　　　D′ *God helps* you!

This answer seals the union. Since they come in peace, peace, peace to help, help, David's heart is knit to theirs. He is already bone and flesh with Israel (11:1). Now, they are united not only in flesh but also in heart by the Spirit (McConville 1984: 30, 32–33).[5]

---

5. This scene exhibits what Hahn has called a "pattern of camaraderie":

　All that David accomplishes he does in consultation and cooperation with the people. The word used again and again is "all" (*kol*)—all Israel, all the assembly, all the people, all the rest of the people. Reference is made to the perfect sympathy of the people with David, their "singleness of purpose" and "single mind" (12:33, 38). . . . Long lists are provided of the names of those who allied themselves with David. Joab is credited with the capture of Jerusalem; David's slaying of Goliath is overlooked while Elhanan's killing of Goliath's brother is mentioned (20:5). The people are not passive investors in David's fortunes; the kingdom is more than one man. The men around David are shown as making considered decisions of allegiance and self-sacrifice

Like Moses, David is frequently seen at the head of an assembly. Like many of the great scenes of Chronicles, the coronation of David ends with joy (Boda 2010: 123). The kingdom transfers from Saul to David not by violence or the sword but peacefully and joyously, as Israel forms a *qahal* (assembly) in the wilderness in the presence of Yahweh (Japhet 1993: 267).

David and the Ark (1 Chronicles 13–16)

First Chronicles 13–15 describes two ark processions, while chapter 16 describes the erection of the ark tent and the organization of worship in Jerusalem. The first section, chapters 13–15, is organized as a modified chiasm:

A   First attempt to transport the ark (13:1–14)
   B   David's house (14:1)
      C   David's exaltation (14:2)
         D   David's sons in Jerusalem (14:3–7)
            E   Two victories over Philistines (14:8–16)
      C'   David's name goes out (14:17)
   B'   David's house (15:1a)
         D'   List of Levites (15:1b–10)
A'   Second attempt to transport the ark (15:11–29)

The D/D' sections are anomalous and perhaps should be incorporated into other sections—David's sons included in C and the list of Levites included in A'.

The latter portion of the passage (15:2–16:3) is itself a modified chiasm:

A   David's intent to bring the ark to Jerusalem (15:2)
   B   David's assembly of all Israel (15:3)
      C   Priests and Levites (15:4–11)
         D   David's speech to priests and Levites (15:12–15)
      C'   Organization of the Levites (15:16–24)
A'   Procession of the ark to Jerusalem (15:25–29)
   B'   David's blessing and dismissal of the assembly (16:1–3)

---

and impassioned oaths of loyalty; according to the Chronicler, they offer indispensable help to the king and his kingdom. The message to the Chronicler's audience is clear: their own zeal and devotion to rebuilding the kingdom will be remembered. (2012: 48)

First Chronicles 16:1–3 both concludes the ark's ascent and begins the following chapter. Chapter 16 has a roughly chiastic structure:

A David places the ark in the tent (16:1–3)
  B David appoints Levites to minister to the ark (16:4–6)
    C Asaph and Levites sing a psalm of thanks (16:7–36)
  B' David arranges for the ark and the Mosaic tabernacle (16:37–42)
A' David dismisses the assembly (16:43)

These chapters initiate a pattern that is replicated, with variations, in later parts of 1 Chronicles. In chapters 13–16 the sequence is this: David plans to bring the ark into Jerusalem; David attempts and fails; David's house is built and Yahweh wins battles; then David successfully brings the ark, organizes the priests and Levites, and installs the ark in Jerusalem. With the temple, the sequence is similar: David plans to build a house for Yahweh; Yahweh sends Nathan to arrest the plan; through Nathan, Yahweh promises to build David a house; then David organizes the priests and Levites in preparation for the temple. In the first sequence, David eventually achieves his plan; in the second, he prepares for a project that will be left to Solomon. David brings Yahweh's throne to Zion; Solomon builds a palace for the throne. Though David leads, the work is not the king's alone. "All Israel," nobles and people together, gather to bring the ark into Jerusalem (Williamson 1982: 113; Pratt 2006: 127; Japhet [1993: 278] notes that this is a change from 2 Sam. 5).

Johnstone (1998a: 175) notes an overlapping pattern involving house-building and international recognition. The sequence first appears in chapters 14–15: David installs the ark with Obed-edom, and then Huram of Tyre helps him build a palace. It is replicated on a larger scale over the reigns of David and Solomon: David intends to build a temple (1 Chr. 17), and then he is recognized by the nations (1 Chr. 18–20). David prepares and Solomon builds the temple (1 Chr. 21 to 2 Chr. 7), and then Solomon is recognized by Sheba and others (2 Chr. 8–9). At a very general level, this is a figure of the two-generation establishment of the new covenant and the Christian temple. First the greater David takes the throne; then the apostles, playing the role of Solomon, build a house for the throne.

Overarching these sequences is a sabbatical theology. Yahweh commanded Israel to take rest every week, but in taking rest they were also to give rest to their manservants and maidservants, their children and cattle. Yahweh follows his own sabbatical regulations. He will eventually take his rest when he occupies his ark-throne in the temple. But before he takes rest, he *gives* rest to David. Before he dwells in his own house, he builds a house for David. It is a movement of gracious humility. First Yahweh exalts and establishes David's kingdom; then the *meshiach* David establishes Yahweh's throne. First the Son is enthroned at the Father's right hand; at the last day, God will be all in all.

The chapters follow the fortunes of the ark. As soon as David becomes king (1 Chr. 13), he wants to bring the ark of God into Jerusalem (1 Chr. 14). His plan comes to an abrupt halt when Yahweh kills Uzza for stretching out a hand to touch the ark. The ark disappears from view for a chapter, and then David successfully brings the ark into the city in 1 Chr. 16. In between, David goes to war, a sign of the "fusion" of David's wars and Yahweh's kingship (Japhet 1993: 275). Prayer is the key to David's victories. He asks and seeks Yahweh before each battle (14:10, 14; Boda 2010: 134; Japhet 1993: 287). In this the Chronicler continues his habit of setting David and Saul in contrast (Throntveit 2003: 378; McConville 1984: 40; Pratt 2006: 133–35). Each time, he uses the verb *sha'al*, the basis for the name Saul (*sha'ul*). David proves a better Saul than Saul; Saul was the asked-for king who did not ask God or seek him (10:13–14), while David is the king who asks God for help.

Because David exalts Yahweh's ark, Yahweh exalts him among the nations. The name of Huram, king of Tyre, is "related to the root of *herem*, 'devoted thing,'" and would have been understood by the Chronicler's readers as a "devoted one." Huram fulfills the demand placed on Israel, "the absolute requirement on Israel to devote to God everything that is due to him. Huram, the 'righteous Gentile,' does just that" (Johnstone 1998a: 176). Gentiles are going to be *herem* one way or another: they may, like the Canaanites, be subjected to the ban, a war of utter destruction, or they may subject themselves utterly to the God of Israel. They are devoted to God either way, as Paul indicates when he describes himself as a priest offering the Gentiles to God (Rom. 16). Contra John Calvin (*Sermons on Second Samuel*, in Cooper and Lohrmann 2016: 549), David does not sin by allying with a "miserable pagan."

The story of David's installation of the ark in Jerusalem can be told as a series of "outbursts" (see Johnstone 1998a: 169; McConville 1984: 41). The verb *parats* is used four times in chapters 13–15, and the noun *perets* five times, twice by itself (13:11; 14:11) and three times in place names. The story begins with an outburst from David. He says to the assembly of commanders and princes, "Let us burst [*parats*] out and send" (13:2 AT). Johnstone (1998a: 169) suggests that the verb highlights the impetuous nature of David's plan. David does not assemble Levites; he does not consult the law of Moses; he just bursts out with a plan.

The plan is upset when Uzza reaches for the ark and Yahweh bursts out (*parats*) against him (13:11), leading David to call the place "Outburst of Uzza" (*perets 'uzza'*, 13:11). This series of events repeats the establishment of the Mosaic tabernacle: as soon as it was erected, Aaron's sons offered strange fire and were killed (Lev. 10). David places the ark in the house of Obed-edom and goes off to fight Philistines.

Instead of destroying Obed-edom's house, the Lord blesses it, and eventually David is able to bring the ark to the capital, using Levites this time (1 Chr. 15). Obed-edom's ethnicity is ambiguous. Though identified as a Gittite, he is also included in lists of Levites (15:24; 16:5, 38). Obed-edom may have been a member of the tribe of Levi born in Philistia or resident in Philistia for a time. It is possible that his family was among the exiles who joined David in Ziklag, a city under the hegemony of Gath. Obed-edom's name ("servant of Edom") suggests otherwise, and there is another explanation: he was ethnically Philistine, a Gentile who was adopted into the Levitical clan after successfully caring for the ark. Just as Joshua conquered the land with a "mixed multitude" of Israelites and Gentiles, so David reconquers the land and raises up the Lord's throne only with the assistance of Gentiles. Israel was never supposed to be isolated from Gentiles; incorporating Gentiles was essential to the success of Israel's mission.

One detail of 1 Chr. 13 supports this, or is at least consistent with it. Typically, the ark is identified as "ark of the covenant" or even "ark of the covenant of Yahweh of Hosts." Both names highlight the unique relationship between God and Israel because they use the term "covenant" and the covenant name Yahweh, the name that is Yahweh's presence with Israel (Pratt 2006: 128). In 1 Chr. 13 it is the "ark of *God*" (*elohim*), a more universal designation (Johnstone 1998a: 170). The ark-throne of *Elohim* is established not just by Israel but by all humanity, Jews and Gentiles. God's kingdom comes when Jews and Gentiles unite around the throne.

While the ark rests at the house of Obed-edom, David wins a battle at Baal-perazim, summarized in 14:11, which uses the Hebrew *parats/perets* four times:

A They came to Baal-*peratsim*
  B Yahweh has burst out (*parats*) against my enemies
  B' Like the outburst (*perets*) of waters
A' So they called the place Baal-*peratsim*

David learns his lesson. If he wants the Lord to burst out against the enemies and not the servants of the Lord, he needs to seek the Lord according to his ordinance (15:13). In the end, he proves to be a true son of "Perez," Judah's son who "broke through" to become preeminent over his brother Zerah.

As noted above (→ 1 Chr. 7–9), the Hebrew word *ma'al* is a key term in Chronicles. It means "act of unfaithfulness" or "sacrilege" and is the sin that leads to Saul's fall (he *ma'al*-ed a *ma'al*; → 1 Chr. 10:13) and to the exile of Judah, whose officials and priests *ma'al*-ed a *ma'al* (2 Chr. 36:14). David does not commit a *ma'al*. Instead, because of his faithfulness in seeking Yahweh, his kingdom is "highly exalted" in the eyes of Gentile rulers like Huram (1 Chr. 14:2). "Highly" translates the Hebrew *lema'lah*, which contains the same consonants as *ma'al* (sacrilege). The verb *'alah*, "to ascend or go up," is the root of the word for "ascension offering" (burnt offering) and a commonly used term for social, spiritual, or physical ascent. As "sacrilege" is a leitmotif in the brief account of Saul's reign and for the reigns of other unfaithful kings, so the punning term for "exalt" recurs throughout the Chronicler's account of the reigns of David and Solomon. David says that the temple will be "exceedingly magnificent" (1 Chr. 22:5), his contributions to the temple are elevated (1 Chr. 29:3), and Solomon himself is highly exalted (2 Chr. 1:1). Other faithful kings are also lifted up (Jehoshaphat, 2 Chr. 17:12; Uzziah, 2 Chr. 26:8). The choice before Israel's kings is between *ma'al* and *ma'alah*, between sacrilege and exaltation. Unfaithfulness brings kings down; faithfulness lifts them up on high.

After defeating the Philistines, David turns his attention to the ark. His war against Philistia recapitulates Yahweh's war on Egypt and its gods. Like Moses, David is Yahweh's instrument for victory, and then, again like Moses, he becomes the hyperactive builder of an ark-tent and omnicompetent organizer of an ark-cult. After the first attempt ends in Uzza's death, David determines that Israel violated the ordinance, the word of God through Moses (1 Chr. 15:13, 15). He makes sure they do not make the same mistake a second time. David prepares a place for the ark (15:1; 16:1). David declares that only Levites can bear the ark (15:2). David assembles Israel (15:3). David summons priests and Levites (15:4). David instructs priests and Levites about their duties, and they obey (15:11–15). David tells Levitical princes to appoint musicians (15:15). David, with elders and captains, brings the ark (15:25). David leaps before the ark (15:29). David leads the offering of ascension and peace offerings (16:2). David blesses the people (16:2). David apportions bread and raisins to Israel (16:3). David appoints Levites and priests as permanent ministers before the ark (16:4). David leaves Asaph and his brothers in charge of the ark (16:37). David returns home to bless his own house (16:43). David, David, David—it is all David. He does not work alone, but he initiates nearly everything. David does not construct the temple, but he constructs the priests and Levites around the ark as a human house of God.

David gathers eight chiefs of seven clans of priests and Levites: Zadok and Abiathar of Aaron, Uriel of Kohath, Asaiah of Merari, Joel of Gershom, Shemaiah of Elizaphan, Eliel of Hebron, and Amminadab of Uzziel (15:4–11). The last three groups are subdivisions of the clan of Kohath, which is responsible for the transport of the ark (Num. 4:1–20). The total number of Levites is 862, the gematria of *tabnit*, the word for "pattern" in tabernacle and temple texts (cf. Exod. 25:9, 40; → 1 Chr. 28:19). The priests form the pattern for the house. Under Yahweh's inspiration, David forms a human temple of living stones.

David instructs these "heads" (*rosh*; 15:12) to consecrate themselves to bear the ark. Yahweh's throne rides on the shoulders (15:15) of the consecrated heads of Israel as they "bring up" the ark. The verb is *'alah*, "ascend." God's throne ascends to its place on the shoulders of holy priests, functionally angels who hold up the throne. The ark ascends through the cloud of sacrificial smoke (15:26) and through an aural cloud of sacrificial song (15:16–24). Yahweh ascends as the Levites "lift up [*rum*] a voice of joy" (15:16 AT).

David organizes the Levites to form this path of song. The text is a complicated, repetitive list, but has an order to it—three sections punctuated by references to gatekeepers:

1. Three leading singers, fourteen secondary musicians, *gatekeepers* (15:17–18)
2. Three cymbal players, eight harpists, six players of lyres, Chenaniah the prince, *gatekeepers* (15:19–23)
3. Seven priests with trumpets, *gatekeepers* (15:24)

The numerology is dense. There are a total of seventy gatekeepers (Boda 2010: 147), which is the number of Gentile nations (Gen. 10) and the number of Israel when it represents the Gentiles (Exod. 1:5). There are seventeen names in the first list, the gematria of *kabod*, "glory." Yahweh is enthroned within his radiant glory; now he comes to be enthroned in the musical glory of Israel. When the seven priests are added, we have twenty-four, and a "chief," Chenaniah. That anticipates the eventual structure of the priesthood, with its twenty-four clans and single high priest, as well as the organization of the Levitical singers into a permanent structure of twenty-four groups.

Chenaniah's ("Yah is gracious") role is puzzling (15:22, 27). He is a prince (*sar*) of the Levites who is skillful and gives direction in *massaʾ*. In Torah, the word *massaʾ* is typically used to refer to the physical labor of transporting/bearing the tabernacle, but in 1 Chr. 15 it has to do with music. It is one of a number of priestly and Levitical terms that take on new meanings; the physical bearing of the ark is transformed into the work of "bearing up" Yahweh's throne in song (see Kleinig 2009: 47). The Chronicler's contrast of Saul and David continues to the end of chapter 15. David seeks God, Saul does not. David cares for the ark that Saul neglected. Saul's daughter Michal despises David's celebration (15:29), continuing in the tradition of her neglectful father (Japhet 1993: 305). We recall that she was barren (2 Sam. 6), marking an end of Saul's family (Boda 2010: 142).

Once the ark is securely in Jerusalem, David appoints a permanent set of musicians. Ten are appointed under the leadership of Asaph, and then the Chronicler informs us that Asaph plays cymbals (16:5) and the priests blow trumpets (16:6). Lyres and harps drop out for the moment, and the music reduces to brass and percussion, without strings. In total, twelve musicians, gathered to *yudah*—to give praise to Yahweh (16:7). They represent all Israel carrying out the royal-Judaic task of praise. The musicians are eventually split into two groups: those who remain in Jerusalem to serve the ark (16:37–38) and the priests and Levitical musicians who serve the Mosaic tabernacle at Gibeon (16:39–43). That double house of music will eventually become one in Solomon's temple. David proves himself a good shepherd by constructing a holy house of musicians, a place for Yahweh's throne filled with the glory of song, a refreshing pasture for the sheep.

First Chronicles 16:8–36 is a long sample of praise. As commentators point out (e.g., Japhet 1993: 312), the psalm consists of three psalms from the fourth book of the Psalter (which begins at Ps. 90). First Chronicles 16:8–22 matches Ps. 105:1–15; the following verses, 16:23–33, are taken from Ps. 96:1–13; and the last few verses of the Chronicler's psalm, 16:34–36, are from the first and final verses of Ps. 106, which closes the fourth book of the Psalter.

It is no accident that the psalm draws from book 4 of the Psalter. Book 3 (Ps. 73–89) ends with a lament over the fallen house of David: "Where are Your former lovingkindnesses, O Lord, / Which You swore to David in Your faithfulness?" (89:49). Psalm 90 turns attention away from the Davidic covenant; it is the only psalm of Moses in the Psalter, and it speaks of God as eternal Creator. A number of the following psalms, including Ps. 96, celebrate Yahweh's kingship, which persists even when David's kingdom has faltered. The composite psalm of 1 Chr. 16 is appropriate to the Chronicler's time period, after the collapse of the house of David, a period of restoration *without* a Davidic king when Israel will have to depend on the eternal King, the God of heaven who stirs the spirit of Gentile protectors. When the Levites first sing the song at the ark-shrine, they do not yet know the depth of its truth.

First Chronicles 16 is an *act* of praise. It is also, perhaps more, an *exhortation* to praise. The opening section, drawn from Ps. 105, contains an "all-Israel" collection of twelve imperatives to worship. It begins with a dense cluster of commands, six in the first two verses, a thesaurus of praise:

1. Praise (*yadah*) Yahweh (16:8a).
2. Call (*qara'*) on his name (16:8b).
3. Make known (*yada'*) his deeds (16:8c).
4. Sing (*shir*) to him (16:9a).
5. Sing praise (*zamar*) (16:9b).
6. Speak (*siakh*) of his wonders (16:9c).

Over the next two verses, four more imperatives are added:

7. Glory (*halal*) in his name (16:10a).
8. Be glad (*samakh*) in heart (16:10b).
9. Seek (*darash*) Yahweh (16:11a).
10. Seek (*baqash*) his face (16:11b).

In sum, there are ten commandments of praise in four verses.

The remainder of the excerpt from Ps. 105 is divided into two exhortations to "remember":

11. Remember (*zakar*) his deeds (16:12–14).
12. Remember (*zakar*) his covenant (16:15–22).

These last sections contain a brief review of Israel's history. Yahweh's wonderful works are the works of exodus, and the covenant is explicitly the covenant with Abraham, Isaac, and Jacob, the covenant pledge of the land of Canaan. The exhortation means "remember and praise"; it also means "memorialize in praise," that is, "remind Yahweh of his deeds and covenant so that he will do it again and again."

In 16:23–33 the scope expands to encompass Gentiles. They are already in view in the opening section; by giving thanks and calling on God's name, Israel makes Yahweh's works known among the peoples (16:8b). But the following section exhorts the nations to join the praise of Israel. Again, the psalm is both an act and an exhortation, now to the nations:

1. Sing (*shir*) to Yahweh (16:23a).
2. Proclaim good news (*basar*) of salvation (*yeshu'ah*) (16:23b).
3. Record (*saphar*) his glory (16:24a).

Yahweh does "wonderful deeds" (*niphle'otaw*) among the Gentiles (16:24b), as he does for Israel (16:12a), and so is a great God, greater than the idols in his splendor, majesty, strength, and joy (16:27). The call to praise is thus simultaneously a call to abandon idols (16:26a). Verse 28 returns to imperatives:

4. Ascribe (*yahav*) to Yahweh (16:28a).
5. Ascribe (*yahav*) glory and strength (16:28b).
6. Ascribe (*yahav*) glory due his name (16:29a).
7. Bring (*nasa'*) tribute (*minkhah*) (16:29b).
8. Come (*bo'*) before his face (16:29c).
9. Prostrate (*shakhah*) to Yahweh (16:29d).
10. Tremble (*khul*) before him (16:30a).

In this psalm, then, there are twelve liturgical commandments for the twelve tribes and ten for the nations, a total of twenty-two commands, matching the number of letters in the Hebrew alphabet. The psalm is an *aleph*-to-*tav* of praise.

The variation of terms is doubtless significant. Israel is called to *yadah*, the root of the name Judah; Israel's peculiar role is to make the Lord known among the nations and to seek him; Israel is the people of remembrance, keeping alive the memory of God's deeds and covenant, so that the nations can praise him and ascribe glory. Yet the nations are not left at a distance. They draw near with their tribute offerings and are called to prostrate to Yahweh, Gentiles dressed like priests "in holy (!) array" (16:29b).

At 16:31 the scope of the exhortation widens further: first Israel, then Gentiles, now the entire creation gets into the act, praising the coming of the judge. Again, the psalm is an exhortation to praise:

1. Be glad (*sameakh*), heavens (16:31a).
2. Rejoice (*gil*), earth (16:31b).
3. Say (*amar*), Yahweh reigns (16:31c). (The "them" in "let them say" is "heaven and earth.")
4. Roar (*ra'am*), sea (16:32a).
5. Exult (*'alats*), field (16:32b).

The closing snatch from Ps. 106 begins with another exhortation to worship, returning to the terminology of the initial exhortation in 16:8: give thanks (*yadah*) to Yahweh (16:34a). We are back to Israel/Judah, the people who above all can declare Yahweh's *hesed*, his covenant loyalty and family love. It is the twenty-eighth (7 × 4) exhortation to praise. Praise is multiplied through seven days and to the four corners. Sabbatical praise stretches to the ends of the earth, turning the entire world into a four-horned altar.

The final verses, also taken from the end of Ps. 106, turn the imperatives around. Instead of calling Israel, the nations, and the creation to praise, the psalm ends with a triple plea to Yahweh:

1. Save (*yasha'*), God of our salvation (*yish'enu*) (16:35a).
2. Gather (*qavats*) us (16:35b).
3. Deliver (*natsal*) (16:35c).

Salvation is not an end in itself, and the psalm gives the reason for asking Yahweh to save, gather, and deliver: "To give thanks [*yadah*] to Your holy name, / And glory [*shavakh*] in Your praises [*tahillah*]." Israel wants another exodus so that they can come to the Lord's mountain to serve him. Israel wants to be saved so that they can become Judah, so they can fulfill their vocation of praise/*yadah*. The psalm traces a great circle of praise: Israel praises Yahweh so that he is praised among the nations; Israel praises Yahweh so that he will remember his covenant and gather Israel from the nations, gather them as a choral host, gather them for praise. Israel praises so they can keep praising, incorporating more and more of humanity and of creation into their sacrifice of thanks. A people that sings like this will not be alarmed when salvation comes in the form of a Gentile emperor who builds the house of Israel's God.

The psalm is not a one-off. David leaves Levites behind to carry out a continuous round of praise. Everyone who has read Gen. 1 knows that Hebrews reckoned time from night till day. "Evening and morning, one day" is a refrain of the creation week (Gen. 1:5, 8, 13, 19, 23, 31). Lamps in the tabernacle burned continually (*tamid*), that is, from evening till morning (Lev. 24:3; cf. Exod. 27:21), and the cloud of the Lord's presence remained above the tabernacle "from evening until morning" (Num. 9:21). During Passover, no yeast was to be found in Israelite homes from the sacrifice of the evening of the first day until morning (Deut. 16:4).

That pattern is thrown into reverse midway through the Old Testament. As Israel enters the Davidic era, nearly every passage that uses "evening, morning" in tandem places morning first. Goliath comes to taunt Israelite troops every "morning and evening" (1 Sam. 17:16). Ravens bring bread and meat to Elijah— like worshipers winging their way to offer sacrifice to God—"in the morning ... [and] in the evening" (1 Kgs. 17:6). Ahaz offers ascensions and tributes on his illegitimate altar—ascensions in the morning and grain offerings at night (2 Kgs. 16:15).

In Chronicles, this reversed pattern is explicitly used to describe the work of priests and Levites. During David's reign, Zadok and his brothers are left at the Mosaic tabernacle to offer ascensions *tamid*, "morning and evening" (1 Chr. 16:39–40). David establishes Levites to offer praise and thanks every morning and evening (1 Chr. 23:30), and once Solomon builds the temple, ascensions are offered "every morning and evening and on Sabbaths, at the New Moons and at the appointed festivals of Yahweh our God" (2 Chr. 2:4 AT; cf. 2 Chr. 13:11; Ezra 3:3).

There are anomalies in both the Mosaic and Davidic eras. Moses sits, making decisions for Israel from morning till evening (Exod. 18:13–14), and the grain offering at the ordination of Aaron is split into morning and evening offerings (Lev. 6:20). On the other hand, Daniel reckons visionary time as a collection of "evenings and mornings" (Dan. 8:14, 26). Still, the reversal is too dramatic and the pattern too consistent to be accidental. Moses's tabernacle operated by the time of the old creation—from darkness to light—but the tent of the new Moses, David, ticks to a new temporality—from light to darkness. Once the sun of kingship has risen on Israel, it enters a new day, so that its days begin not in darkness but in brilliant light. Already within the old covenant we have a glimpse of the new era of morning.

4

COVENANT WITH DAVID

1 Chronicles 17–20

David has become king. He has conquered the capital city of Jerusalem. He has brought the ark of Yahweh into the city and placed it in a tent. He has stationed Levites at the tent to offer sacrifices of praise. An anomaly hits him: he lives in a cedar-paneled palace, and the Lord is still enthroned within tent curtains. He consults the prophet Nathan, who endorses his desire to build a house for the Lord: "Do all that is in your heart, for God is with you" (1 Chr. 17:2).

It is a typical thing for an ancient king to do: conquer, and then build a house for the god who gives victory. Nathan's is a typical reaction for an ancient prophet in a king's court. Ahab wants to go to war with the Arameans, and his prophets assure him of success. Prophets are there to give a divine stamp to "whatever is in the king's heart."

But the God of Israel is not like other gods, and his prophets are not like other prophets. That night, the word of Yahweh comes to Nathan to correct him. When Nathan delivers the oracle, David is a new Abraham, to whom the "word of the LORD came" to promise the land (Gen. 15:1, 4). Nathan is a Samuel, who is also given a word to correct a king (1 Sam. 15:10). Nathan is the first to be designated a "prophet" within Chronicles, linking him with the later writing prophets to whom "the word of the LORD came." Nathan tells David he will not build the house, which signals yet another link between David and Moses. Moses led Israel from Egypt but did not bring them into the land. David leads Israel from Philistine slavery and establishes Yahweh's throne, but he does not complete the conquest by building the temple. That task will be left to his successor, Solomon, the new Joshua. David remains within the Mosaic tradition of tent shrines.

The oracle is part historical review, part reminder of Yahweh's commitment to David, and part promise. It is framed by "go and tell David My servant" (1 Chr. 17:4) and "according to all these words and according to all this vision, so Nathan spoke to David" (17:15). Within that frame is a chiasm:

> A   You shall not build a house; I have never dwelt in a house or asked for one (17:4–6)
> > B   Yahweh has been with David; promises a great name (17:7–8)
> > > C   Promises to Israel: appoint a place, plant, no more waste (17:9–10a)
> > B'   Promise to David: I will subdue enemies (17:10b)
> A'   Yahweh will build a house for David, and his son will build a house (17:10c–14)

"House" appears three times in 17:4–6 and another three times in 17:10–14. The whole oracle is enclosed by "not build a house" (in 17:4, a prohibition to David; at the end of 17:6, part of a question). B describes Yahweh's commitment to David, and the reference to victory in 17:10 links back to those promises. The promises to David circulate around the central section, which contains promises not to David but to Israel.

After the initial "you shall not build me a house," section A forms a small chiasm of its own:

> a   I have not dwelt in a house,
> > b   but have gone from tent to tent.
> > b'   In all my walking with Israel
> a'   have I asked any shepherd-judge, Why have you not built me a house of cedar?

A' is also a chiasm:

> a   Yahweh will build a house for David (17:10c)
> > b   Yahweh will establish kingdom of David's son (17:11)
> > > c   David's son shall build a house for Yahweh (17:12a)

b′ Yahweh will establish his throne as his own son (17:12b–13)
a′ Yahweh will settle David's son in Yahweh's own house and kingdom (17:14)

Along the way, Yahweh moves from speaking of "your house" to speaking of "My house" (Pratt 2006: 25).

The nighttime oracle is actually two oracles (noted by Johnstone 1998a: 201–6). Each has the basic structure of a covenant formula: Both begin with a "thus says Yahweh" (17:4, 7). Both review Yahweh's history with Israel. Both summarize the demands of the covenant. The first briefly recounts the Lord's peripatetic life from the exodus through the time of the judges, walking with Israel, moving from house to house (17:5–6). The second oracle focuses on Yahweh's history with David himself: he took David from the pasture, elevated him to be prince, and has gone with David wherever he has walked (17:7–8).[1] The second oracle continues in this covenantal vein by stating Yahweh's perpetual commitment to Israel, David, and David's seed (17:8–13).

This promise is multilayered: Yahweh builds a house for David, a people house, and David's son will have his throne in that house. David's son will build a house for Yahweh, the temple, and David's son will have a place in that house as well, since Solomon's palace is part of the temple complex in Jerusalem (cf. 1 Kgs. 6–8). This is not simply a promise that David's house will continue to rule Israel; it is a promise that David's seed will fulfill the destiny of the human race, royal sonship to Yahweh. It is a promise that Yahweh's kingdom will be bound up with David's (Hahn 2012: 76).

Why the double form of the oracle? Why not just get to the covenant commitment in the second oracle? Why not just present the theology of temple reciprocity—Yahweh builds a house for David, David's son builds a house for

---

1. Everyone who has sung a Christmas carol knows that "Immanuel" means "God with us," but centuries of singing about Immanuel have domesticated and sentimentalized the word. "Immanuel" has a history before Isaiah applies it to a child Messiah (Isa. 7). Yahweh's covenant with David forms an important part of the background. In 1 Chr. 17, the Lord reminds David, "I have been with you wherever you walk," and then specifies *how* he has been with David: "I have been with you wherever you have gone, and have cut off all your enemies from before you; and I will make you a name like the name of the great ones who are in the earth" (17:8). David, in short, has been the recipient of the promises to Abraham: Yahweh has cursed those who curse David and has given him a great name. In Isa. 7 the birth of a child identified as "Immanuel" is a sign to King Ahaz, and a sign that reiterates the promise of this Davidic covenant. Do not fear the kings of Aram or Israel, Isaiah tells the king, because the Lord will cut them off. The birth of a child will be the sign of God's presence to give this victory. God is with Jesus, the greater David, for the same purpose: to cut off his enemies and to give him a name above every name. Jesus with us is God with us to realize the Davidic promise among us. He is with us to give us a share in his victory and his great name.

Yahweh, Yahweh places David's son in his house? The question is sharper when we realize that, for all its formal similarities to a covenant decree, the first oracle ends with a *question*. Most covenants are of this form: I am the king; I have done this and that for you; so, you do this and that for me. Here it is: I am Yahweh of Hosts; I have been with Israel; would I ever ask for anything from *you*?

That question is essential if we are going to get the temple theology right. As Johnstone (1998a: 202) points out, the passage highlights the ultimate absurdity of reciprocity in dealings with God. By reminding David that he needs no house, Yahweh reminds David of the utter asymmetry of their relationship. That is an essential point of theology proper if Israel is to perform the temple services rightly. Yahweh's needlessness, his aseity, sets him radically apart from the gods of the nations, who depend on temple-building kings and their offerings of food and service. The first oracle thus establishes a "sacramental" principle of temple theology (Johnstone's term). Will Yahweh be in the temple? *Yes*, his name is there; but *no*, no house, including the house of the cosmos, can contain him. He is / is not there, *in loco*.

Both poles of the paradox are essential. To deny the "is" is to call God a liar, for he has pledged to make himself available to his people. To deny the "is not" is to call God a liar, because a God who can be contained within a temple is no God, not the Lord and Creator of the universe. Without this "sacramental" framework, Israel will inevitably fall into pagan idolatry, confident that they can manipulate and control the God who cannot be controlled. This prototemple theology is an essential foundation for the temple theology itself.

Now, think incarnation. Think ecclesiology. Think real presence. All are founded on the Chronicler's prototemple theology.

All this takes place at night, "the same night" after David proposes the building project (1 Chr. 17:3). Many of God's acts of deliverance begin at night. Jacob escapes from Laban at night (Gen. 31). Passover occurs at night (Exod. 12). Sleepless in Susa, King Ahasuerus listens to the chronicle of his reign and remembers Mordecai (Esth. 6). In his night visions, Zechariah sees the high priest Joshua cleansed and the temple liturgy rebooted (Zech. 4). And Nathan receives this message about David and his descendants at night. In the Passover setting, Solomon is the "firstborn of Israel," the king who represents the entire people delivered from the angel of death and planted in the land.

The nighttime message points to a new exodus setting, and the rest of the chapter confirms that. The word "house," referring to the house of Israel and the house of David and the temple-house, is used fourteen times and brings to mind

Yahweh's deliverance of the house of Israel from the house of bondage in Egypt (Hahn 2012: 71). As Yahweh brought Israel to Sabbath rest in the exodus, so he brings them to share in his own rest when he is enthroned in his house. The word "servant" is used twelve times, the number of Israel, and reminds us of Israel's hard yoke of service in Egypt and the easy yoke that the Lord places on them. Israel is not finally the "servant" of Yahweh. Rather, Israel is Yahweh's "son." That is the reason Yahweh demands that Pharaoh let Israel go: "Israel is My son, My firstborn. . . . Let My son go that he may serve me" (Exod. 4:23). In his prayer of grateful response, David makes an explicit reference to the deliverance from Egypt, which displayed God's uniqueness, and Israel's, when he took one nation from another by doing great and terrible things (1 Chr. 17:21). The covenant with David is a new exodus, a renewal and specification of the covenant at Sinai, focused now on a specific clan within Israel, the family of David. David is a new Moses, but surpasses Moses insofar as he "incarnates" Israel in his own person.

The roots of this promise extend all the way back to creation. David's excited prayer uses a form of God's name twenty times (Japhet 1993: 336). In particular, he prays to Yahweh God, *Yahweh Elohim*, the name used throughout Gen. 2, the account of the Lord's creation of Adam, Eve, and the garden of Eden. The promise goes beyond David's imagination, and it involves more than his own house. "Who am I, O LORD God, and what is my house that You have brought me this far?" (17:16). But this is "a small thing in Your eyes." Yahweh's promise is not merely about David's immediate descendants but about "the distance" (17:17 AT). It does not just pertain to one people or nation. It involves all humanity. The word for "man" in 17:17 is *adam*, and the verb is *'alah*, "ascend." Yahweh makes David "an Adam ascended." By his elevation to kingship, to sonship, to membership in Yahweh's own household and family, David is not only a new Moses but a new Adam, and through David Yahweh pledges to bring humanity as a whole to its fulfillment. David responds by sitting "before Yahweh," perhaps in the ark-shrine in Jerusalem (Merrill 2015: 225). It is a sign of his exaltation that he can *sit* in the presence of Yahweh, something no priest was ever privileged to do.

The gospel announces the fulfillment of this promise. Jesus comes as the son of David, the Son of God, to take the throne and to fulfill Yahweh's pledge to David. From the perspective of the Davidic covenant, the gospel is about God keeping his commitment to the house of David: to make David's house great, to build a house for David, a house out of David, and to display his glory among the nations. It is about the ascent of Adam, the glorification of humanity in Jesus, the son of David. Glimpsing this climax of the covenant leaves David breathless

(17:14). In the covenant with David, Yahweh discloses the good news: Adam, the last Adam, has ascended. Adam, the last Adam, is enthroned as son of David and Son of God. Adam, the last Adam, ascends to his throne so that we might become a kingdom of priests and reign with him on earth.

David's Wars (1 Chronicles 18–20)

Chapters 18–20 bring together David's conquests into a neatly packaged unit.[2] By the end of chapter 20, David has established control over greater Israel, the ideal kingdom promised to Abraham (Gen. 15), stretching from the Euphrates (1 Chr. 18:3) south into Edom, near the brook of Egypt (18:12–13). Though the bulk of these chapters is devoted to describing David's battles, the structural center sums up David's administration of Israel. Domestic justice is the aim of David's war-making. He also fights to ensure domestic prosperity, as he takes control of the trade routes in and out of Israel (Boda 2010: 160–61).

The chapters are organized chiastically, beginning and ending at Gath (Boda 2010: 170):

 A War with Philistia and Moab (18:1)
  B War with Ammon, Aram, and Edom (18:2–13)
   C David reigns with justice and righteousness (18:14–17)
  B' War with Ammon and Aram (19:1–20:3)
 A' War with Philistia (20:4–8)

There are good reasons to conclude that B and B' describe the *same* war. Both involve both Aram and Ammon; in both, David captures 7,000 charioteers (18:4; 19:18); the number of infantry is somewhat confusing, but the 20,000 + 22,000 of 18:4–5 is roughly equal to the 40,000 of 19:18.[3] The chapters also follow a geographic pattern. David conquers Philistia, Moab, Ammon/Aram, and Edom. Philistia is on the Mediterranean coast, to the west of Israel; Moab is east of the Jordan; David fights Hadadezer in Hamath in the far north, and Edom is south, toward the border of Egypt. David's conquests move west to east, north to south.

---

2. In Samuel, the same wars are scattered over several chapters; Japhet (1993: 343) calls this section a "mosaic" drawn from Samuel.

3. Johnstone (1998a: 214) points out that it would have been impossible for Hadadezer to mount a *second* campaign after a defeat as devastating as that described in 18:3–4. Putting the two accounts together clarifies some details. David defeats Hadadezer when he goes to establish his hand at the Euphrates (18:3), and 19:16–19 explains what Hadadezer was doing there: he was organizing an alliance to fight David.

At the least, the geography establishes a four-corner theme, as David prefigures the universal rule of a future Davidic king. One wonders if something else is going on too. The world of the Old Testament takes its symbolic orientation primarily from Israel's sanctuaries, built on an east-west axis with the doorway to the east and the inner sanctuary to the west. Key temple furnishings are at each point of the compass: the bronze altar to the east, the ark to the far west, the menorah to the south, and the table of showbread to the north.[4] David establishes his throne in the west; conquers peoples who pay tribute from the east; sets up watch towers and garrisons to the north; and brings the treasures of the conquered lands to the center, to the sanctuary. David's four-cornered kingdom sets up a "sanctuary" land that replicates on a macro scale the microcosm of Yahweh's house.

David fights just wars, in obedience to Yahweh, in the strength of Yahweh. The Chronicler highlights David's obedience by showing how he conforms to the Torah, especially with regard to plunder. David captures chariot horses but does not use them to create a chariot force. He obeys the prohibition against multiplying horses and chariots (18:4; cf. Deut. 17). David is no Achan. Achan was the Judahite who seized plunder from Jericho, booty that belonged to Yahweh. Achan's *ma'al* led to a humiliating defeat at Ai, which was erased only after Joshua executed Achan and his complicit family (Josh. 7; → 1 Chr. 2:7). When David conquers Gentiles and seizes armor and treasure, he sends it back to Jerusalem, to Yahweh (18:7, 11).

His wars bring peace. He forcibly seizes much of the plunder, but Tou, king of Hamath, gives his tribute *voluntarily*, out of gratitude. Hadadezer had been at war with Tou, and when David defeats Hadadezer, he also liberates Tou. David fights in order to defend Israel (cf. 19:13), but his wars bless Gentiles who are

---

4. James Jordan has argued that spatial orientation in the Bible is also linked to the faces of the cherubim. Working from Ezekiel's vision of the *merkabah*, Yahweh's chariot, he sketches this arrangement: the lion is on the west, facing east; the bull east, facing west; the eagle is south, facing north; the man to the north, facing south. To these he adds another overlay: the lion is royal ("lion of Judah"), the ox is priestly (sacrificial), the eagle is prophetic, and the man unites all three. Now, what might this have to do with David's conquests? David begins with a westward conquest. That is the position of the ark-throne and the lion. He establishes his royal dominion over Gath, setting up his throne toward the sunset. Then he moves east to Moab, to the ox and the altar; fittingly, the eastward Moabites are the first to bring tribute, a "bovine" sacrifice to the lion of Judah. After Abishai conquers Edom in the south, David sets up garrisons (18:13), lamps, and watchers over the southern territory. Overall, David's movement is from throne-lion to ox-altar, then from table-man to lampstand-eagle: lion, ox, man, eagle. That is, interestingly, the same order as the cherub faces in Rev. 4. It is not, however, the movement of Israel's history generally, which moves from priest to king to prophet, finally coming to a climax in the man Jesus. Perhaps the order lion-ox-man-eagle is an order of conquest, while the arrangement ox-lion-eagle-man is a liturgical order. Jordan, "Behind the Scenes: Orientation in the Book of Revelation," 1995, Biblical Horizons Occasional Paper No. 19, Niceville, FL: Biblical Horizons.

willing to befriend him. Like Huram of Tyre later in Chronicles, Tou is a type of the kings who, the prophets promise, will someday stream to Jerusalem, bringing their treasures to the house of God (cf. Rev. 21:24). He is an Epiphany figure, a prototype of the magi, and like the other Gentile kings in Chronicles he anticipates Cyrus ($\rightarrow$ 2 Chr. 36).

Nestled within chapters that describe David's wars, 1 Chr. 18:14–17 explains the purpose of those wars: David's wars mediate Yahweh's justice to the nations in order to establish Yahweh's order of justice in Israel, an order of justice that David himself administers and mediates. Having conquered Philistia, Moab, Ammon, and Edom, David reigns over "all Israel" (18:14), and his reign is a righteous one.

Justice and righteousness mean conformity to Torah. David fights obediently, and he is also Torah-observant in peace. David gives equal justice to all, which brings particular advantages to the weak and vulnerable who, lacking resources of their own, rely on the king's protection (cf. Ps. 72). "Doing justice and righteousness" (*mishpat, tsedaqah*) is explicated with a list of David's officials in the military, court, and temple—officers of war, law, and worship. Though the king "does justice" as the representative of the just God, the king carries out his justice through subordinates. *Mishpat* (like many similar terms in ancient languages) implies the establishment of order, and so doing justice involves organizing institutions and installing personnel. David does justice by setting up an orderly bureaucracy ($\rightarrow$ 1 Chr. 23–27).

David's justice is numerologically represented in the list of names in 18:15–17. Seven officers are mentioned by name (noted also by Boda 2010: 162): Joab is over the army, Jehoshaphat ("Yah judges") is recorder or court historian, Zadok and Abimelech are priests, Shavsha is secretary, Benaiah is over David's personal guard, and David's sons are "chiefs." David is the "eighth" over the entire kingdom. A seven- or eightfold bureaucracy hints at a new-creational theme. The administrators also represent Israel: the Chronicler identifies the administrators by naming their fathers, which expands the list to twelve. David's is a twelvefold court for the twelve tribes.

It may not excite those social justice advocates who prefer grand public gestures to the hard work of seeking justice, but Chronicles shows that orderly administration is essential to doing justice. Think of the roadblocks that a clogged, corrupt, or stagnant bureaucracy throws up, and you have an idea of why David's justice involves appointing righteous men to head up sectors of his kingdom.

As noted above, 19:1–20:3 describes in more detail the circumstances that led to the Ammonite war briefly recounted in 18:2–8. That longer account is also arranged chiastically:

A War with Ammon begins (19:1–5)
>   B Ammon allies with Aram (19:6–9)
>   C First war with Aram: Joab wins (19:10–15)
>   C′ Second war with Aram: David wins (19:16–18)
>   B′ Aram makes peace with David (19:19)
> A′ Joab takes Rabbah of Ammon (20:1–3)

Though the frame records the cause (Hanun's insult of David's messengers) and conclusion (David wears the Ammonite crown) of the Ammonite war, the center is concerned with Ammon's alliance with Aram. The Arameans provide the overwhelming chariot force (32,000, 19:7; think *tanks*), and they are the ones who regroup to fight again (19:16). Joab's and David's battles both focus on fighting Arameans (19:14, 18). David's handling of Arameans is essential to his victory over the Ammonites.

In Samuel, this is the war that is going on when David stays back in Jerusalem, commits adultery with Bathsheba, and covers it up by killing Uriah. There is nothing of that in the Chronicler's version. Instead, he focuses on the war itself, its origins, conduct, and conclusion. In the absence of the Bathsheba incident, the war story has a very different significance.

The war begins with a public insult. When King Nahash of Ammon dies, David sends his condolences to his son Hanun (1 Chr. 19). Saul defeated Nahash (1 Sam. 11; Boda 2010: 165), and at some unspecified time David allied with him. Nahash showed love-and-loyalty (*hesed*) to David, so David returns *hesed* (19:2). Hanun does not believe it, and the princes (apparently young advisors; → 2 Chr. 10) stoke up his suspicions (19:3). David sends messengers not to honor his father but to spy out the land; David *obviously* thinks that Ammon is vulnerable during its interregnum. David thinks Hanun is a boy ("tennis balls, my liege"), and so he tries to leverage Nahash's death to Israel's advantage. From Hanun's perspective, David wants to spy out the new king to see where the soft spots are. Hanun and his youthful advisors *assume* this is David's intent because that is what they would do if David died. The Chronicler tells us differently. David is returning kindness for kindness, loyalty for loyalty, gift for gift.

Hanun has to demonstrate his strength to show David that he is not to be messed with. He has to prove his manhood, and he does it the old-fashioned way, by humiliating other men. To prove he is a man, he acts like an adolescent. He shaves and disrobes David's ambassadors. Hair is a glory-crown; a man's hair signifies his manhood. Second Samuel 10 specifies that Hanun shaves half of the messengers' beards. The Chronicler is less specific: Hanun simply "shaved them" (19:4), implying that they were shaved from head to toe-hairs. Shaved, the men are feminized, stripped of their male glory and reduced to a state of mourning (Merrill 2015: 236). Clothing is also a glory, and for royal messengers clothing signifies their high status at court. Hanun strips that glory, too, cutting the messengers' robes up to the hips and sending them back to David bare-bummed (again a feminization). Hanun cannot believe David, the warrior-king of Israel, could show kindness and political love. He treats David's royal messengers as slaves and POWs. He inverts all the standards of hospitality that one king typically shows another (Japhet 1993: 356).

An assault on David's messengers is an assault on David himself. This is the kind of incident that, still in our high-minded world, becomes an international *cause célèbre*, the kind of scandal that can spark a shooting war. Insulted, his *hesed* greeted with contempt, David ... *does nothing* (Japhet [1993: 357] emphasizes David's restraint). He sends the messengers to Jericho to wait for their hair to grow back (19:5), but nothing more. He makes no war preparations, plots no retribution. David does not return insult for insult, evil for evil.

David's inaction is one of the most surprising things in the story, so subtle we can miss it. It is surprising, but perfectly in character for David. He had long practice in bearing humiliations and unjust treatment. It is the story of his life, at least during Saul's reign.

At this point, Hanun could let it go too. After all, he is one up on David: he has humiliated David's messengers, sent a macho message back to Israel, and protected his turf and his crown. He is getting good PR from the David-hating Ammonite press. He does not let it go because he again misjudges David. He cannot believe David would sincerely send condolences for his father. He does not believe that David will accept the insult without reacting. He *anticipates* that David will punish Ammon for the insult, so he hires Aramean mercenaries and besieges Medeba (19:6–7), a city in the tribal area of Reuben (Josh. 13:9). This is no longer an insult but an attack, and David responds by sending Joab to protect and liberate the cities (1 Chr. 19:9–10). The insult turns into a shooting war—*entirely* because of Hanun's folly.

The war with Aram is cosmic, holy war. "Hadadezer" contains the divine name Hadad, the proper name of the god often known as Baal (a title, "Master"); his name means "Hadad helps." But Hadad *does not* help; nor are Hadadezer's hired warriors much help to Ammon (18:5; 19:19). On the other hand, Yahweh helps first Joab and then David. Both defeat the Arameans, causing them to break their alliance with Ammon and seek a covenant of peace with David. David's divide-and-conquer works: once Aram allies with David, Ammon can no longer resist. David defeats the Ammonites because he makes peace with their mercenaries. He wages war by making peace.

In the end, David attacks the Ammonite capital city of Rabbah. He takes the city and the crown. The very thing that Hanun feared—that David would take advantage of the interregnum and seize power, that David would take Hanun's crown—happens. Hanun tries to protect his crown by humiliating David's ambassadors and by starting a war with David. He does everything a heroic king should do, and he loses his crown anyway. David takes the crown not by vicious response, not by taking vengeance, not by returning evil for evil. David's kindness and restraint is a trap for the Ammonites. He is not intentionally setting a trap, but it becomes a trap.

Operating by the code of warrior cultures—defend honor above everything, defend it by shaming others and, if necessary, by killing—the Ammonites cannot make sense of David's behavior. David's *un*-heroism makes them stumble; they fall into the hole they dug for David. David returns kindness for Nahash's kindness, curbs his passion for revenge, lets things go, and ends up with another crown in his collection. One would think that David's unheroic conduct would make him a loser, but David is a political winner. *Somebody* is defending David's honor, but it is not David. The whole affair is suffused with the irony of Yahweh.

Throughout the episode, David is a type of the greater David. Jesus, too, becomes king of kings not by cruelty and conquest, but by submitting to insult and assault and by doing nothing in return. Jesus resists, but not in any of the normal, expected ways. He resists by turning the other cheek and absorbing beatings and mockery, the crown of thorns and the whip, the nails, and the brutal suffering of the cross. He resists by entrusting himself entirely to his heavenly Father, by trusting his heavenly Father to vindicate him, by relentless, unswerving obedience to his Father. That obedience gets him into trouble in the first place, but he does not shrink back when his obedience is met with murderous hatred. He continues in the painful way of obedience because of the joy set before him.

It is astonishing that the world works this way. It is shocking that apparent defeat is the way of victory. But the gospel makes an even more astonishing claim: Jesus is the revelation of the Father's glory, most especially on the cross. It is not just that the world works this way. The world works this way because this way is *God's* way. We cannot put God off his game. We are powerless to change his mind and his purpose, no matter how murderously we respond to him. He will save his own; he will put his world back to rights. If he is determined to love and forgive and restore, he will.[5] Since this is the way of Jesus and his Father, it must also be our way.

---

5. As Rowan Williams has put it, "You can do what you like: but God is God." Deal with it. As Williams says, "Here is a divine love that cannot be defeated by violence: we do our worst, and we still fail to put God off. We reject, exclude and murder the one who bears the love of God in his words and work, and that love continues to do exactly what it always did. The Jesus who is dying on the cross is completely consistent with the Jesus we have followed through his ministry, and this consistency shows that we can't deflect the love that comes through in life and death." *The Sign and the Sacrifice: The Meaning of the Cross and Resurrection* (Louisville: Westminster John Knox, 2016), 8.

5

THE PATTERN OF THE TEMPLE

1 Chronicles 21–29

David and Satan (1 Chronicles 21)

First Chronicles does not mention David's sin against Bathsheba and Uriah (cf. 2 Sam. 11–12). Bathsheba is mentioned in Chronicles very briefly (1 Chr. 3:5), and Uriah only once, in a list of David's warriors (1 Chr. 11:41). In the Chronicler's account, David's great sin is taking a census of Israel (1 Chr. 21; cf. 2 Sam. 24). It is inspired by Satan (1 Chr. 21:1; see below), provokes the Lord's displeasure (21:7), and leads to a plague that kills seventy thousand (21:13–14). With Satan in the vicinity, it is like another fall of man (McConville 1984: 69). Clearly, the Chronicler considers it a great evil, like the sin of Moses at the rock (Num. 20). But why?

We can begin by asking, Who is the "Satan" who provokes David's census? First Chronicles 21:1 is a curious statement, especially in the light of 2 Sam. 24, which attributes David's census to Yahweh's anger (2 Sam. 24:1). Wright (1993: 87–105) points out that the Hebrew *satan* means "adversary" and could refer to a human adversary (as in 1 Kgs. 11:14, 23, 25, where "satans" assail Solomon). The Hebrew text of 1 Chr. 21:1 lacks the definite article; this is not "*the* Satan" but "a satan" (Japhet 1993: 374–75; Boda [2010: 174] appeals to Num. 22:22–23). It seems best to conclude that David musters the army because of an attack from an enemy, most likely a foreign power.

That makes sense of both 2 Sam. 24 and 1 Chr. 21. In the former, Yahweh's anger burns, and he incites David to take a census. That might mean that Yahweh implanted a desire in David (Yahweh does "stir the spirits" of kings; 1 Chr. 5:26; 2 Chr. 21:16; 36:22). But it might also mean that in his anger Yahweh sent an enemy to attack David as a test of David's faith. David flunks; instead of pacifying the Lord's anger by seeking reconciliation and atonement, David relies on military power. Similarly, in 1 Chr. 21 David is moved to muster the troops when an adversary attacks.[1]

A census is a military act, but David does not follow the procedure laid out in Exod. 30, where Yahweh requires each man who is mustered to give a half-shekel "ransom" to "make atonement" before going to war (Johnstone 1998a: 228–29). Johnstone explains the intention of this rule: "War is not being glorified: military service is only legitimate within the context of fighting the LORD's battles as the LORD's host. Killing on the field of battle is an inevitable consequence of war: but taking the life of another human being immediately warrants the payment

1. Commentators, Wright (1993) says, have read the Chronicler's narrative through the lens of 2 Sam. 24, which recounts the same event. Wright argues that the Chronicler does not retell the story of Samuel but subverts it. For the Chronicler, the problem is not the census but Joab's failure to complete the census. Joab should carry out the commands of the king, but he stops the census because of his own scruples. Wright points out that "God was displeased with this thing" (1 Chr. 21:7) immediately follows the notice that "[Joab] did not number Levi and Benjamin" (21:6), suggesting that in this case *post hoc* does mean *propter hoc*: "this thing" is Joab's cessation rather than David's original command. Joab's question to David—"Why does my lord seek [*baqash*] this thing?" (21:3)—is a loaded one (as pointed out by Gard [2006: 233–52]). The verb has been used several times in the previous chapters of 1 Chronicles, most notably in the psalm performed by the Levitical choir at the ark-tent in Jerusalem. David should remember the song: "Let the heart of those who seek the LORD be glad. / Seek the LORD and His strength; / Seek His face continually" (16:10–11). David *does not* seek the Lord's strength; he seeks strength in numbers. And he is *not* glad. Further, Wright has to argue that David is wrong to confess sin (21:8); he confesses to a sin he did not commit. And it requires Wright to say that Yahweh "plays along" with David's unnecessary confession by offering the king three judgments to choose from (21:9–12; Wright 1993: 100). The chapter idealizes David. Faced with an ambiguous, impenetrable God, David takes responsibility even for sins he did not commit. But it leaves Yahweh looking manipulative, a wanton god who treats people like flies, accusing for sport. Wright's point about David's responsibility can be partially rehabilitated. David is himself responsible for the plague. He is not wrong to say, "I have sinned greatly." He is atoning for his own sin, but he *also* acts on behalf of the entire nation. He pays for the threshing floor, buys the wood and animals for sacrifice, and bears the cost of the sacrifice. As king, he knows he cannot use someone else's property to offer atonement on Israel's behalf.

Wright (1993: 95–96) notes that Joab leaves two tribes out of his census: Benjamin and Levi (1 Chr. 21:6). Joab's sin is failing to carry out David's command. But if we assume that Joab acts righteously, we might speculate on why the mustering of these particular tribes makes David's command abhorrent to Joab. Benjamites risked everything to join David while Saul was king (1 Chr. 11–12); they are Yahweh's gift to David, stirred up by the Spirit to join him instead of clinging to Saul (cf. 12:16–18). For David to lay hands on this tribe is a particular offense against Yahweh. Even more so it is an offense against the Levites, who belong to Yahweh in a unique way, his own special possession. In seizing this tribe and deploying them for his own purposes, David lays claim to Yahweh's prerogatives.

of life for life" (228). Exodus 30 provides the "necessary sacral preparation for war," the half-shekel serving as "the indemnity laid up as a perpetual reminder before the LORD for the life of '*you* all,' that is, not just of the combatants, but of the community at large, on whose behalf the host sallies forth and which might suffer because of the blood shed by the host" (228). The half-shekel atones; that is, it maintains "the oneness between community and God, which will otherwise be broken even by acts of necessary bloodshed" (228). The atonement is not a repair but prophylactic, a set of "precautionary, prospective measures, which anticipate the possibility of bloodshed" (228–29; cf. the similar conclusions of Hahn 2012: 88; Boda 2010: 175–76).

David does not prepare the troops in this way, just as he did not observe the protocols for the transfer of the ark (1 Chr. 13). Going to war without paying the atonement is like attempting to enter the sanctuary without the protective veils that screen human beings from the holy God. David also bypasses the Levites, who are normally essential to the conduct of war. Having foregone the prophylactic atonement, David has to prepare a retrospective atonement, which repairs Israel's relation to Yahweh.

Other details fill out the nature of David's sin. The appearance of the *mashkhit*, the death-angel, is a clue. In Exod. 12:13, 23, the *mashkhit* slaughters the firstborn of Egypt in retribution for Pharaoh's enslavement of Yahweh's son Israel. Now the death-angel is back, slaughtering *Israelites*. The typology assigns David the role of Pharaoh, seizing God's people for his own purposes. He has turned Israel into an Egypt, and a Passover sacrifice is needed to stay the plague. David is also an Adam, seizing forbidden fruit, God's host. The census is a sacrilege, an intrusion on Yahweh's realm and his host. It is a sign that David has slipped into Saul-like royalty; he does not "seek Yahweh" and so brings '*asham* (guilt) on Judah (21:3; cf. Gard 2006: 233–52). But he does not remain in that condition. When he fails to bring the ark into Jerusalem, he corrects his infractions and tries again. When he sinfully numbers the people, he repents and becomes the un-Saul, a model of penitence and restoration (Hahn 2012: 93).

Contrary to what some commentators say, the Chronicler does not whitewash David's reign. The census is as great a sin as adultery and murder, because it is a direct and flagrant trespass onto Yahweh's rights. It is a variation of David's sin with Bathsheba, but on a national scale: in 2 Samuel, David seizes the wife of a single warrior; in 1 Chronicles, David seizes the host of Yahweh and treats it as if it were his own. With Bathsheba, David committed something resembling statutory, if not actual, rape. The census is worse: he rapes the bride of Yahweh.

Yahweh offers David three options for punishment: three years of famine, three months of defeat, or three days of the "sword of Yahweh," defined as "pestilence" (21:11–12). The numerology hints that these are mitigated punishments: Yahweh does not threaten a full-scale sevenfold punishment, but a "half week" of discipline. Because David confesses his guilt (21:8), Yahweh shows mercy.

When David sees Yahweh's angel devastating the land, he reiterates his confession of responsibility: "Is it not I who said to muster the people?" (21:17 AT). Like Moses, he offers himself in place of the people, acting a Melchizedekian part as a priest-king. Yahweh hears his plea and sends the prophet Gad to instruct David to build an altar on the threshing floor of Ornan the Jebusite (Araunah in 2 Sam. 24). Though Ornan is willing to gift David both the threshing floor and the sacrificial animal, David refuses; he has brought the pestilence on Israel by seizing, and he refuses to seize again. The offering must be made from dedicated land, and land can only be dedicated by its owner. It is significant that David offers the atoning sacrifice on a threshing floor. Uzza died at a threshing floor when he touched the ark (1 Chr. 13:9), and Solomon will later build the temple on this very site, which is on Mount Moriah (2 Chr. 3:1). A threshing floor is where wheat and chaff are separated and sifted, and thus becomes a symbol for judgment. Threshing is an early moment in the process of bread making, and now the threshing floor of Ornan becomes a part of the festive site, the house of bread, the temple.

When the tabernacle was completed, Yahweh's fire burst out from the most holy place to consume the sacrifices of the priests (Lev. 9:24), and the Lord repeats this action when Solomon finishes the temple (2 Chr. 7:1; cf. also 1 Kgs. 18, Elijah's altar on Mount Carmel). Fire from Yahweh is a sign of acceptance and approval. Yahweh lights his altar to show that David's prayer has been heard, his sacrifice accepted. Israel has been delivered, and David has not had to make good on his offer to give himself for the people (1 Chr. 21:17). Like the first sacrifice on Mount Moriah, Abraham's offering of Isaac (Gen. 22), the Lord provides the sacrifice. Following the typology of Genesis, David's sacrifice on Moriah is linked to the purchase of a plot of land (Gen. 23; Hahn 2012: 90–91, 94). David is a Moses figure; he is also a new Abraham.

David numbers the people, then repents of his sin. Yahweh begins to destroy the people, then "repents" of the evil (McConville 1984: 72). Wright (1993: 100) makes much of the fact that the Lord has already paused the plague before David sacrifices (1 Chr. 21:15). For Wright, this is playacting: David's sacrifice does not actually *do* anything, since the threat has already passed. The Chronicler's point is different. The story makes an essential point about temple service, consistent with the Chronicler's "prototemple theology" (→1 Chr. 17). Building an altar or a temple does not secure Yahweh's mercy but is a provision of mercy. Yahweh's mercy is prevenient. But that prevenient grace must be secured and perpetuated. In the space and time opened by the angel's pause, David purchases the temple site, constructs an altar, and offers sacrifice. His sacrifice *is* effective: it causes the angel to sheathe his sword (21:27), and so makes the pause permanent. Just so, the temple is built *within* God's mercy as a provision for continuing mercy.

Chapter 21 ends with an odd note about the tabernacle of Moses, still pitched at Gibeon. David did not seek God there because "he was terrified by the sword of the angel of Yahweh" (21:30). The Mosaic tabernacle has become an Eden, guarded by a cherub with a flaming sword. David's sin has blocked that old path to Yahweh. But that does not leave David exiled from Yahweh's presence. The Mosaic Eden is closed, but David has purchased a place of sacrifice, and Yahweh has received it. David's sin results in a crucial turning point in the history of Israel's worship (Hahn 2012: 95). There is no going back to paradise, but the offering on Moriah promises a new paradise to come.

Planning the Temple (1 Chronicles 22–29)

The final section of 1 Chronicles is neatly framed by speeches by David (Boda 2010: 210–11). Chapter 22 contains David's speech of encouragement to Solomon, concluded by a brief exhortation to "all the leaders" (22:17–19). Chapters 28–29 record several public speeches, marked by "David said" and interspersed with descriptions of temple furnishings:

1. Speech #1: David addresses officials, princes, commanders, and overseers (28:1–10).
2. David gives to Solomon the *tabnit* (pattern) for the temple and its furnishings (28:11–19).
3. Speech #2: David exhorts Solomon to be strong and courageous (28:20–21).
4. Speech #3: David details his contributions and calls for contributions (29:1–5).
5. Rulers, princes, commanders, and overseers bring contributions (29:6–9).
6. Speech #4: David blesses Yahweh (29:10–19).
7. Speech #5: David calls on the assembly to bless Yahweh (29:20).

How fitting that the last recorded words of David are, "Now bless Yahweh your God" (29:20).

Between these two sets of speeches are several chapters concerned with David's organization of the personnel of the temple. In these chapters, the physical temple fades from view. David mentions the gold he has gathered in his initial speech (22:14); gold is not mentioned at all in chapters 23–27 but is a major concern of David's final speech (28:14–18; 29:2–5, 7). The same pattern is evident with bronze (22:14, 16; 29:2) and silver (22:16; 28:14–17; 29:2–5, 7). The verb "build" appears eight times in chapter 22 (vv. 2, 6, 7, 8, 10, 11, 19), never in chapters 23–27, and another seven times in chapters 28–29 (28:2 [2×], 3, 6, 10; 29:16, 19). David's speeches are concerned with the temple; David's *actions* between the speeches are entirely concerned with people.

First Chronicles 23–27 may look like a digression (Wright 1991: 229–42). David delivers an exhortation to Solomon (1 Chr. 22) and makes him king (23:1). Then there is a five-chapter digression as the Chronicler describes, in excruciating detail, the numbers and duty assignments of Levites, priests, and royal officials. In chapter 28–29 we are back where we started, with David addressing Israel's leaders, exhorting Solomon, and making him king "a second time" (29:22). Why couldn't we move from chapter 22 to 28 without the distractions? Yet, given its length and place in 1 Chronicles, chapters 23–27 appear to be central to the Chronicler's depiction of David, not a digression at all.

We can grasp the significance of these chapters by noting that "Davidic assignment formulas" (Wright 1991: 234) are used elsewhere in Chronicles in the context of a national renewal. In 2 Chr. 23, for instance, "Jehoiada re-establishes the correct temple personnel following the debacle of Athaliah (vv. 18–19; see 2 Chr. 24:15–16). A Davidic assignment formula legitimates the new system that accompanies the change in regimes, referring to 1 Chr. 23:28–24:19 and 26:1–19" (Wright 1991: 235). The same formula is used in the Chronicler's accounts of Hezekiah (2 Chr. 29:25) and Josiah (2 Chr. 35:4, 15). Wright (1991: 237) concludes that 1 Chr. 23–27 describes the "foundational establishment of temple personnel" and provides "the basis of a motif that runs throughout Chronicles: the establishment of temple personnel during the reigns of 'good' royal figures." Good kings repair the physical temple; good kings also provide for the maintenance of ongoing temple service. Since Israel is called as a priestly nation, the reorganization of temple personnel is essential to restoring Israel to its proper calling among the nations.[2]

---

2. Citing Persian documents that indicate that kings are legitimized by their attention to the gods' temples and temple servants, Wright (1991) concludes that David's attention to priests and Levites

As is typical of the Bible's down-to-earthness, high concepts like "national renewal" involve quotidian realities like the restoration of faithful political and religious leadership. One of the chief signs of Israel's resurrection is a re-shuffling of temple bureaucracy. It is a lesson for the Christian church, since the gatekeepers and temple personnel figure the pastoral offices of the new covenant (cf. Johannes Piscator, *Commentarii in omnes libros Veteris Testamenti*, in Cooper and Lohrmann 2016: 575). Revivals in the church last only when they affect the mundane operations of church administrators. The Chronicler anticipates the Pauline claim that administration is a gift of the Creator Spirit (1 Cor. 12:28). Protestants, who often reduce church leadership to one or two functions, may find an enriched theology of office in 1 Chronicles (contra John Mayer, *Many Commentaries in One*, in Cooper and Lohrmann 2016: 570, who contrasts Protestantism and Catholicism on this point). Like Israel, churches assign individuals to lead worship, to teach, to play music and sing, to collect and distribute funds, and to oversee operations and ensure that the church's ministries run efficiently. Churches sometimes denigrate the more material dimensions of the church's ministry, but the Chronicler teaches us that the church secretary or administrative pastor is as essential to God's work as preachers and teachers.

David's organization of personnel is structured chiastically:

A Levites (23:1–32)
   B Priests (24:1–31)
      C Musicians (25:1–31)
   B' Gatekeepers (26:1–32)
A' Laity (27:1–34)

The arrangement is perhaps better described as an architectural-literary structure. The outer edges of the text list those who function in the outer parts of the temple: Levites (A) who assist with sacrifices in the court but never enter the house, and lay Israelites (A') who also enter only the court. Priests (B) work in the house itself, and gatekeepers (B') guard entrances and exits. If you were to enter the temple precincts, you would first pass through the court with its Levites and lay

---

"legitimates the rule of David himself. A comparison of the motif of the establishment of temple personnel to autobiographical writings of the Persian period suggests that the passage functions to further the idealization of David in Chronicles. David is the founding king of Israel, whose legacy commands the respect of both the Judean society and its god" (242). Because David organizes the Levites as preparation for the installation of Solomon as king, the same effort legitimizes Solomon.

worshipers, then the gatekeepers, and then enter the temple proper, where the startled priests would wonder how you got past the gatekeepers.

At the center of the literary structure is a list of Levitical musicians. Music is the center of the text, as music has become the center of Israel's worship. The architectural-literary structure places music in the inner sanctuary, at the ark. It is a literary portrait of the fact that Israel carried on with the worship of the Davidic tabernacle—song offered at the ark—even after the temple was finished. Song becomes the ark-throne, as Ps. 22:3 indicates: "You are holy, / O You who are enthroned upon the praises of Israel." This music-centered segment forms a neat enclosure with 1 Chr. 1–9, which also centers on musicians. Israel is a choral people, and the house of their God is a concert hall, with music in the middle, a new form of sacrifice (cf. John Mayer, *Many Commentaries in One*, in Cooper and Lohrmann 2016: 571).

New Moses to New Solomon (1 Chronicles 22)

First Chronicles 22:6–16 records David's hortatory speech to Solomon about building the temple. It is divided into two large sections, each marked by the phrase "my son" (22:7, 11). The first section repeats Yahweh's oracle to David explaining why he will not build the house and promising that David's son will complete the project. Based on Yahweh's commitment to Solomon, David exhorts his son to build. The exhortation is framed by a chiastic *inclusio*:

A   Yahweh be with you (22:11a)
   B   Build the house (22:11b)
   B′ Arise and work (22:16b)
A′ Yahweh be with you (22:16c)

Within this frame, David deals with two main concerns. First, he prays (or pronounces) that Yahweh will give Solomon wisdom to keep Torah (22:12), which is the way of prosperity. That section ends with a fourfold command: be strong, be courageous; do not fear, do not be dismayed (22:13). Second, in 22:14–16a David reminds Solomon of the preparations he has made, assembling vast supplies (22:14, listed in descending order of value, gold, silver, bronze, iron, timber, stone, from the inner sanctuary to the outer walls) and wise workmen (22:15). Yahweh's presence will make Solomon successful, but David makes preparations too. "Yahweh be with you" and "look at all the stuff I've gathered" are not incompatible.

The final verses of 1 Chr. 22 record a brief speech of David to the leaders, an exhortation to help his son (22:17–19). After reminding them of the rest Yahweh has given, David says (22:19),

A Set heart and soul to seek Yahweh your Elohim.
  B Arise and build the sanctuary of Yahweh Elohim
    C to bring in the ark of the covenant of Yahweh
    C' and the vessels of Elohim
  B' into the house built
A' for the name of Yahweh.

The chiasm is precise down to word level: B has "build the sanctuary" and B' has "house built." "Yahweh" appears four times, "Elohim" thrice. The exhortation begins with the creation name Yahweh Elohim, a combination of the covenant name Yahweh and the more universal title Elohim. The two names split in the middle of the verse, Yahweh attached to the ark of the covenant and Elohim linked with other vessels. Yahweh of Israel is Lord of the four corners; altogether, God's names constitute a creation-week seven.

The shape of the text mimics the exhortation. In the outer layers, David refers to the "sanctuary" and "house" that are to be built, but the interior verses name the objects that are in the interior of the house. Yahweh's name is at the outer frame; the building of the house, where the ark and vessels are, is for the sake of God's name and fame (cf. 22:5). The exhortation is fundamentally not about building but about the "hearts" of the leaders. The structure also implies a certain form of piety: as Israelites, the leaders wear Yahweh's name, but they will succeed only if the throne of God is set up in their hearts and only if their hearts are devoted to worshiping Yahweh Elohim, Creator and Lord. The form of the text reminds Solomon and the leaders that they are dealing with a God who does not look on the outward appearance but on the heart.

David is to Solomon as Moses was to Joshua (Boda 2010: 182–83, 214), addressing a successor who is young and needs the guidance of his "father." The first part of the speech (22:8–11) reviews David's interactions with Yahweh about the temple project. In 1 Chr. 17 Yahweh stops David from building a house, promising instead to build a house for David. In chapter 22 (as in chapter 29), David says that the Lord prohibits him from building the temple because he is a man of blood (22:8). Below (→ 1 Chr. 29), we will consider the significance of this rationale, but here we can at least note the contrast between David's warfare and Solomon's peacefulness.

The latter is a man of rest (*menukhah*; cf. the name Noah) and peace (*shalom*, which puns on Solomon's own name; 22:9). Solomon has entered the rest of Yahweh and so is qualified to facilitate Yahweh's rest. First the prince rests (23:25), then the throne of the High King rests in the temple (22:18). As son, Solomon is a "head of his father," a builder who makes a house for his father, as he will for his Father.

The speech is analogous to the book of Proverbs, in which Solomon gives instructions to his son the prince. Especially in 22:11–13, David delivers a speech of wisdom. That formal analogy with the Wisdom literature is supported by the speech itself, which is full of wisdom terminology. David exhorts Solomon to be wise (*sekel*, used eight times in Proverbs) and to pursue understanding (*binah*, fourteen times in Proverbs). Later, Huram of Tyre confirms that David's wishes come to pass, when he declares that David is blessed in having a wise and discerning son (2 Chr. 2:12). The Hebrew *binah* resonates punningly in the context. David addresses his son (*ben*) about building (*banah*) a house, work that requires *binah*. In building with wisdom, Solomon proves himself a true son of David. Building wisely is what sons are built for.

David reminds Solomon that he, David, has already gathered 100,000 talents of gold and one million of silver (22:14), along with bronze, iron, wood, and stone. He has assembled the workers, all of them "wise" (*khakam*, "skillful," 22:15). This is the first and only use of this key word for wisdom in 1 Chronicles, but it is used another six times in 2 Chronicles (2:7 [2×], 12, 13, 14 [2×]). Like Solomon himself, the craftsmen who work on the temple must possess a sevenfold wisdom suitable to the new creation of Yahweh's house. Together, king and craftsmen build a house of wisdom.

To say that the temple is a house of wisdom is *not*, however, to leave Torah and Moses behind. In the very context where David exhorts Solomon to cultivate wisdom and understanding, he also urges him to guard the commandments and judgments that Yahweh delivered to Moses (22:13). Solomon needs wisdom and understanding precisely to guard Torah (22:12), and only then will he succeed. David exhorts Solomon to be strong, as Moses exhorted Joshua; Solomon's temple will complete the conquest Joshua began, and peaceable building will require as much courage as war. In David's mind there is no tension, much less contradiction, between Torah and wisdom.

Dividing the People (1 Chronicles 23–27)

Plato said that purification is a science of division. So is creation. In Genesis, God forms the formless by separating. He divides (*badal*) light from darkness to form a temporal structure of evenings and mornings (Gen. 1:4), and waters from water to create a vertical spatiality (Gen. 1:6–7). He delegates the creative work of dividing day and night to the heavenly bodies, which rule and signify in part by separating (Gen. 1:14, 18). After Genesis 1, the Hebrew verb *badal* is not used again until Exodus, when the Lord instructs Moses to erect a veil as a "divider" between the holy place and the most holy (Exod. 26:33). It is another creative act, delegated this time to a human being: by erecting the firmament boundary between holy and most holy, Moses re-forms the world. A world that previously was not mapped by the separation of holy and profane is now mapped by that separation.

Torah requires not only the creative division of space but also the creative division of persons. Israel is separated (*badal*) from the peoples as Yahweh's own (Lev. 20:24, 26; cf. 1 Kgs. 8:53). Within Israel, Levites are separated from the other tribes (Num. 8:14), and priests are distinguished from the rest of the Levites (Num. 16:9). Priests are guardians of created order because they are responsible for creating and maintaining the divisions between holy and profane, unclean and clean (Lev. 10:10). They create holiness boundaries by rites of consecration; they create purity boundaries by pronouncing people clean or unclean, like Yahweh forming the creation by word.

Chronicles records yet another re-creative division. First Chronicles 23:13 repeats Torah's claim that the sons of Aaron were divided off (*badal*) as most holy. Like the veil separating the holy place from the most holy place, Yahweh's choice of Aaron is a separating choice, a division within the holy people that consecrates one family as most holy. First Chronicles 25:1 presents an innovation. Within the tribe of Levi, David and the commanders of the hosts set apart (*badal*) the sons of Asaph, Heman, and Jeduthun for the ministry of song. In Chronicles, only the priests and singers are "set apart," a datum that calls attention to the parallels of priestly and musical ministry, of sacrifice and the sacrifice of praise. More, the division of singers from the rest of the Levites is yet another fresh creation within the new creation that is Israel. Forming a specialized company of singers and musicians at the heart of the temple repeats the first moments of creation, when the morning stars sang together. Inspired by the Spirit, they are seer-singers (Japhet 1993: 463; Boda 2010: 195–96).

Already in 1 Chr. 23:30–32 David innovates by including song in the daily round of temple worship. Levites "stand and sing" ("stand and serve" is a description of priestly ministry; Deut. 18:7) morning and evening. "Thanks and praise" has been added to the "service" (*'avodah*) of the Levites: given the usage in the Pentateuch, we expect the text to say that the Levites are to "stand every morning to serve," but instead we read that they are to "stand every morning to thank and to praise." Song has become a form of priestly "service"; the ascent of sound before Yahweh delights him just as the ascending smoke soothes his anger.

The Levitical singers are organized into *mishmeret* or "watches" (1 Chr. 25:8; Kleinig 2009: 41–42). The Hebrew noun comes from the verb *shamar*, which means "to guard," and the noun and verb are used together in several passages in Numbers to refer to the guard duty of priests and Levites at the Mosaic tabernacle (Num. 1:53; 3:7; 8:26; 18:3–5; Milgrom 1970: 8–16). At the tabernacle, the Levites literally guarded doorways, armed to prevent unauthorized Israelites from intruding on holy space. David also assigns Levites to guard duty, but the form of guard duty has been transformed. Instead of (or perhaps in addition to) killing intruders, the Levitical guards now "do guard duty" by singing and playing musical instruments. Musical performance is described under the metaphor of guard duty.[3]

First Chronicles 25 encapsulates the Chronicler's theology of music. By placing Levitical singers in the center of the genealogies that begin with Adam, he indicates that music encapsulates the vocation of human beings. In 1 Chr. 25 he indicates that human beings are made to be singers because we are made to be priests, kings, and prophets.

Levites are the primary singers, and their song is a form of priestly ministry. In Leviticus, priests turn animal flesh to smoke that ascends as a soothing aroma to the Lord. In Chronicles, priests offer their own life breath as a pleasing sound to Yahweh. Chronicles marks an advance in the history of sacrifice: instead of offering animals, Levites offer themselves as living sacrifices.

At the same time, music is a royal activity. David the *king* organizes the Levitical choir and orchestra. It is fitting business for David, sweet psalmist of Israel, harpist of Saul's court, inventor of musical instruments, whose hands fight with the sword while his fingers fight with the lyre (Ps. 144). It is fitting business for *any* king. Lamech, scripture's first king, was father to Jubal, himself "the father of all those who play the lyre and pipe" (Gen. 4:21). The link between music and kingship is not accidental. To sing, we have to rule our bodies and breath. To enhance our singing with musical instruments, we cut and trim trees, pull guts into strings, and train our fingers to pluck. We mine metals, shape them into

---

3. For further discussion of the role of music in the Chronicler's temple, see Kleinig 2009 and Leithart 2003.

flutes and pipes, and learn to blow melodically. Music is a signal of dominion accomplished. Every orchestra is a royal assembly, every choir a company of kings and queens. A musical instrument is an effective sign of the end of all things: it is an instance of creation remade into an instrument of praise, a glimpse of the future destiny of creation intruding into the present.

Music also *makes* us into kings and queens. The Spirit evokes music: "Be filled with the Spirit, speaking to one another in psalms and hymns and spiritual songs, singing and making melody with your heart to the Lord" (Eph. 5:18–19). And it works the other way around: music inspires spirit. Soldiers march and sing to prepare for battle, to train them to act as a unit. The pounding beat of the warm-up music fills athletes with the spirit of the game. Martyrs go to the arena singing psalms and hymns. Music channels spirit, also *the* Spirit.

That is Elisha's assumption when he calls for a minstrel to help him prophesy (2 Kgs. 3). Song can be a form of prophecy (1 Chr. 25:1), and prophecy can become song. Isaiah sings Yahweh's love song to his vineyard, Israel (Isa. 5). Like a soprano shattering a champagne glass with a high C, Jeremiah's dirge plucks up and breaks down, destroys and overthrows (Jer. 1). Prophets hear and deliver God's word. Caught up into God's presence, they catch his melody and sing it to Israel. To say God made Adam to make musicians is to say that God made Adam to produce priestly singers, royal musicians, and Spirit-mad prophetic chanters. God made us to make music and to be made by the music we make.[4]

After musicians come gatekeepers, the guardians of the inner sanctuary of song (1 Chr. 26:1–19). The passage is framed by references to the "allotment" or "apportionment" of assignments to Korahites (26:1) and sons of Korah and Merari (26:19). Within this frame, the text moves in a complex parallel fashion

---

4. How is music *prophetic*? First, prophets enter the divine council (Jer. 23:16–22) to hear the Lord's judgments and report them. Music is a stairway ascending into the Lord's court. Second, prophecy consists of human words with the power to create and destroy (cf. Jer. 1:10). Songs can have prophetic power. Samson's songs made the Philistines look ridiculous. Wagner and rock 'n' roll subverted traditional mores. Third, the Spirit moves prophets to speak (2 Pet. 1:20–21), and the Spirit inspires music (Eph. 5:18–19). Music and prophecy are linked by the work of the Spirit. Fourth, there is a real link between music, creation, and history. Genesis 1 sets out a melody: the *act* of creation is musical, a patterned, recurring sequence of speech acts. As a *product* of God's creating activity, creation has musical qualities—melody, rhythm, harmony, form, and texture. Creation is not a fixed and static object. It is made in movement, and it *moves*. The sevenfold melody of the world's making is the recurring melody of its history. The week of creation establishes the recurring rhythm of world history (cf. the sevens in Revelation). Creation is to history as theme is to variations. Prophets tell the future because, guided by the Spirit, they have a mature feel for the music of time. They sense when things are moving to a crescendo, when a "movement" begins to resolve, when the key is about to change. Finally, music gives a glimpse of the end of all things. Creation is destined to unite in praise, and by putting creation to work praising God, music-making anticipates that future.

through different subclans of gatekeeping Levites, with a few verses in the center describing the casting of lots:

   A Meshelemiah (Kohathite) and sons (26:1b–3)
      B Obed-edom (Kohathite), sons, and grandsons (26:4–9)
         C Hosah (Merarite) and sons (26:10–11)
            D Casting lots (26:13)
  A' Assignment for (Me)Shelemiah and son (26:14)
     B' Assignment of Obed-edom and sons (26:15)
        C' Assignment of Hosah and sons (26:16)

There is a wrinkle in the text at 26:9, which returns to Meshelemiah (26:1–3) after listing descendants of Obed-edom. First Chronicles 26:1–9 thus forms a small chiasm of its own: A. Meshelemiah; B. Obed-edom; A'. Meshelemiah. (Boda [2010: 198] suggests that Meshelemiah is treated as "firstborn" by being given a double assignment.)

The Levitical subclans form one of the structural principles of 26:14–16; geographic designations form another, as the text moves from east ([Me]Shelemiah) to north (Zechariah, son of Shelemiah) to south to west. The next verses, 26:17–18, run through those same positions in the same order, now enumerating the assigned Levites in each position. Thus, 26:14–18 is a parallel-patterned text that spins off from the parallel pattern of 26:1–16:

1 Chronicles 26:14–16	1 Chronicles 26:17–18
Shelemiah on east (26:14a)	Six Levites on east (26:17a)
Zechariah on north (26:14b)	Four Levites on north (26:17b)
Obed-edom and sons on south (26:15)	4 + 2 Levites on south (26:17c)
Hosah on west (26:16)	Four on west (26:18)

We can correlate these positions and Levitical clans with the furniture of the sanctuary (cf. Leithart 2018): on the east, Shelemiah is associated with the court and the altar; stationed to the north, Zechariah is linked with the table of showbread; positioned to the south like the lampstand, Obed-edom and sons are a menorah clan of the Levites; Hosah on the west is connected with the ark-throne. The overall liturgical movement of the list is from east to west, from altar to throne, from court to inner sanctuary (perhaps marked by the reference to the "ascent" on the west in 26:16). The four-faced tribe of Levi takes the position and task of Eden's cherubim, guarding the holy place. As human cherubim, the

Levites administer the house, receive tithes and gifts, and care for the temple (Boda 2010: 200).

First Chronicles 27:25–31 lists the officials in charge of David's stores and lands. Twelve men are named, and each has an area of responsibility:

1. Azmaveth, king's treasuries (27:25a)
2. Jonathan, treasuries in the field (27:25b)
3. Ezri, supervisor of field workers (27:26)
4. Shimei, vineyards (27:27a)
5. Zabdi, treasury of wine (27:27b)
6. Baal-hanan, olive and sycamore trees (27:28a)
7. Joash, treasury of oil (27:28b)
8. Shitrai, herds in Sharon (27:29a)
9. Shaphat, herds in valleys (27:29b)
10. Obil, camels (27:30a)
11. Jehdeiah, donkeys (27:30b)
12. Jaziz, flocks (27:31)

Most of these supervisors or foremen are paired: Azmaveth is in charge of the treasury of the capital city ("the king's storehouses," 27:25), but there are royal treasuries and storehouses in every region of the land, overseen by Jonathan. Shimei is in charge of the vineyards, but he is not in charge of the finished product, wine—Zabdi is. Olive trees and oil are likewise split between Baal-hanan and Joash. The allotment of responsibility divides phases of production; farming is a distinct subdivision from wine- and oil-making. This division of labor also splits production from storage and distribution; one group under Shimei cares for the vines and grapes, while Zabdi's crew makes wine, stores it, and presumably determines where it goes when. Animal husbandry is also doubled, for less obvious reasons. Bovine herds are divided between those on Sharon and those in the valleys. Camels and donkeys—both unclean animals used for heavy work— seem to form a pair. Only Ezri, foreman of "servants of the *'adamah*," and Jaziz, overseer of ovine flocks, work solo. The Chronicler continues his vindication of bureaucracy. David rules by organizing the temple administration. The whole land is Yahweh's, and so the land, too, must be administered as quasi-holy space.

These twelve supervisors and their subordinates are engaged in an Adamic task of dominion. Ezri is over those who "serve the ground" (*la'avodat ha'adamah*) and work in the "field" (*sadeh*). *'Adamah* takes us back to the creation account. Adam was commissioned to "serve" (*'abad*, Gen. 2:15) the garden, and the phrase "serve the ground" appears several times early in Genesis (2:5; 3:23; 4:2; cf. 9:20, where Noah, the "man" ['*ish*] of the *'adamah*, is the first to plant a vineyard). Further, 1 Chr. 27 works within the frame of days three and six of creation. Vines and fruitful trees appeared on day three, and on day six God made land animals. David has both clean (herds and flocks) and unclean (camels and donkeys) on his land, a signal of his authority over both Israelite and Gentile.

David's arrangement of his agricultural lands is a concrete implementation of Israel's status as a kingdom of priests. David's land supplies the court and the army, but the army is the host of Yahweh, devoted to fighting his wars and protecting the land of his house. More directly, the king's lands supply materials for temple worship: grain for tribute offerings, wine for libations, oil for the lampstand and bread, herd and flock animals for sacrifice and feasts, and unclean animals to transport the goods from the field to the city to the temple. First Chronicles portrays a nation of worshipers, of sacred housekeepers. It portrays an entire new-Adamic kingdom liturgically arranged.

The Pattern of the Temple (1 Chronicles 28–29)

In the final chapters of 1 Chronicles, David delivers a series of speeches to the *qahal* (assembly) of Israel, the officers and princes of his court and army. The *qahal* consists of the "princes" (*sar* is used six times) and warriors (*gibborim*). The first speech is structured chiastically:

A   Hear (*shema*) (28:2a)
    B   David says, It is in my heart to build (28:2b)
        C   God says, You shall not build (28:3)
            D   Yahweh chooses David and Solomon (28:4–5)
        C'   Solomon will build (28:6)
    B'   Solomon's kingdom is established (28:7)
A'   Guard and seek God's commandments (28:8)

The Torah frame is notable: David begins with a Deuteronomy 6-ish "Hear, brethren and people" and ends with an exhortation to keep the Lord's commandments as a condition of retaining the land. That sets the context for David's talk about temple-building. A successful temple project does not depend on mere skill ("wise" men, men of *khochmah*, 28:21). It will succeed if the leaders of Israel "listen" and "guard and seek" God's commandments.

In 1 Chr. 17 Yahweh prohibits David from building a house for Yahweh because Yahweh first will build a house for David. In chapter 28 (as in 1 Chr. 22), David says he was prevented from building the temple because he shed copious blood (22:6-11; 28:2-7). Though his wars were legitimate and just, they disqualify him from building a "house of rest" (28:2 AT), the house where the ark "rests" (Japhet 1993: 487). The sharp distinction between wartime and peacetime kingship is remarkable, especially as David's exhortations to Solomon have a military ring to them ("be courageous and act," 28:10; "be strong and courageous, and act," 28:20). There is a time for war and a time for peace; there is also a king for war and a king for peace, a king who breaks and a king who builds. Though peacetime politics requires the military virtues of strength, cunning, and courage, politics is *not* war carried on by other means.

Commentators should be more shocked at David's self-accusation than they are. Murray notes that the phrase "shed blood" (*shaphak dam*) is used thirty-three times in the Hebrew Bible, fifteen times with reference to violent death. The phrase typically refers to murder or man-slaying: in the "overwhelming majority of instances the expression designates lethal violence perpetrated by ordinary citizens in civil-religious life against other ordinary members of the community not deserving of death." Shedding blood "constitutes a heinous offence that merits both human and divine condemnation, and incurs the penalty of death for the perpetrator" (Murray 2001: 464-65). Solomon accuses Joab of "shedding blood" (1 Kgs. 2:5), emphasizing that he sheds the blood of war in peace. Executing Joab is *not* "shedding blood."

That David would confess to a crime is itself surprising. Equally surprising is the fact that his guilt for bloodshed is linked to war. Only three instances of the phrase refer to violent killing in war, as Murray notes: "The warriors in Ps 79,3.10 are the nations, God's enemies, and the context is one of appeal to YHWH to avenge the undeserved slaughter of his not-so-guilty servants. In Joel [3:19] Egypt and Edom are threatened with desolation for their bloody violence against the innocent of Judah." That is to say, the phrase is "never, outside of Chronicles, used to denote killing by Israelite warriors in the context of war." Typically, killings in war are "conceived of as belonging to a sphere of their own where they are not criminal offences, and thus neither incur bloodguilt nor are subject to the process of blood-vengeance" (Murray 2001: 465-66). Israelite warriors smite, kill, strike, and gain victories. Apart from David's usage in Chronicles, they never "shed blood."

To explain David's terminology, Murray turns to Numbers. Numbers 35:33–34 says that "shedding blood" pollutes the land and requires atoning cleansing. Executing the blood-shedder is the solution: blood will have blood, blood cleanses blood. Since the land is Yahweh's, the land of his dwelling, blood pollution is a particular danger. If it is not cleansed, Yahweh threatens to abandon the land. As Murray puts it, blood shed is "a religious pollution that banishes the presence of YHWH from his land and his people." This is one reason why David cannot build the temple: it is "absolutely imperative that such an offence should not be built as it were into the very foundations of the building that is supremely to manifest YHWH's presence among his people" (Murray 2001: 469).

Why would David's wars lead to this danger? Murray points to Num. 31:19–20, which prescribes a "decontamination" rite for warriors who have killed in war. The rite requires purification on the third and seventh days, a rite that resembles the purification from corpse defilement in Num. 19. Murray infers that "the law in Numbers 19, as the details in 19,14–18 indicate, applies to those contaminated by a corpse in civil life; the law in Numbers 31,19–24 to those so contaminated in a military situation" (2001: 471). Numbers 35 defines "shed blood" as "anyone who strikes someone dead," while Num. 31 uses essentially the same expression to describe warriors defiled by corpses.

Murray's argument has the virtue of highlighting the oddity of David's words and the severity of the charge. His appeals to Numbers are persuasive. But he doesn't answer some obvious questions: What prevents David's bloodshed from being purified? If a warrior can be cleansed from corpse defilement, why not David? Besides, how much of the blood David shed was shed *on the land*? He pushes back Philistines from their incursions into Israel (1 Chr. 14:8–17), but the main wars (recorded in 1 Chr. 18–20) take place elsewhere. Finally, David sets up an ark-shrine in Jerusalem and seems to have direct access to the Lord's presence (1 Chr. 17:16), at least on one occasion. If he can do that, and lead Israel's processions and acts of worship, why can't he build a temple? Can he be too impure to build and yet pure enough for his other acts of cultic leadership?

David's inability to build the temple is part of a Moses typology that, as I have noted, runs through the Chronicler's depiction of David: as Moses was not permitted to enter the land, so David is not able to build the temple (Hahn 2012: 99). The two situations are more deeply analogous than they might appear, given that Solomon's temple completes the conquest and given the analogies between Moses/Joshua and David/Solomon (e.g., Moses/David says "be strong and courageous" to Joshua/Solomon). Moses dies with the rebels and does not enter the rest of the land; David does not enter into the rest of the temple. Neither Moses nor David is cut off from Yahweh. Their personal sins are forgiven. But both are cut off from enjoying the full fruit of their labors. David dies, as it were, on the plains of Moab, on the far side of Jordan.

David's exclusion from temple-building anticipates the end of 2 Chronicles. The exile interrupts the Davidic dynasty. In the Chronicler's own time, a second temple is being built, not only without David's help but without the help of *any* Davidic king (though Zerubbabel is descended from David). David's exclusion from building the first temple is matched by the exclusion of Davidic kings from the second temple. And this exclusion is linked, if somewhat loosely, to abuse of the land. In Chronicles, the abuse is a failure to give the land rest (→ 2 Chr. 36:20–21). Because David sheds blood, he is not allowed to build the temple; because the Davidic kings failed to give the land rest, they are not allowed to reenter as kings when Israel recovers the land. The analogy is closer if we incorporate Kings, which emphasizes that the Davidic dynasty falls because of the shedding of innocent blood (2 Kgs. 24:4).

Though the practical issue of David's speech has to do with building the temple, it is centrally about election—Yahweh's choice of David and Solomon (mentioned four times in 1 Chr. 28; Boda 2010: 212). The election is multilayered, both communal and individual. In the background is the Deuteronomic truth that Yahweh chose Israel; in choosing a king, Yahweh chooses an Israel-in-flesh. David explicitly names four levels of election: God chose Judah from among the tribes, Jesse's house within Judah, David from among his brothers, and Solomon from among David's sons (28:4–6; *bachar* four times). God chooses a nation, a tribe, a family, and, within that family, individuals.

David varies the language at the end of 28:4. Among the sons of Jesse, the electing God "took pleasure" (*ratzah*) in David. The verb is a sacrificial term for the "acceptance" of an offering that meets the requirements of wholeness (Lev. 1:4; 7:18; 22:23, 25). That sacrificial allusion furnishes a basso continuo underneath David's speech. Saul was chosen by lot in a similar multilayered, telescoping process: Benjamin is taken, Kish's house is taken, Saul is taken (1 Sam. 10:20–21). And we can hardly read about Saul's selection without thinking of Achan, who is revealed as the cause of Israel's defeat at Ai by a similar process of lot casting (Josh. 7:16–18). Saul is designated as king and Achan unveiled as a criminal by the same process that determines the scapegoat on the Day of Atonement. Both Saul and Achan are "sacrificial," though in different ways. Saul's death is a scapegoat death that clears the land and makes way for renewal. David, too, is a choice sacrifice.

Saul is selected by lot, but there is no mention of an extension of Yahweh's choice beyond Saul. Yahweh's choice of David, though, does not terminate with David. David is chosen from his father's sons, and then Solomon is further chosen from among David's sons. That both David and Solomon are "chosen" is consistent with the Chronicler's overall presentation: he sees David and Solomon as co-founders of a new order, virtually co-builders of the temple. At the very least, this means that David's line has a future that Saul's did not. Yahweh's choice of David is an intergenerational election. David is chosen father of a chosen son.

Yahweh's choice of both David and Solomon is an election to privilege. David is chosen "to be king over Israel" (28:4). Solomon appears to have an even higher status, chosen to "sit on the throne of the kingdom of Yahweh over Israel" (28:5). As man of peace and royal builder, Solomon is a "sacrament" (Johnstone 1998a) of Yahweh's kingship in a more overt way even than David. He shares Yahweh's throne because he is chosen as Yahweh's son (28:6). Sonship is everywhere in the passage.[5] David repeatedly refers to Jesse's sons and his own: "among the sons of my father . . . of all my sons . . . many sons . . . chosen my son Solomon . . . your [David's] son Solomon" (28:4–6a). Then *boom*—in the sixth use of "son" in the speech, Yahweh breaks in to claim David's son as his own: "I have chosen [Solomon] to be a son *to Me*" (28:6; emphasis added).

A chosen son is a privileged son who sits on Daddy's throne. A chosen son is also a son with a task. Yahweh's *ben* (son) will *banah* (build) a house for his Father. That is what sons do; indeed, that is what sons *are*. A man is a father only if he has children, so his sons and daughters are the house-builders for the father. Sons can, of course, make a muck of it. A foolish son destroys his father's house, legacy, wealth, and reputation. But a wise son builds and *is* a house for his father. We are back to the genealogy, with its lists of "heads of the fathers" (→chap. 1, pp. 10–11).

Barthians have already anticipated the denouement. Yahweh elects David and Solomon and so determines *their* status, task, and future. Yahweh's election of David, and especially of Solomon, is also a *self*-determination. Once he has chosen David—freely, out of his delight in David—he is determined as God of David. More intimately, he determines himself as Father by his choice of Solomon as his son. Yahweh's election is determinative for Israel and the nations. Yahweh's election is likewise determinative *for Yahweh*. Once he elects, he cannot abandon Israel or David without denying himself, something he *cannot* do, for "the gifts and the calling of God are irrevocable" (Rom. 11:29).

---

5. *Ben* is used seventeen times in chaps. 28–29, and seventeen is the gematria of *kabod*, "glory." The word appears seven times in David's opening speech alone.

David gives Solomon the "plan" (*tabnit*) for the temple. *Tabnit* is used four times in 28:11–12, 18–19, the only uses in Chronicles. The word is used twice in Exodus (25:9, 40) to describe a model or blueprint for the tabernacle. Deuteronomy 4:16–18 uses the word five times, not of a "model" or "plan" but of likenesses made according to a plan or model. Yahweh prohibits Israel from making and venerating a *tabnit* of male or female, animals, birds, creeping things, or fish (note the Gen. 1 classification of creatures). In Deuteronomy, the living creature—the woman or the calf or the snake—is the model, and the graven thing is the *tabnit*. The word *tabnit* is used for the copy rather than the original (cf. the similar use in Ps. 106:20; Isa. 44:13; Ezek. 8:10).[6]

Derived from *banah* (build), *tabnit* embraces the whole process of building or making. It names the initial conception, the plan or model, *and* the finished object, a copy of the model or execution of the plan. It is both exemplar and instance, model and product, an ideal thing-to-be-built and the particular, concrete built-thing (usually an idol). Both idea and object are designated as *tabnit*.

Unlike Moses, David does not have to climb a mountain to get the *tabnit* (cf. Exod. 25:9, 40; Japhet [1993: 494] cites Ezek. 43:11). It comes from "the spirit [*ruakh*] with him" (1 Chr. 28:12 AT) and from a "writing" from the Lord that comes "by His hand upon me" (28:19). The *ruakh* is Yahweh's, and he stirs David to produce a written plan (Boda 2010: 230–31). David's *tabnit* comes from Yahweh as much as Moses's does, but David is a more active agent. He does not simply see a pattern and replicate it; the pattern comes from within him and he writes it, though only because Yahweh's hand is on him. David thus marks a step forward in the progress of human creativity: the first creation was by Yahweh's unmediated word; the second creation came through Moses's conformity to the *tabnit* he saw on the mountain; the *tabnit* for the new creation of the temple is imprinted in David's heart, written, and then passed to Solomon. Yahweh's Spirit hovered over creation to give it form and fullness; now Yahweh's Spirit hovers over *David* so *he* can form and fill a new world.

Another shift is implied as well: Moses saw a portrayal of the tabernacle (a model, or the true heavenly sanctuary); David's plan comes by writing or is expressed in writing. With David, the *tabnit* becomes verbalized. Moses is a "classicist" who builds by imitating a model; David is more a "Romantic" who

---

6. It is doubtless significant that the tabernacle and temple are never described as *tabnit*. They *could* be, since they are likenesses of Yahweh's glory. But only false likenesses—idols—are described as *tabnit*. The tabernacle and temple are rightly built because they are built *according to* the "made thing" that Moses saw on the mountain, the made thing that David received in his heart by the Spirit.

formulates a plan by expressing what the Spirit places on his heart. It appears that David understands the pattern *by* writing it. Writing is a coming-to-know, not merely an expression of something already known. That is neither classicist nor Romantic, but baroque.

We might infer this: for the Old Testament, a conception is as much a construct as the construction. Conceiving a plan is as much a making or building as physical making or building. And we can perhaps surmise an interaction between the two: the ideal construct or plan takes *polished* form in the execution of the plan. We do not conceive and *then* build; we build a conception that matures as we build the thing conceived. In the new covenant, we are all Romantic and baroque creators, indwelt by the Spirit, who implants the pattern of God's temple in our hearts and writes it in the scriptures so that, equipped by the Spirit, we can build in step with the Spirit's plan, so that *by building* we can come to know what we build.

David's *tabnit* is partly a floor plan, the pattern for the "porch" and its associated buildings, treasuries, rooms, and courts (1 Chr. 28:11–12). The plan also includes instructions for organizing the priests and Levites (28:13a) and for the utensils of service for the temple (28:13b–18). In Exodus, *tabnit* is directly applied only to the tabernacle and its furnishings (25:9), specifically the lampstand (25:40). In Chronicles, priests and Levites are more explicitly included as part of the design, living furniture in Yahweh's house. We are moving toward the new covenant in which the temple and its furnishings are *entirely* humanized. The latter includes designs for lampstands and lamps (28:15); tables (28:16); forks, basins, and pitchers (28:17); the altar of incense (28:18a); and the cherubic chariot (28:18b; the only such reference in scripture; Japhet 1993: 497). In each case, presumably, David's plan describes the form and shape of the utensils of service, but the accent falls on the weight of the materials (*mishqal*, "weight," used eight times in 28:14–16). The *tabnit* prescribes both form and material.

David's summary of the contents of the *tabnit* is arranged chiastically:

A *Tabnit/tabnit* (28:11–12)
 B Rooms and buildings (28:12)
  C Priests and Levites (28:13a)
   D Utensils (28:13b–14)
    E Lampstands and lamps (28:15)
    E' Tables (28:16)
   D' Utensils (28:17)

C' Altar (where priests turn incense to smoke) (28:18a)
B' Cherubim spread wings over ark (28:18b)
A' *Tabnit/tabnit* (28:18–19)

One of the striking changes from the tabernacle is the new prominence of silver (noted by Japhet 1993: 496). The tabernacle had silver sockets that held the posts and boards of the gold-dominated sanctuary (e.g., Exod. 26:19, 21, 25, 32), as well as silver hooks and bands on the pillars around the bronze-dominated court (Exod. 27:10). Silver was an intermediate metal between the bronze of the courtyard (altar, laver) and the gold of the inner sanctuary (table, menorah, incense altar, ark). Silver was the icing between the two layers of tabernacle cake.

In the temple, the use of silver dramatically expands. Solomon makes additional golden utensils *and* silver ones (1 Chr. 28:13). He expands the number of golden lampstands from one to ten, but also adds silver lampstands with silver lamps (28:15). The Mosaic table of showbread was gold, but Solomon's temple has silver as well as gold tables (28:16). In Kings, Solomon's age is a golden age, when silver was worth no more than common stones. For the Chronicler, Solomon's is a golden age because it elevates silver into the sanctuary itself.

What does this change mean? In the tabernacle, silver, unlike bronze and gold, does not have its own space, serving only as a thin barrier between bronze and gold. The bronze and gold spaces are the spaces of people and priests, respectively. Only priests can enter the golden regions of the holy and most holy places; lay Israelites are confined to the bronze courtyard. In this construction, Levites form the "silver" cordon between people and priests, guardians of the sanctuary who are not allowed to enter; they are ordained to draw nearer to the tent than lay Israelites but not as near as priests.

Thus, the elevation of silver in Solomon's temple is a material representation of the elevation of the Levites. That latter elevation is obvious in Chronicles: Levites are still deacons to the priests, but they are responsible for purifying holy things, doing the work of the house, taking care of baked offerings, and offering ascensions of praise morning and evening (23:28–31). They are still gatekeepers, but now they offer sacrifice—not the sacrifices of the altar but the new sacrifices of song. That elevated status is symbolized by the inclusion of silver furniture. David does not indicate where the silver lamps and tables are placed; perhaps they are in adjoining buildings and not in the sanctuary proper. Still, the fact that there are silver furnishings means that Levites are represented in the temple plan as lights and tables, as those who illuminate and feed. Solomon's is an age of silver because the Levites come into their own.

In David's final speech, he offers a fivefold praise of God's perfections (29:11): Yours is . . .

1. Greatness (*gedullah*)
2. Power (*geburah*, related to *gibbor*, "mighty man")
3. Glory
4. Victory
5. Majesty

He adds an expansive note (6. Yours is . . . everything in heaven and earth) and then ends with two clauses:

7. Yours is dominion (*mamlakah*).
8. You exalt yourself as head over all.

This eightfold praise is followed by a carefully arranged statement about God's power (29:12):

A Riches and glory (*kabod*) from you
  B You rule (*mashal*) over all
    C In your hand
  B' Power (*koakh*) and *geburah*
    C' In your hand
      D To greaten (*gadal*) and strengthen all

David does not separate God's attributes from the actions of his hand. Nor are the two simply parallel, as if God were, on the one hand, great and, on the other hand, a God who makes great. The two are more intimately connected. God does not need the world to be great, powerful, and so forth. Yet, having made the world, he is great, powerful, and so forth, *in relation to* that world.

And the relation is a particular one: he is great, powerful, glorious, and so forth, in *conferring* these same attributes on creatures. The linguistic parallels are close. God is great, but he does not reserve greatness to himself. He is great by "greatening" all. He is powerful, but he does not reserve power to himself but strengthens all. Everything in heaven and earth comes from him, yet he gives riches and honor. He is great by greatening, strong in his strengthening, rich in enriching. For human beings, too, greatness comes by greatening, power by empowering, wealth by dispossession, glory by glorifying.

David's ecstatic prayer—the last words he speaks in Chronicles—includes this notable verse: "Who am I and who are my people that we should have strength to volunteer offerings like this? For from you comes all, and from your hand we give to you" (29:14 AT). David refers to the vast outpouring of resources for the temple—thousands of talents of gold, silver, bronze, and iron (29:6–8). That is the "voluntary gift" that David celebrates. He commends the people for their generosity, but, more fundamentally, he acknowledges that *their* generosity is from Yahweh.

The second clause is a dense five-word piece of Hebrew poetry, alternating words that end with the second-person pronominal suffix, *-k*:

A From you (*mimmeka*)
  B the all
A' and from your hand (*miyyadka*)
  B' we give
A" to you (*lak*).

Yahweh is on both sides of the exchange. Everything comes from him, and what Israel gives back is only what has come from Yahweh's hand. That formulation does not quite capture the depth of David's confession, since it suggests that God hands things over into our possession, and then we, by some power of our own, return gifts to him. David suggests a tighter relationship between the giving God and Israel's return gift. Yahweh is the source of Israel's generosity, so that the capacity to make a return gift, the impulse to give back to the Giver, also comes from the Giver. It is not merely that the return gift comes from the hand of Yahweh; the return *giving* is also from him.

The use of "hand" highlights another dimension of Israel's gift-giving. David calls on the people to make donations to the temple by asking who will "fill his hand this day to Yahweh" (29:5 AT). "Fill the hand" is *malloʾot yado*, a Mosaic idiom for "ordination" of priests. Aaron and his sons were ordained by having their hands consecrated for tabernacle service and filled with food-gifts to offer on Yahweh's altar. In Chronicles, Israel does not receive anything. They fill their hands by donating gold, silver, and other precious metals. They are consecrated as a priestly people by handing over goods; they fill their hands by emptying them.

This consecration, too, is an act of God: Yahweh claims them as holy by giving the gift of generosity.

First Chronicles 29:14 is set within a somewhat larger chiastic structure that stretches from 29:14 to 29:16:

A *From* you all
   B from your hand we give to you.
      C We are sojourners, tenants;
      C′ our life is shadow, we have no hope.
   B′ Abundance from your hand
A′ *to* you all.

From him and to him are all things—this has a familiar ring to it. It is as if nothing ever leaves the hand of God, and yet the things that we receive become genuinely ours, subject always to a double possessive (*his* things and *mine*). For creatures there *is* no possession but double possession. The Lord encircles the entire process of gift and return gift. He underwrites our exchanges and reciprocity.

When we finally get to it, Solomon's coronation (a "second time") seems almost an afterthought. It is less the cause of the celebration than a consequence (Japhet 1993: 513). David received the kingdom in a similar setting (Japhet 1993: 409). For the Chronicler, the gift of political power is not a grim necessity to secure public order. Kingship is conferred as an outflow of joy.

6

THE LAND AT REST

2 Chronicles 1–9

Solomon is Joshua to David's Moses. David leads Israel from Philistine slavery, constructs a tent, organizes Levites, and prepares for the completion of a project that he will not live to see. Solomon is a man of peace rather than war, but his building projects complete the conquest of Joshua. Though Solomon never goes into battle, he does conquer through his wise administration of the kingdom, his glorification of Yahweh's house, and his testimony to Gentiles. Joshua conquers by the sword, while the new Joshua, Solomon, carries on a form of "sapiential imperialism."

Solomon receives more coverage in Chronicles than any king other than David. David's life and reign covers more than half of 1 Chronicles (chaps. 11–29), while Solomon's covers the first nine chapters of 2 Chronicles. Yet the Chronicler's treatment of Solomon is compressed by comparison with that of 1 Kings. He devotes half as many verses to Solomon as Kings does (201 to 434), and he omits a number of crucial episodes that are included in Kings: Solomon's wise judgment with the two prostitutes (1 Kgs. 3:16–28), details of his building projects (1 Kgs. 7), and, most strikingly, his harem and the idolatry it produced (1 Kgs. 11). One result of these editorial decisions is that Solomon becomes the only flawless king in Judah's history. David is nearly flawless but stumbles by taking a census of the people (→ 1 Chr. 21). Hezekiah, too, is nearly flawless but is criticized for failing to show sufficient gratitude after the Lord healed him (→ 2 Chr. 32:25). Solomon alone is above criticism.

Kings begins with Solomon's reign (1 Kgs. 1–11) and places the ministries of Elijah and Elisha at the center of its history (1 Kgs. 17 to 2 Kgs. 10). The Chronicler begins with a lengthy genealogy and includes new information about the reign of David. Solomon's reign thus occupies the structural center of Chronicles. The Chronicler also rearranges the internal structure of Solomon's reign. Material from 1 Kgs. 10:26–29 is placed at the beginning of Solomon's reign (2 Chr. 1:14–17), and details of Solomon's administration (1 Kgs. 5:23–26) are moved to the first part of the Chronicler's account (2 Chr. 2:1–18). The effect of these rearrangements is to organize the reign of Solomon into a smooth chiasm, with Solomon's dedication prayer central (cf. Pratt 2006: 206; Dillard 1981):

A Solomon's wealth, wisdom, power (1:1–17)

  B Huram of Tyre aids Solomon (2:1–18)

    C Solomon builds temple and its furnishings (3:1–5:1)

      D Ark enters temple, glory fills temple (5:2–6:11)

        E Solomon's prayer (6:12–42)

      D' Yahweh accepts sacrifice and house (7:1–22)

    C' Solomon builds cities and completes house (8:1–16)

  B' Huram and Sheba (8:17–9:12)

A' Solomon's wealth, wisdom, power (9:13–28)

The corresponding sections share common words, characters, and themes.

A/A': The Chronicler's narrative begins with an assembly of Israel's leaders at Gibeon (1:2). During the night, Yahweh appears to Solomon and grants his request for wisdom (1:7–13). "Wisdom" (*khokmah*) appears three times in the scene (1:10, 11, 12) but then disappears from the narrative for several chapters. It reappears only in chapter 9, in Sheba's audience with Solomon (9:3, 5, 6, 7) and at the close of the entire Solomon narrative (9:22–23). (As in 1–2 Kings, "wisdom" then disappears *entirely* from the history of the monarchy.) Because Solomon's request for wisdom pleases Yahweh, he promises to give Solomon riches and honor, too, "such as none of the kings who were before you has possessed nor those who will come after you" (1:12). On cue, the final section of the narrative indicates that Yahweh's promise comes to pass: "King Solomon became greater than all the kings of the earth in riches and wisdom" (9:22).

The opening and closing sections are also united by their attention to Solomon's chariots. Second Chronicles 1:14 records that he had 1,400 chariots and 12,000 horsemen; 9:25 indicates that he had 4,000 stalls for the chariots and horses of his 12,000 horsemen. And 1:16–17 indicates that the horses were imported from Egypt, which is confirmed in 9:28.

B/B′: These sections highlight the assistance of King Huram of Tyre (2:3, 11–12; 8:2, 18; 9:10, 21; another Huram is introduced in 2:13). Though B′ is concerned mainly with Sheba's royal visit to Solomon, that story is framed by references to Huram of Tyre (8:18; 9:10). These sections are also dramatically linked by Gentile confessions of Yahweh's supremacy. Huram says, "Blessed be Yahweh, the God of Israel, who has made heaven and earth, who has given King David a wise son" (2:12), addressing God as "Yahweh, God of Israel," a divine title that is unique in scripture (Japhet 1993: 544). Sheba echoes Huram: "Blessed be Yahweh your God who delighted in you, setting you on His throne as king for Yahweh your God; because your God loved Israel . . ." (9:8). Strikingly, only Huram and Sheba speak explicitly about Yahweh's love for his people (Ben Zvi 1999: 219).

C/C′: The chapters covered by C detail the construction of the house of Yahweh and the new furnishings that Solomon makes for the temple. The verb "build" (*banah*) occurs eleven times in chapters 2–3. The temple construction section is closed out with 5:1, which declares that the work was "finished."

C′ is also an account of Solomon's building. The verb *banah* reappears, used eight times in chapter 8. Chapter 8 begins with a reference to the building of Yahweh's house (8:1) but details other building projects—fortified cities, an altar, a house for Pharaoh's daughter. That narrative of building also ends with a notice that Solomon finished (*kalah*) and completed (*shalam*) the house of Yahweh (8:16).

D/D′: Second Chronicles 5:2–6:11 describes the celebration of the feast of the seventh month (5:3), the transport of the ark into the house (5:4–10), and the descent of the glory on the house, which prevents the priests from entering to minister (5:11–14). It closes with Solomon blessing Yahweh for fulfilling his promise to David (6:1–11). Second Chronicles 7:1–22 begins with another notice about the glory of Yahweh filling the house (7:1–2) and the Lord's acceptance of the sacrifices on the altar (7:1). It ends with another dream in which Yahweh verbally confirms that he has accepted the house and will be attentive to prayers offered in and toward it (7:11–18) and warns about the consequences of forsaking him (7:19–22).

The structure puts Solomon's dedication prayer at the center of the narrative, reinforcing a concentric cosmology: Gentiles at the edges (Huram, Sheba), the king's building projects in the land inside that large circle, Yahweh's descent into the house within the account of those building projects. And at the very heart of the heart of the story—at the center of the cosmos, its holy of holies—is a prayer offered from an altar-like platform (6:13) by the king of Israel. For the Chronicler, the world is mapped from this center, Yahweh's house of prayer.

And Solomon's prayer draws on all the other major topics and themes of the narrative. Though the prayer does not use the word "wisdom," prayer is one of the most dramatic demonstrations of the king's wisdom. In both the blessing that precedes the prayer and the prayer itself, Solomon repeatedly refers to the house that he has "built" (6:2, 5, 7, 8, 9 [2×], 10, 18, 33, 34, 38).

Wisdom among Gentiles (2 Chronicles 1–2)

Yahweh hears and answers David's prayers for Solomon, and David's exhortations have their effect. David hopes the Lord will make his son strong, and Solomon's kingdom is "established . . . securely" (2 Chr. 1:1). He hopes that his son will have a glorious kingdom, and Solomon's kingdom is highly exalted. The Hebrew *lema'lah* stands in contrast to *ma'al*, the sin of Saul and of all other unfaithful kings (→1 Chr. 10). Solomon's strength and glory are Yahweh's gifts. He is established because Yahweh is with him. His words are potent for the same reason. Like David, he "seeks" God (1:5) and prospers.

Following Kings, Chronicles records Solomon's prayer for wisdom and the Lord's answer. In contrast to Kings, the Chronicler records that this takes place in a public setting (Japhet 1993: 525–26). Solomon has gone up to Gibeon, where the Mosaic tabernacle is located, for a festival. Even after David brings the ark into the tent in Jerusalem, the Mosaic tabernacle continues to function (Japhet 1993: 576). This is typical of the Chronicler, who frequently depicts kings acting as heads of an all-Israel *qahal* (assembly). Israel's entire life flows from festive assemblies; their entire political order takes shape in the joy of worship. One thousand ascensions are offered (1:6), smoke signals to catch Yahweh's attention. Those ascensions anticipate Solomon's own progress as he "goes up" from Gibeon after the festival to reign over Judah from Jerusalem (1:13).

When Solomon asks for wisdom, Yahweh responds chiastically (1:11–12):

> A   Because you did not ask for riches, wealth, honor, the life of those who hate you, or long life,
> 　　B   but asked for wisdom and knowledge
> 　　　　C   to judge this people over which you are king,

B′ therefore wisdom and knowledge are given to you
A′ and I will also give riches, wealth, and honor beyond all kings before and after you.

Solomon's request is specific, and he gets what he asks. But the Lord also responds positively to *unasked* prayers. Solomon is not promised the lives of his enemies or a long life, but he is promised riches, wealth, and honor to go with the wisdom and knowledge that he requests. Yahweh gives beyond what Solomon asks or imagines, gives not according to need but according to the riches of his glory. Intriguingly, the gift of wisdom and knowledge is stated passively ("is given"), while the gifts of riches, wealth, and honor are explicitly from Yahweh ("*I* will give"). The center of the Lord's speech indicates the point of it all: Solomon needs wisdom and knowledge to judge Israel. That dimension of wisdom has less prominence in Chronicles than in Kings (Japhet 1993: 531), but it is more prominent than we might guess. Solomon's temple project is the great expression of wisdom in judgment, the royal wisdom of rule. Only a king who can inspire loyalty and commitment to a great cause could complete a construction project on this scale. As in David's speeches (→ 1 Chr. 22, 28–29), wisdom is linked punningly to sonship and building. Solomon is David's *ben*, his son; as such, he builds (*banah*) a house for David and for his heavenly Father. To accomplish that task, he needs wisdom (*binah*). Wisdom is skill to rule (1:10), but in Chronicles it is primarily the skill of a royal son to build.

Yahweh's gift of riches, wealth, and glory enables Solomon to rule well. Riches may corrupt, but they can also be a protection against corruption. A king who is wealthy can resist the lure of bribes. Wealth can also expand the imagination. Projects that a man of modest means will dismiss as pipe dreams are within the imaginative range of a wealthy man. A king with riches and wealth can act out dreams of justice. Glory can corrupt (→ 2 Chr. 26), but glory can also be used to promote justice, and it does in Solomon's case (2 Chr. 9:8; cf. 1 Chr. 18:14; Japhet 1993: 637). Solomon's glory attracts kings and queens to Jerusalem. They hear his wisdom, the wisdom that begins with the fear of Yahweh. Without the awesome radiance of glory, Solomon would not have attracted an audience of kings. Glory gives him a platform to encourage kings to walk in Yahweh's ways.

The temple project requires, above all, wise management of a large workforce. Second Chronicles 2 shows that the workforce is not confined to Israel. Solomon enlists the aid of Huram of Tyre, king of one of the main Canaanite cities to the north of Israel. From the beginning, the tribe of Judah has been enlivened by

Gentiles (→ 1 Chr. 2–4). Huram anticipates later Gentile assistants, and especially the liberating Persian emperor Cyrus, who sends the people back to the land with treasure and protection (→ 2 Chr. 36). Solomon's interaction with Huram is described in symmetrical speeches:

A Workforce (2:1–2)
   B Solomon's request (2:3–10)
   B¹ Praise of God (2:3–6)
   B² Send a man (2:7–9)
   B³ I will send food (2:10)
   B' Huram's response (2:11–16)
   B'¹ Confession of Yahweh (2:11–12)
   B'² Sends Huram-abi (2:13–14)
   B'³ Requests food (2:15–16)
A' Foreign workforce (2:17–18)

The temple is an international project, a house of prayer for all nations that is built by Israel and their Gentile helpers. The temple project exemplifies the ideal relationship between Israel and the nations: they do not join to construct a tower of Babel (Gen. 11) or a house of Baal (→ 2 Chr. 18); rather, Israel takes the lead in establishing a house for Yahweh, and Gentiles pitch in with material and skill. The ideal is specifically embodied in Huram-abi (whose name means "my father is devoted"). He is omnicompetent, capable of working in every sort of temple material with skill in every sort of craft. King Huram lists six minerals, in descending value (gold to wood), and four classes of fabric that Huram-abi knows how to work with, and adds that he can make engravings and design designs. There are twelve items on the list. Huram-abi is a one-man temple-builder, with all-Israel range of competence. A child of a Danite mother and a Tyrian father (2:13–14), he encompasses Gentile wealth and skill, being himself a Jew-Gentile, one new man made from the two. That Huram-abi bears the same name as the king of Tyre emphasizes King Huram's personal involvement in the work (Ben Zvi 1999: 217). He is Oholiab to Solomon's Bezalel (Exod. 31; Boda 2010: 226).

Solomon and Huram make a covenant. Solomon promises food, and Huram offers skillful workmen and cedars of Lebanon (2:16). Israel is the land of bread, wine, and oil. It is an Eden full of the sacramental foods. Huram's gifts of people and treasure anticipate later prophetic visions of Jerusalem as the destination of the pilgrimage of nations. Huram is a prototype for the nations who bring their wealth into new Jerusalem, where a crystal river flows (Rev. 21).

Huram stands to profit from the arrangement, but he is not doing it for the food. He begins his response to Solomon by confessing Yahweh's love for Israel and blessing him as the maker of heaven and earth (2:11–12; →2 Chr. 36). He knows that the good rule of Solomon is a gift from the Creator who governs the nations and distributes power as he wishes. If we are tempted to dismiss this as diplomatic rhetoric, the parallel with Solomon's own confession (2:3–6) indicates otherwise. Solomon claims, "Greater is our God than all the gods" (2:6), and Huram does not dispute the claim. More generally, it is unlikely that an ancient king would help build a temple for a god he does not acknowledge. Solomon's wisdom "conquers" the Canaanite king of Tyre, making him a servant of Yahweh.

Yahweh's House (2 Chronicles 3:1–5:1)

Like many ancient Near Eastern kings, Solomon devotes himself to building a temple for his God (cf. Boda 2010: 227–31). David begins the project by purchasing the site and organizing personnel; Solomon completes the task (Boda 2010: 268). In terms of Cappadocian trinitarian theology, David is the Word, Solomon the Spirit. If we include the dedication ceremony, the temple section of 2 Chronicles runs from 3:1–7:22. It is framed by dates (3:2; 8:1), and within this frame the temple is built, the ark-throne installed, and the house dedicated.

David purchased a threshing floor in Jerusalem and built an altar there (→1 Chr. 21). It is not until we arrive at the temple construction that we learn this threshing floor stands on Mount Moriah (2 Chr. 3:1). Moriah is the mountain where Abraham was sent to sacrifice Isaac (Hahn 2012: 112; Williamson 1982: 204; Japhet 1993: 551–52), and the placement of Israel's worship on such a location is significant. Every worshiper who draws near to the temple knows he follows the steps of father Abraham. Every time a worshiper slides the knife along the throat of a victim, he knows that the animal is a substitute for his beloved son. Every worshiper is an Abraham, every victim an Isaac. And for that reason, every worshiper is also reenacting the Passover, when a goat or lamb is slaughtered and its blood displayed to stave off the angel of death. Worship on a threshing floor means worship that involves sifting and judgment, but also love: Solomon's ancestor Ruth met her husband in a nighttime tryst on a threshing floor (Ruth 3).

The Chronicler's account of Solomon's temple construction (2 Chr. 3:1–5:1) is arranged chiastically:

A Solomon begins to build (3:1–2)
   B What Solomon makes (3:3–4:10)
      C What Huram-abi makes (4:11–17)
   B' What Solomon makes (4:18–22)
A' Solomon completes (*shalam*) the work (5:1)

The long section in B is itself a chiasm:

A Foundations and dimensions (3:3–7)
   B Most holy place (gold; house, cherubim, veil) (3:8–14)
      C Doorway and court (bronze; pillars, altar, sea, ten basins)
         (3:15–4:5)
   B' Holy place (gold; ten lampstands, ten tables, one hundred bowls)
      (4:6–8)
A' Court of priest and great court (4:9–10)

Exodus 25–31, which describes the plan for the tabernacle, is organized as seven speeches of Yahweh, which follow the seven days of the creation week. The Chronicler's account of the construction of Solomon's temple (2 Chr. 3:1–5:1) also follows the creation week of Gen. 1 in general and in specific details. In general, the account moves from a description of the dimensions, materials, and adornments of the three zones of the temple (porch, palace, most holy place, 3:1–9) to a description of the items of furniture that are placed in each room (3:10–4:10): first empty rooms, then stuff to fill them. This mirrors the movement of Gen. 1 from forming (heaven and earth divided by firmament, earth and sea divided) to filling (lights in the firmament, fish in the sea, animals and humans on land).

When the Chronicler gets to his "filling" section, he follows the creation account in specific detail and in order:

1. Within the most holy place (corresponding to heaven) Solomon places two cherubim, heavenly beings (3:10–13). Day one, when "God created heaven and earth."

2. The veil separates the most holy place from the rest of the temple (3:14). This corresponds to the firmament of day two.

3. The bronze altar (4:1) and sea (4:2–6) are earth and sea, corresponding to day three.

4. Ten lampstands (4:7) are like the lights placed in the firmament on day four.

5. Perhaps the ten tables and one hundred bowls (4:8) correspond to the creation of teeming things on day five. As is often the case, the correspondences of day five are the most elusive.

6. Solomon made the court of the priests and the great court, for the new Adamic priests and people (4:9). Day six.

7. Huram "finished" (*kalah*) the work for Solomon (4:11), employing a verb first used in Gen. 2:1. Day seven.[1]

Some things in 2 Chr. 3–4 do not fit this scheme, most prominently the description of pillars in 3:15–17. Given their placement in the creation-week scheme, they are connectors between the firmament-veil of 3:14 and the bronze earth-altar of 4:1. They are the pillars on which the heavens rest, corresponding conceptually to the twelve oxen that hold up the sea of heavenly water (4:4). Genesis 1 says nothing about such a structure connecting heaven and earth. Perhaps we are to link the pillars with the altar as part of the earth that is separated from the sea; they represent the "high places" of earth. Or perhaps we are to infer that the temple represents something *new* in creation, the establishment of a link of heaven and earth that did not previously exist. From that perspective, we might surmise that the pillars are a vertical representation of the temple itself, the capitals corresponding to the most holy place, the bases to the furniture of the court, and the pillars themselves the columns of sacrificial smoke that lead from earth to heaven.

Solomon's temple thus does not merely represent *old* creation, as closely as its construction follows Gen. 1. It is a *new* creation, the introduction of an innovative

---

1. Alternatively:
    1. "Solomon began to build the house" (2 Chr. 3:1), parallel to Gen. 1:1.
    2. Solomon makes the most holy place and the cherubim (3:8–14), parallel to the firmament of day two.
    3. Solomon makes pillars and the sea (3:15–4:6), mimicking the separation of land and sea on day three.
    4. Solomon makes the lampstands (4:7), a solar system of lights within the heavenly house.
    5. Solomon makes other implements (4:8–16), which swarm around Yahweh's throne like the creatures of day five.
    6. Temple implements are cast in the *'adamah* and then brought to the temple (4:17), like Adam formed from dust and placed in the garden. Temple vessels represent Israel gathered to serve Yahweh in his house.
    7. Solomon "finishes" (*shalam*) the house (5:1), as Yahweh "finished" (*kalah*) heaven and earth (Gen. 2:1).

element into the world. It is not incarnation, but it is a step toward the advent of a human Pillar who unites heaven and earth in his one Person.

The Chronicler begins with the dimensions of the house itself. The sixty-cubit length (3:3) includes the most holy place, which is twenty cubits long (cf. 1 Kgs. 6:17). The *ulam* (porch) extends another ten cubits in front of the house and is, the Chronicler says, 120 cubits high (3:4). Viewed from the side, the temple would extend much higher in the front than in the rear, giving the impression of a "crouching lion," according to rabbinic tradition. The house is adorned with precious stones and gold. Carvings of palm trees and cherubim adorn the walls, suggesting an Edenic setting or the oasis of Elim with its seventy palm trees (Exod. 15). With the gold overlay, the temple is a glorified garden, no longer simply wood or stone but the fiery color of gold.

Though the most holy place is included in the dimensions of the house, the Chronicler describes it as a separate "house" (3:8), figuratively if not literally detachable. Within the inner sanctuary are two new cherubim, each ten cubits high with a two-cubit wing span. Their wings "cleave" and "spread" (3:12, 13 AT), forming a covering for the ark. Both terms have marital connotations. Adam was to cleave to his wife so as to become one flesh; in marriage a man spreads the "wing" of his garment to cover his bride. The ark is the throne of Yahweh, but his inner sanctuary is the inner room where he has intimate communion with his bride.

After a description of the dimensions and materials of the house of Yahweh, the Chronicler enumerates the items that Solomon "made" (*'asah*) for the temple (cf. Pratt 2006: 57–59 for a list of temple furnishings). There are thirteen made-things, the list marked by the repetition of the phrase "and he made":

1. House of the inner sanctuary (3:8)
2. Cherubim (3:10)
3. Veil (3:14)
4. Pillars (3:15)
5. Chains for pillars (3:16a)
6. Pomegranates for chains on pillars (3:16b)
7. Altar (4:1)
8. Sea (4:2)
9. Ten water basins (4:6)
10. Ten golden lampstands (4:7)
11. Ten golden tables (4:8)

12. One hundred golden bowls (4:8)
13. Court for priests and the great court (4:9)

The Chronicler lists things that Huram-abi makes (4:11–17), using *'asah* ("make") six times, and then returns to Solomon to describe three additional things he makes: "all these utensils" (4:18), "all the things that were in the house of God" (4:19), and "all the work" (5:1). Gold items are reserved for Solomon, but the Israelite-Gentile Huram assists with bronze work. In sum, there are 13 makings of Solomon + 6 makings of Huram + 3 makings of Solomon = 22 makings, 22 being the number of letters in the Hebrew alphabet. The text presents an alphabet of construction, from *aleph* to *tav*.

Everything is bigger and better in Solomon's temple than in the tabernacle of Moses. Solomon's altar (20 x 20 x 10 cubits) is far bigger than the Mosaic altar (5 x 5 x 3 cubits; Exod. 27:1). The altar has expanded to become the size of the most holy place. Like the pillars, it is a sign that the secrets of the inner sanctuary are being put on display in the outer court. The laver has grown up too, into a sea, ten cubits in diameter and thirty in circumference (4:2). According to the Chronicler, oxen are cast around the circumference of the sea (4:3; 1 Kgs. 7:24 has "gourds"). Twelve large oxen hold up the sea, which represents the waters of heaven, the waters above the firmament, which fall to the earth to make it fruitful. The twelve oxen represent Israel, the Atlas nation, holding the firmament, guardians of the heavenly waters. The sea is Yahweh's "cup" (4:5), from which he pours both refreshing rains and catastrophic floods. It has a lily lip, a connection with the Song of Songs (2:1, 2, 16; 4:5; 5:13; 6:2, 3; 7:2). The sea is feminine, the delight of the husband of Israel.

If we exclude the final item, the list above divides neatly into four groups of three items each. Each group is associated with one of the zones of the temple. The Chronicler begins in the most holy place, with the room itself and the freestanding cherubim; that group ends with the veil (*paroket*, 3:14) that separates the inner sanctuary from the palace (*hekal*, 3:17). He skips the holy place and describes the pillars that stand at the doorway of the temple. Three items are "made": the pillars and capitals themselves, the chains strung on the capitals, and the pomegranates that are attached to the chains. Though we are not told in 2 Chronicles, we know from 1 Kings that the pillars are bronze. From the doorway, the Chronicler moves out to the court to describe three items: a new and larger bronze altar, a great sea resting on the backs of twelve oxen, and ten water basins for washing ascension offerings and priests. Finally, he moves back into the temple, describing the furnishings of the *hekal*: ten lampstands, ten tables, and one hundred bowls.

The items in each group are parallel and mutually interpreting. Though the Chronicler does not explicitly inform us that the cherubim stand on the right and left of the ark, that is the clear implication of the complex description of their placement (3:11–12). In every other list, there are things "right and left"—pillars (3:17), basins (4:6), lampstands, and tables (4:7–8). Second Chronicles 4:10 clarifies what orientation the Chronicler is using. The sea is to the right, and that is explained as "southeast." Since the temple is oriented on an east-west axis, and the south is to the right, right and left are being described from the perspective of someone within the temple looking out. That is, right and left are designated from the perspective of Yahweh enthroned in the inner, western sanctuary, facing the eastern front door.

The repetition of "right and left" suggests that the pillars, basins, lampstands, and tables are joined up with the cherubim in the inner sanctuary. What the cherubim represent is elaborated by the items that are visible right and left; cherubim stand at Yahweh's right and left as pillars, basins, lamps, tables, to cleanse, illumine, and feed. Since king and priest function as human cherubim, guardians of Yahweh's throne, this architectural structure also lays out their responsibilities within the house of Israel.

Another odd detail reinforces that linkage of inside and outside. Second Chronicles 3:16 states that Solomon made the chains "in the inner sanctuary" and then set them on the capitals of the pillars. If we take this at face value, the inner sanctuary functions as a foundry. It is a strange idea, and many have taken the phrase as an interpolation or a scribal error. Perhaps we can make theological sense of it. Even if the chains were not literally forged in the inner sanctuary (which is undoubtedly the case), the chains are understood to emerge from the inner sanctuary and then are placed like crowns on the pillars' "heads" (Heb. *ro'sh*; and, of course, our English word "capital" is also etymologically a *caput, capita*, head). If we throw Zech. 4 into the mix, perhaps we have this picture: the two cherubim in the inner sanctuary are anointed ones who serve as the source of the visible glory of Solomon's kingdom. And if we remember that the temple is an architectural man (pointing to the temple that is Jesus), then the Chronicler's temple might offer some fuel for reflection on the relation of a public "face" to the inner workings of the heart. In Solomon's temple, the exterior is true to the interior: the pillars and capitals, visible to everyone in the court, manifest the secrets of the inner chambers. The temple represents the man who enters its courts with clean hands and a pure heart (cf. Ps. 15).

We arrive at a similar conclusion through another line of argument. Mary Douglas (2001: 70) notes the "house that Jack built" quality of the Levitical descriptions of sacrifice. Priests put animal parts on the wood that is on the fire that is on the altar. Douglas takes this as a sign that Leviticus describes sacrifice as a "construction" within the altar. A small tabernacle is reproduced—the animals representing priests, the wood the tabernacle itself, formed around Yahweh's fiery presence. The Chronicler borrows the same stylistic flourish to describe Huram-abi's construction of the two bronze pillars set at the doorway of Solomon's temple (4:12–13):

1. Two pillars
2. Bowls and capitals on top of the pillars
3. Two networks to cover the bowls of the capitals on top of the pillars
4. Four hundred pomegranates for the two networks to cover the bowls of the capitals on the pillars

The order moves vertically, and moves from structural features to ornamental features: pillars, then capitals on the heads of the pillars, then chains/networks to adorn the heads of the pillars, then pomegranates for the networks/chains. Pillars could exist without capitals, capitals without networks, and networks do not need pomegranates.

The analogy with Leviticus hints that the pillars are replicating the structure of the temple as a whole. The Chronicler's initial description of the temple moves from the porch (outside, earth) to the nave to the most holy place (interior, heaven). That provides a rough parallel with the construction of the pillars: pillar (corresponding to porch and perhaps nave) to capital (corresponding to the most holy place). This connection is strengthened by the claim (3:16) that the chains on the capitals of the pillars were made "in the inner sanctuary." We might force (or nudge) the analogy with Leviticus and see the pillars as an architectural representation of sacrifice. The pillars are bronze, like the altar, and set on the ground. They extend upward, like sacrificial smoke, to an adorned capital that is linked to the most holy place. The last thing Huram adds is pomegranates (*rimmon*), a fruit most prominent in the Song of Songs (4:3, 13; 6:7, 11; 7:12; 8:2). At the top of the pillars one finds the fruit of love; ascending in sacrificial smoke, the worshiper enters the inner chamber of the Husband of Israel to enjoy a love feast in his throne room. Pomegranates are among the fruits of the land (Deut. 8:8) and here a sign of the land brought to fulfillment.

House of Prayer (2 Chronicles 5–7)

The Chronicler's account of the completion of the house of the Lord (2 Chr. 5–7) is arranged in a fairly neat chiasm:

A Solomon finishes (*shalam*) work (5:1)
  B Solomon celebrates the feast in the seventh month (5:2)
    C Levites take the ark into the house, with sacrifices and music; glory fills the house (5:3–6:11)
      D Solomon offers a prayer of dedication (6:12–42)
    C' Fire falls from heaven, glory in the house, with sacrifice and music (7:1–7)
  B' Solomon keeps the feast of the seventh month (7:8–10)
A' Solomon finishes (*kalah*) the house (7:11)

A and A' both speak of a completion of the house, but only the latter uses the key word *kalah*, the verb used to describe the completion of creation (Gen. 2:1–4) and of the tabernacle (Exod. 40:33). The house is not finished when the architectural shell is finished, or even when the ark and other furnishings ascend into the house. The house is fully finished only when it has been dedicated by prayer as a house of prayer. C and C' share several of the same elements—the glory of Yahweh fills the house, Levites and priests play music, priests cannot enter the house, sacrifice. But they run in reverse order. In C the sequence is as follows:

  a Congregation slaughters sheep and oxen (5:7)
    b Levites and priests play music and sing (5:11–13a)
      c House filled with cloud of glory (5:13b–14)
        d Solomon prays (6:1–11)

In C' the order is this:

      c' Fire descends and glory fills the house (7:1–2)
    b' Israel responds with praise (7:3)
  a' King and people offer sacrifice (with music) (7:4–7)

Note that the praise in b/b' is stated in identical terms: "Truly He is good, truly His lovingkindness is everlasting" (5:13; 7:3). And in both c and c' the priests cannot "stand to serve" or "enter" the house because "the glory of Yahweh filled the house of Yahweh/Elohim." We can fill out the sequence if we include the long prayer in chapter 6; it matches Solomon's prayer of praise in 6:1–11 and reinforces the centrality of prayer in the dedication. In c, Yahweh's descent in glory is a response to the sacrifices and songs of the priests and Levites; in c', praise, sacrifice, and music are a response to Yahweh's descent. Overall, Israel praises → Yahweh descends → Israel praises. 'Tis the story of Israel in a nutshell.

Solomon prays from a bronze platform with dimensions of 5 × 5 × 3 cubits, the same dimensions as the Mosaic altar. His prayer is a form of sacrifice, coming from Solomon, who is a living royal sacrifice. Sacrifices and song surround the event; without sacrifice and song, the Lord does not come near. But animal sacrifice exists to facilitate, to open a path for, the sacrifice of prayer. Solomon dedicates a house of prayer for Israel and the nations.

The central importance of prayer is reinforced by another structural detail. Second Chronicles 7:12–22 dangles outside the chiasm. It does not belong to the following section of 2 Chronicles (8:1 marks a structural break with "it came about at the end of the twenty years in which Solomon had built the house"), but it does not fit into the previous section either. Its structural awkwardness catches attention. In some sense, *this* is the climax of the whole dedication. And 7:12–22 records the Lord's response to Solomon's prayer—his promise to place his "eyes" and "heart" in the temple (7:16) and his threat, "If you turn away and forsake My statutes . . ." (7:19). If the temple is a house of prayer, it is also a house where Yahweh receives and assesses prayers, blessing those who keep covenant and cursing those who do not.

Solomon's initial prayer is structured as a double chiasm (6:14–21). The first runs from 6:14 to 6:17:

A   Yahweh, God of Israel, you keep covenant (6:14a)
   B   to servants who walk before you (6:14b)
      C   You have kept (*shamar*) what you spoke to David (6:15a)
         D   You spoke with your mouth, fulfilled with your hand (6:15b)
      C'   Yahweh, God of Israel, keep (*shamar*) what you spoke to David (6:16a)
   B'   You shall have a man on the throne, if your sons walk as you walked (6:16b)
A'   Yahweh, God of Israel, confirm the word you spoke (6:17)

Solomon uses some name of God fourteen times in the prayer (Hahn 2012: 11). If we follow the three uses of the title "Yahweh, God of Israel," the prayer breaks down into two sections, the first a declaration that God *is* loyal to his covenant and the second a request that he *be* loyal to his covenant. The prayer moves from indicative to subjunctive. Both sections begin with the divine name, and the prayer ends with a third use of his name. The logic of the prayer's argument is this: you keep covenant; you have kept your word to David; therefore, keep your word to David. At the center of the prayer is a statement about Yahweh's integrity. He has mouth-hand coordination; what he speaks he performs. His hand is the "amen" to his word (*'aman* is "confirm" in 6:17).

The second portion of the prayer (6:18–21) is also a chiasm:

A Heaven cannot contain Elohim, much less this house (6:18)
   B Turn your face to prayer and supplication of your servant (6:19a)
      C Hear the cry and prayer your servant prays (6:19b)
         D Open your eyes toward this house, put your name there (6:20a)
      C′ To hear the prayer of your servant (6:20b)
   B′ Hear the supplications of your servant and your people when they pray (6:21a)
A′ Hear from heaven (6:21b)

While Yahweh cannot be confined to the house (A), the house amplifies prayer so that he hears in heaven (A′). Solomon asks that Yahweh "*my* Elohim" would hear *his* prayer ("your servant," 6:19 [2×], 20, 21), but in the end all Israel's prayers are gathered up with Solomon's: "Hear the supplications of Your servant and Your people Israel" (6:21 AT). Yahweh is not just the king's God but "Yahweh, God of Israel" (6:14, 16, 17). But this is redundant: Solomon is Israel-in-person, and so his prayers are the prayers of the people.

The center of this second chiasm resembles that of the first; both speak of the organs of Yahweh's body. The first states that Yahweh's *hand* follows up to accomplish what he commits to with his mouth, and the second is a prayer that the Lord's *eyes* would be open *to hear*. Putting them together, we have this scenario: Yahweh's eyes and ears (cf. 6:40) are open to the temple; he has said he will respond to the prayer of his people; when he hears their prayer, he stretches out his hand to accomplish what he has spoken.

Solomon's theology of prayer depends on understanding the relation of heaven and earth (*shamaim* frames both chiasms, 6:14, 18 [2×], 21; cf. 6:23, 25, 26, 27, 30, 33, 35, 39; eight times in the seven petitions, twelve times in the entire prayer).

Heaven is above earth, and Yahweh is greater than heaven (6:18). Heaven is the source of help, the help Israel needs in every distress—just judgment, defeat, drought, plague, exile, and, above all, sin. Only the God who exceeds heaven itself can supply such help. Earth is not autonomous; it is not buffered, immune to influence from outside. On the contrary, events on earth depend on the fact that earth is porous to heaven. Yahweh, the incomparable God of heaven, is not remote from Israel or from Gentiles who hear the fame of Israel's heroic God.

The seven sections at the center of Solomon's prayer move from center to periphery, from the temple that is the axis mundi to the edges of the universe (cf. the chart in Boda 2010: 262):

Prayer "before the altar" and "in the house" (6:22–25)

Prayer "toward this place" (6:26–33)

Prayer "toward this city" from the battlefield (6:34–35)

Prayer toward land, city, house from a distant land (6:36–39)

Yahweh hears prayers uttered in the house, but he also hears the cries of his people when they are expelled from the land. His kingship is universal, which means that Israel can appeal to him from anywhere.

Solomon speaks as Yahweh's "servant" (6:19, 20), but the house of prayer is open to everyone. As representative of the people, Solomon bundles their prayers so that they can pray as well. Prayers come from "Your servant and Israel" (6:21). The recurring request is that the Lord "hear" (6:21, 25, 27, 30, 33, 35, 39) and, in hearing, "forgive" (6:21, 39). Forgiveness restores good relations between Yahweh and Israel, the harmony on which Israel's prosperity depends. *Shema* is the demand on Israel: "Hear, O Israel." Israel survives if they listen to the word of Yahweh through the prophets. Because Israel fails, their future depends more fundamentally on *Yahweh's* hearing, his ability and willingness to respond. Israel's entire hope rests on this: He who planted the ear, does he not hear?

Petitions to the temple are legal petitions (6:22–23). When two people take an oath to resolve a dispute, Solomon asks that Yahweh intervene to ensure that justice is done. "Maintain their cause" (6:35, 39; "cause" is *mishpat*) means "take up their legal case." The prayer comes to a climax with a list of seven disasters (6:28–31; Japhet 1993: 596). Prayer is the solution to all of Israel's ills, but it is not *pro forma*. It must be accompanied by full-scale repentance, involving thought, verbal confession, supplication, and a "return" of heart and soul (6:36–38; Japhet 1993: 599). When Israel is taken captive (*shabah*), they must turn (*shub*) in order to be restored. They will "turn back" to the land if they "turn" from sin toward Yahweh (Boda [2010: 265] notes the pun; Williamson 1982: 225–26). At the very close of the prayer, Solomon blesses God in words drawn from Ps. 132 (cf. Japhet 1993: 601–3). The psalm takes us back to Yahweh's "ark of might" and reminds us that the house is a "house of the *kapporet*" (1 Chr. 28:11; Japhet 1993: 495), a house to house the ark-throne and footstool of the God of heaven.

After Solomon's prayer, the Lord responds with fire from heaven. The temple is "finished," like the completion of a new creation (Gen. 2:1–4; cf. Hahn 2012: 115–16). People pronounce it "good," echoing the divine evaluation at the beginning of all things (2 Chr. 7:3). The completion of the temple replays the consecration of the tabernacle (Lev. 9). Once again, the glory fills the house. Once again, the priests cannot minister because the glory is too intense. Once again, fire comes from before the Lord to light the sacrifices on the bronze altar. This time, though, the house is consecrated by the king and people (2 Chr. 7:6) rather than by priests. Solomon oversees a wholesale slaughter of sacrifices, but the Lord responds as much to song and prayer as to the smoke of sacrifice. Fire came from the most holy place of the tabernacle (Lev. 9:24), but the temple altar is lit by fire from heaven (2 Chr. 7:1). The house is in more direct contact with heaven than the tent was.

When the fire "eats" (*'akal*) the sacrifice, the temple becomes a "house of sacrifice" (7:12). Sacrifice (*zavakh*) implies not only the slaughter and burning of victims but also the preparation of feasts. To "sacrifice" is to prepare a banquet of meat, so the temple is a house of sacrifice by being a house of festivity. When Yahweh descends in fire on Sinai, the people fear; when he sends fire from heaven to consume the temple sacrifice, the people respond with joy and reverence (Japhet 1993: 610). They fall on their faces on the "pavement" (7:3), a word that elsewhere refers to a stove-stone (1 Kgs. 19:6), fiery marble (Esth. 1:6), or a glowing coal (Isa. 6:6). With their faces to the pavement, they become living sacrifices. It is no accident that the court of the temple is used as an altar platform (2 Chr. 7:7). Every worshiper who stands in the court to pray and sing has become a sacrificial offering to Yahweh; every priest who enters the stone temple, its interior glowing with light and gold, has walked into a giant altar. The people rejoice because they have entered the flame of Yah, his passionate love for Israel.

The dedication is a Pentecostal moment, when the Lord descends in fire from heaven. It is Hanukkah, a temple dedication. In literal fact, the temple is consecrated in the *seventh* month, at the time of the Feast of Booths, which Solomon celebrates twice over (2 Chr. 7:8–11; on the complications of timing, see Boda 2010: 270). The Feast of Booths commemorates Israel's sojourn in the wilderness but also anticipates a final harvest of nations. By dedicating the temple in the seventh month, Solomon expresses the hope of Israel, that the house would be a house of prayer for all nations, a house of sacrificial festivity for Israel and the Gentiles. By dedicating the temple in the seventh month, Solomon anticipates the second house, which will be not just used but *built* by a Gentile king.

In addition to sending fire from heaven, the Lord responds verbally to Solomon's prayer. The promise is chiastically arranged:

A I have heard prayer and chosen this place (7:12b)
  B If I shut heaven, command locust, send pestilence (7:13)
    C And my people humble themselves, pray, seek, turn (7:14a)
  B' I will hear, forgive, heal (7:14b)
A' My eyes are open and ears attentive to the chosen place (7:15–16)

Yahweh's promise turns on Israel's humility, expressed in prayer, seeking the Lord, and repentance. Humility becomes a keynote of kingship. Even the worst of kings can be redeemed by humble repentance; even the sickest of kingdoms can be healed if the king will seek the Lord (→2 Chr. 12:6–7; →30:11; →32:26; →33:23; →36:12). One of the remarkable things about this promise is that the Lord incorporates Solomon into the founding of the Davidic dynasty. Israel's future depends not only on the Lord's faithfulness to his promise to David but also on his promise to Solomon (7:17). In Chronicles, the founding of the temple takes two generations—David to prepare and Solomon to build. And only when the Lord is enthroned in his house is the Davidic covenant fully founded. This reaches back to the two-generation founding of the Mosaic order (Moses to Joshua) and points ahead to the two-stage founding of the new covenant (Jesus to apostles).

Yahweh's promise is followed by a warning:

A If you turn; forsake statutes; go, serve, worship idols (7:19)
  B I will uproot you from my land (7:20a)
    C I will cast this house from my sight (7:20b)
      D I will make it a proverb and byword (7:20c)
    C' When people will ask about this house (7:21a)
  B' Why did Yah do this to this land and house? (7:21b)
A' Because they forsook; adopted, worshiped, served idols (7:22)

Healing comes by turning toward Yahweh. Disaster happens whenever Israel moves away from him. Yahweh's warning traces a regress from faithfulness: turn, forsake, go, serve, prostrate (7:19). When Israel forsakes, the Lord will forsake them and forsake the lofty house that Solomon has built. Israel and the temple will become a *mashal*, a proverb and cautionary tale for the nations. When the nations see that the house itself has been uprooted, scattered among the Gentiles like an unclean thing (7:20), they will take note and fear the God of Israel.

Gentiles Ascend (2 Chronicles 8)

To Solomon, Yahweh's house is for the nations: "concerning the foreigner who is not from Your people Israel, when he comes from a far country for Your great name's sake . . . then hear from heaven" (6:32–33). Huram and Sheba can find a place of prayer as much as Solomon. That concern with the inclusion of Gentile worshipers is central to chapter 8, which details Solomon's additional building projects but focuses structurally on his relations with Gentiles:

> A   Solomon builds cities that Huram gave him (8:1–2)
> > B   Solomon "went out" to strengthen Hamath (far north) (8:3)
> > > C   Solomon builds (8:4–6)
> > > > D   Ascent of the Canaanites (8:7–10)
> > > > > E   Ascent of Pharaoh's daughter (8:11)
> > > > D' Ascension offerings, festivals, priests (8:12–15)
> > > C' Building complete (8:16)
> > B' Solomon "went out" to Ezion-geber (south) (8:17)
> A' Huram's ships and sailors (8:18)

The verb *banah* (build) is used thirty-one times in the Chronicler's account of Solomon, mostly with reference to the construction of the temple. Chapter 8, though, uses the verb eight times (8:1, 2, 4 [2×], 5, 6, 11, 12), usually to refer to building projects other than the temple. After twenty years of building the temple and his palace (8:1), *then* Solomon gets busy building—cities, storage facilities, stables, a palace for Pharaoh's daughter. The other key word of the passage is *'alah*, "ascend," used four times (8:8, 11, 12, 13; cf. noun *'olah* in 8:12). The keynote of the chapter is the elevation of Gentiles.

Five cities are named: Hamath-zobah, Tadmor, upper and lower Beth-horon, and Baalath. Solomon does not (contra Japhet 1993: 622) conquer Hamath; he simply "goes out" to it. He is not a man of war. These cities are gifts from Gentiles, a sign that Solomon is a greater Joshua engaged in a peaceful expansion of Israel's territory, engaged in peaceable imperialism. The cities are described as "cities of desire," suggesting an erotic relation between king and city. Jerusalem is queen of the land; the cities of Israel are "daughters of Jerusalem," members of the royal court.

One project arrests the eye: "Tadmor in the wilderness" (8:4). It is arresting, first, because of the wordplay. "Desert" is *midbar*, a word that shares three of four consonants (*mem, dalet, resh*) with "Tadmor." Turn *bet* into a *tav* and rearrange the letters, and you have a city instead of a wilderness. It is arresting, too, because it sums up in four Hebrew words the direction of redemption, from wasteland to city. That image is underscored by the name of the city itself. First Kings 9:18 names the city *tamar*, a feminine name meaning "palm tree." In the wilderness, Solomon builds a city of palms, a fertile oasis. Building another "Elim" (Exod. 12; *elim* also means "palms"), he plants Eden in the howling waste. The king is like rain on mown grass, bringing Tadmor from the *midbar*.[2]

Solomon also builds a house for his wife, the daughter of Pharaoh (8:11). Johnstone notes that this is the only reference to Solomon's marriages in Chronicles, and sees it as "testimony to the recognition which [Solomon] has secured even among the traditionally most threatening of Israel's neighbors, and to the positive relations that can prevail when the nations are in harmony through that recognition" (1998a: 365). Mark Boda is surely correct that the notice about moving Pharaoh's daughter illustrates that Solomon "is passionate for ritual purity" (2010: 278). But *how* does it show that? What regulations of purity and holiness is Solomon obeying?

Some have suggested that ethnicity is the issue: Pharaoh's daughter is excluded because she is a foreigner. That is not what the text says, however; Solomon says that "my *wife*" will no longer dwell in the house of David. Johnstone offers a more plausible explanation: "No wife of Solomon can reside in Jerusalem (cf. the sexual abstinence enjoined on Israel as part of the measures in preparation to encounter God in Exodus 19.14–15 or the legislation on purification from emission of semen or discharge of blood in Lev. 15.16–24). The maintenance of purity at the centre of his rule is an absolute prerequisite for the maintenance of the holiness that is Israel's vocation" (1998a: 366). John Mayer cites Peter Vermigli to similar effect: "Women were unclean by their monthly periods. They were therefore unfit

2. This project becomes all the more enticing if, as some suggest, Tadmor is Palmyra.

to be in the same house as the ark was" (Mayer, *Many Commentaries in One*, in Cooper and Lohrmann 2016: 602). This proves too much, for it implies that *no* women are allowed to live in Jerusalem.[3] Besides, a woman becomes clean after her period. Concerns about the occasional impurity of women cannot explain the *permanent* exclusion of Pharaoh's daughter. Finally, men were as susceptible to impurity as women; involuntary ejaculation polluted a man (Lev. 15).

According to 1 Kgs. 3:1, Solomon brings Pharaoh's daughter into the city of David while the ark is there (1 Kgs. 3:15; cf. 2 Sam. 6:12–17; 1 Chr. 15:1). Solomon builds a house for Pharaoh's daughter *after* he completes the temple (1 Kgs. 7:8; 2 Chr. 8:1, 11), after the ark has been removed from the city of David into Jerusalem. So, the sequence of events is: David brings the ark to the city of David; then Solomon sets Pharaoh's daughter in the city of David, and she lives there as long as the ark is there; after the temple is finished, the ark is brought to the temple on Moriah (2 Chr. 5:2–10); *only then* is Pharaoh's daughter removed from the city of David—the place where the ark *is not*. Yet the reason for removal is that "the places are holy where the ark of Yahweh has entered" (8:11). How can she be disqualified from living in the city of David after the ark leaves when she resides there while the ark is present? The difficulty is intensified by the fact that Pharaoh's daughter is brought *up* (hiphil of *'alah*, "to cause to ascend") from the city of David. There is only one way "up" from the city of David—toward the Temple Mount.[4]

We can solve this puzzle by translating the text more literally than most English translations do: "For [Solomon] said, 'My wife shall not dwell in the house of David king of Israel, because *they are holy* where the ark of Yahweh has entered.'" Instead of declaring the *place* holy, Solomon declares that certain *people* are holy (*ki-qodesh hemmah*) because the ark of Yahweh "has entered to them" (*'asher-ba'ah 'alehem*). His point is that those who live in the city of David when the ark was there are now *too holy* (not too impure) to continue dwelling in the city

---

3. As Shaye Cohen has argued, the evidence that menstruants were excluded from public environments is slight (Num. 5). Cohen, "Solomon and the Daughter of Pharaoh: Intermarriage, Conversion, and the Impurity of Women," *Journal of the Ancient Near Eastern Society* 16–17 (1984–1985): 23–37.

4. One might save Johnstone's explanation in a couple of ways. Perhaps the ark's years in the city of David left behind some residual sanctity; though the ark was no longer there, the place was still too holy for Pharaoh's daughter to live. But this does not explain why she was put there in the first place or why she would follow the ark from the city of David to the upper city. Perhaps Solomon is correcting an error: Pharaoh's daughter never should have been in the same location as the ark, as Solomon belatedly realizes. But that does not explain why he brought her *up*. Sara Japhet (1993: 626) neatly summarizes the problem: "If the queen's living in proximity to the ark in the city of David constituted a transgression, why is this never mentioned in reference to Solomon's initial decision to bring her 'into the city of David until he had finished building his own house...' (1 Kgs. 3.1)?" Japhet agrees that Pharaoh's daughter is excluded because she is a woman, but sees this as a unique prohibition in scripture.

of David after the ark has been removed. Consecrated by proximity to the ark, they belong in a holier place, and so Pharaoh's daughter is "brought up" to live in *closer* proximity to the temple.[5]

The typology of the passage is consistent with this interpretation. Yahweh descends in a cloud and fire to take up residence in the temple with his bride, Israel. Following his heavenly Father's example, Solomon, Yahweh's anointed son, brings *his* bride into the city as well, so that the king and queen together provide an animate image of Yahweh and Israel (as in the Song of Songs). Pharaoh's daughter follows the progression of the ark, from the city of David into the higher temple-city. As Solomon's queen, she is an image of Israel as the throne-people of God, and so her history tracks that of the ark-throne. The deeper typology goes back to Eden: having built the garden-temple and his own palace, Solomon brings his wife into the garden-city to be with him, because it is not good for a king to be alone. And, of course, the Edenic typology reaches ahead to portray a King who not only takes his throne but goes to prepare a place on the throne for his church, the queen of heaven.

Solomon completes the temple and elevates Gentiles. But the temple is nothing unless it is a location for festivals and worship, those outlined in Torah (8:12–16; cf. Num. 28–29; Deut. 16:16). The Chronicler lists the feasts in two triads: Sabbaths, new moons, festivals; then the annual cycle of Unleavened Bread, Weeks, and Booths. It is the most complete listing of the feasts of Israel's calendar outside the Pentateuch. To oversee these festivities, Solomon implements David's plans for a reorganized priesthood:

A Decree (*mishpat*) of David
  B Priests for service (*'avodah*): apportionment
    C Levites for guarding (*mishmeret*) in praise and service before priests
  B′ Gatekeepers: apportionment
A′ David's command

---

5. Can we make sense of a notion of "contagious holiness"? According to Lev. 6:27, anyone who touches "most holy" flesh or blood is consecrated and needs to go through a ritual of "deconsecration" to get back to normal. Within Chronicles, the Levites who sang praise at the ark in the city of David are brought to the Temple Mount to continue their musical worship (2 Chr. 5:11–14; Hahn 2012: 125–35). Pharaoh's daughter receives an analogous consecration that permits her to "ascend" out of the house of David to the Temple Mount. This appears to fit with 8:7–8, where Solomon "raises" (*'alah*) the descendants of the Canaanites to assist with his building projects. That is not presented as a subjection but as an elevation.

Solomon also issues his own commands to priests and Levites (8:15), a sign that he shares founding authority with David. Now that the Gentiles have been elevated, the feasts have been instituted, and the Levites deployed, the temple is fully finished (*kalah*) and completed (*shalam*, 8:16). Now new creation begins.

Queen Sheba and Solomon (2 Chronicles 9)

The state visit of Queen Sheba[6] is embedded within references to Solomon's gold-trading ventures:

A Huram sends ships to Ophir (8:17–18)
    B Queen Sheba arrives with spices, gold, precious stones (9:1)
      C Sheba observes Solomon's wisdom (9:2–4)
      C' Sheba confesses Yahweh (9:5–8)
    B' Sheba gives gold, spices, precious stones (9:9)
A' Huram sends gold from Ophir and algum wood (9:10–11)
    B" Sheba returns home (9:12)

The structural connection is not random. The sea represents the Gentiles, and Solomon's sea ventures symbolize the international reach of Solomon's reign. For ships to travel from land out to sea is for Israel to move out into the world of the Gentiles. There is another typological overlay: by mining and shipping gold from Ophir,[7] Solomon replicates the organization and program of the original

---

6. English translations typically render the Hebrew phrase *malkat-sheba* as "Queen of Sheba," identifying "Sheba" as her kingdom. The Hebrew phrase is a construct form, indicating a genitive relation: "Queen *of* Sheba." But the LXX uses the phrase *basilla saba*, "Queen Saba," and the Vulgate follows suit with *regina saba*. This raises the possibility of a distinct Hebrew text tradition in which "Sheba" is the queen's proper name rather than her realm. Even if the construct form is original, the modern identification of Sheba with an Arabian kingdom is contestable. Isaiah 43:3 links "Seba" with Egypt and Ethiopia, which is at least consistent with the long-standing tradition that Solomon's visitor came from Ethiopia rather than Arabia (cf. Jesus's "Queen of the South," Matt. 12:42). To signal my skepticism about the consensus view of the queen's origins, I adopt the admittedly eccentric convention of calling her "Queen Sheba" and treating "Sheba" as her proper name.

7. David's wars opened trade routes, and Solomon extends trade by cooperating in shipping (Boda 2010: 278). David and Solomon traded in gold from "Ophir." Later, Jehoshaphat attempts to revive the trade route but fails when his ships sink (→ 2 Chr. 20). Ophir—now where might that be? Truth is, nobody knows. In *Seafaring Lore and Legend*, Peter Jeans summarizes some of the tantalizing possibilities:

> The ancient ruins discovered in Zimbabwe have been put forward as a possible site for Ophir, but they do not seem to be old enough. Zanzibar on the east coast of Africa has also been mentioned,

creation. Eden was rich with food, but gold was outside Eden in the land of Havilah (Gen. 2:11–12). Adam was called to follow Eden's rivers to Havilah so he could bring gold into Eden to adorn the Lord's sanctuary. Solomon with his gold-transporting ships is another Adam, fetching gold from distant lands to adorn the glorified Eden of the temple.

Given the Chronicler's interest in Israel's mission and witness to Gentiles, it is fitting that he reserves the most impressive Gentile visit for the final chapter of his account of Solomon's reign. Hearing the hearing of Solomon (*shema* is both verb and object in 2 Chr. 9:1), Queen Sheba visits Israel's king with an impressive retinue (or "very glorious strength"). Solomon has a "hearing heart" (1 Kgs. 3:9 AT), ready to receive others' words. Queen and king speak heart to heart. Their whole encounter is an "apocalypse," a disclosure of hidden things. She comes with "riddles" (*khidah*, 9:1), and Solomon proves himself a riddler on par with Samson (*khidah*, used eight times in Judg. 14), filled with the wisdom to untangle knots (cf. Prov. 1:6), a riddler like Yahweh himself (Ps. 49:4; 78:2). Second Chronicles 9:2 makes the point with a precisely formed chiastic sentence:

A Reported (*nagad*)
   B Solomon
      C all her words/things (*dabar*).
         D Not hidden
      C′ a word/thing (*dabar*)
   B′ from Solomon
A′ which he did not report (*nagad*) to her.

---

but that too is a very doubtful proposition. Because the voyage of Solomon's gold convoy apparently occupied some three years, more distant lands have been sought as an answer to the question of *where?*, such as the delta of the River Indus (near what is now Karachi in Pakistan), Johore in southern Malaysia, Goa on the west coast of India, Malabar on the southwest coast of India, Malacca (earlier, Malaka) on the west coast of Malaysia, and Sumatra—each of these has been suggested as the possible original Ophir; even Spain, Armenia, Phrygia (now Anatolia, central Turkey), and distant Peru have had their supporters. It is interesting to note that on the coast of Abyssinia (modern Ethiopia) there is a people who call themselves the Aphar; it does not take much imagination to derive "Ophir" from "Aphar." One atlas of ancient and classical geography suggests that Ophir might have been located in the region of Ceylon (now Sri Lanka). (*Seafaring Lore and Legend: A Miscellany of Maritime Myth, Superstition, Fable, and Fact* [Camden, ME: International Marine, 2004], 37)

He brings us down to earth by suggesting that Ophir was probably closer to home, somewhere in Arabia. Perhaps. But we can dream dreams of Hebrew-speaking seamen disembarking on the coast of India or Malaysia or Peru, perhaps able to communicate just enough to tell them they serve the Creator God of heaven and earth and promising to return.

The verb *nagad* in A/A′ is the root of *nagid*, "announced one," a term regularly used for a crown prince or for Israel's king who serves under High King Yahweh. Solomon proves himself a genuine *nagid* by his capacity to *nagad* every word or thing that Queen Sheba asks. The Septuagint got it right by translating it with *anēngeilen*, from the same root as *angelos* and related to *euangelion*. This is, after all, a gospel account. Queen Sheba "hears a hearing" (9:1) about a wise king in Jerusalem. Skeptical, she comes to see for herself (9:6) and finds it is better than she imagined. There is good news of a divinely wise king, and this king "announces" hidden mysteries. He provides the keys to the riddles of life, and the queen ends up not only recognizing the blessing enjoyed by Solomon's entourage but also confessing Yahweh the God of Israel (9:8).

Hidden at the center of 9:2 is a negation of the verb *'alam*, "to hide": nothing is hidden from Solomon. Equipped with Yahweh's wisdom, Solomon unveils things hidden from the foundation of the world. Solomon tells/reports to Sheba "all *her* words." *Her* words are not hidden from him. That may seem a rather odd way to describe the interview. Is not the queen coming to make *Solomon* speak, to get him to report *his* words? Part of the solution to the puzzle is in 9:1: she tests him with "riddles" (*khidah*), dark or hidden sayings. She poses a riddle, and he tells her what it means. But there may be another dimension: 9:2 indicates that Solomon tells the queen what she really means. She does not grasp what her own words mean until Solomon reports them to her. If that is what is happening, it points to a radically interpersonal, social understanding of meaning. Say what you mean, says the philosophical Fox in C. S. Lewis's *Till We Have Faces*, but Queen Orual eventually learns that this is a "glib saying." We do not *know* what we mean. Words remain lodged in us, until *someone else* dislodges them. Solomon's wisdom, in short, is apocalyptic in the original sense—it unveils, uncovers. In this, Solomon's wisdom is truly divine. Like Yahweh's, his eyes behold and test. Like Yahweh's, his sight penetrates past the surface to the heart of things—in this case, to the heart of Queen Sheba (9:1).

In Rom. 13 Paul says that the minister of God bears the sword as a "deacon" who ministers God's wrath. We assume that sword is a symbol of coercion, but that is not the only scriptural connotation of "sword." God's word is a two-edged sword that divides between soul and spirit, joints and marrow, and exposes the thoughts and intentions of the heart. Because the Lord bears the sword of his word, everything is uncovered and laid bare before him (Heb. 4:12–13). Yahweh looks at the heart (2 Chr. 6:30; Boda 2010: 264), and by conferring the sword he grants his king a limited ability to cut through to the heart.

Thus, Solomon uses the threat of the sword to expose the hearts of the two prostitutes who bring their case to him (1 Kgs. 3). By threatening to use the sword, he
is able to cut the Gordian knot and distinguish between the true mother and the
false. The threat of punishment can elicit confessions, bringing evidence to light
that would otherwise be inaccessible. In other cases, the ruler's word is his sword,
drawing out others' plans (Prov. 20:5). A clever ruler sets traps and throws out lures
to expose the plots of his enemies inside and outside the court. The ruler's sword
is simultaneously a light. His sword flames like the sword of the cherubim at the
gate of Eden, in order to strip away layers of obfuscation and to shine light into the
darkness. In this sense, *every* exercise of authority, not merely coercion, is an exercise of the sword. Skilled rulers in every sphere untie knots, solve difficult riddles,
and bring secret things out into the open where they can be evaluated and judged.

Queen Sheba's reaction is total. She hears (9:1), sees (9:3, 6), confesses (9:5–8),
and gives tribute (9:9). Her ears are confirmed by her eyes, which leads her to confess Yahweh with her tongue and pay him tribute. Her confession is double. She
blesses the servants of Solomon who always enjoy the privilege she has for a short
time—to stand with Solomon to hear his wisdom. But she knows that this wisdom
comes from heaven, and so her blessing of Solomon's servants leads to her blessing
of Solomon's God. She offers a tribute of gold, spices, and precious stones, which
matches the gold, wood, and stones from Ophir. She gives a tribute of temple materials, becoming, like Huram, a sponsor of the house of Yahweh. Spices have erotic
overtones (Song 4:10, 14, 16; 5:1, 13; 6:2; 8:14). Whether we are to understand
this as a gesture of love to Solomon or to Solomon's Lord does not matter much.
Sheba acknowledges God because she hears his wisdom from Solomon's mouth.
She wants intimate communion with Solomon because Yahweh is "with him."

Queen Sheba sees things that take her breath away (2 Chr. 9:3–4), *seven* things,
which roughly match the seven days of creation:

1. All she sees expresses the wisdom of Solomon, wisdom from God who by
   his wisdom "created the heavens and the earth" (Gen. 1:1; Prov. 8).
2. She is impressed with the house Solomon built. We are not told whether
   this is the house of Yahweh or Solomon's own palace. If the former, it is an
   earthly form of the firmament-tent of Yahweh, from day two of creation.
3. On day three of creation, food sprang from the earth, grasses with seeds
   and trees with fruit. Earth becomes a table set with food for animals and
   humanity. Queen Sheba is impressed with the food (*ma'akal*, the "edible
   things") of Solomon's table.

4. She marvels at the seating of Solomon's servants, who are enthroned (*moshav*) like the lights that rule from the heavens. Day four.

5. Others stand (*'amad*) to serve (*sharat*) at Solomon's table, like the priests who stand to serve at Yahweh's altar-table in the temple. The text calls attention to their "attire" (*malbush*), and clothing is a common day-five theme in the Torah. Swarming things created on day five form clouds and coverings, resembling clouds of incense or billowing robes on a priest.

6. A third category of servant is also named—cupbearers (*mashqeh*). In several places, the word means "well-watered" (Gen. 13:10; Ezek. 45:15) or "drink" (Isa. 32:6). Cupbearers are refreshment-bearers for kings. Perhaps we can see a distant hint of the abundant water of the garden of Eden. And the table servants of the king recall Adam, the original table servant of Yahweh.

7. Sheba is impressed by the ascent by which Solomon ascends (*'aliyyato 'asher ya'aleh*, using a form of *'alah* twice) to the house of Yahweh. Ascent is a Sabbath theme (echoing the rest of day seven), reinforced by the fact that the ascent is to the house of Yahweh.

All this fits the Chronicler's typology of kingship. Solomon's court resembles the courts of Yahweh's house. Like Yahweh, Solomon has servants who stand and a table, food and drink, and festivity. Since the temple is an architectural expression of creation, it is fitting that Solomon's house and court would also conform to the creation pattern. All this leaves Queen Sheba without spirit: "there was no more spirit in her" (9:4 AT). In the context of these allusions to creation, this use of *ruakh* (spirit) is significant. The Spirit of Yahweh initiates and orchestrates the symphony of creation; seeing the skill of Solomon's kingdom, a gift of the Spirit, the queen's spirit departs.

No wonder this scene became archetypal for prophetic visions of the pilgrimage of nations (Isa. 60), which stretch through to the gospel (three kings in Matt. 2) and on to the Apocalypse (kings bring treasures to new Jerusalem, Rev. 21). The gospel is simply this: one greater than Solomon is here, ready to unveil secrets and share the Wisdom that he is with queens and kings.

Sapiential Imperialism (2 Chronicles 9)

The Chronicler's narrative of Solomon ends with a complex summary of his wealth, wisdom, and power. The section is divided into two units:

A   Six hundred sixty-six talents of gold as tribute (9:13–14)
   B   Shields of gold in the house of the forest (9:15–16)
      C   Throne (9:17–19)
   B'   Chalices of gold in the house of the forest (9:20)
A'   Ships to Tarshish (9:21)

A   Kings seek (*baqash*) wisdom (9:22–23)
   B   Kings bring sevenfold tribute (9:24)
      C   Horses and chariots (9:25)
A'   Solomon rules kings from Euphrates to Egypt (9:26)
   B'   Silver is as common as stones (9:27; cf. 1:15)
      C'   Horses brought as tribute (9:28)

As noted in the structural analysis at the beginning of this chapter, the summary reaches back to the beginning of the Solomon narrative, repeating information about Solomon's horses and chariots, and twice reiterating the claim that Solomon's wealth made silver as cheap as stone (1:15; 9:20, 27). Wealth is one of the themes in this concluding section. "Gold" (*zahav*) is used seventeen times between 8:18 and 9:24 (thirteen times in chap. 9; Japhet 1993: 638), and seventeen is the gematria of "glory" (*kabod*), sometimes a gematrial synonym for Yahweh. The Chronicler emphasizes the *sources* of Solomon's wealth. Gold comes not only from merchants and trading missions (9:14, 21) but also from tributary kings in Arabia (9:14) and throughout the territory between the Euphrates and the Nile (9:26). Solomon's wealth is an index of his power.

And his power is an index of his wisdom. Like Queen Sheba, "all the kings of the earth" seek (*baqash*) an audience with Solomon to hear the divine wisdom that God had put in his heart (9:22). Seeking is, as we have seen, a major theme of 1–2 Chronicles. Gentile kings seek Yahweh by seeking Yahweh's king, who gains wisdom by seeking Yahweh. They are willing to pay for the privilege of being in his presence, bringing a sevenfold tribute (9:24; silver, gold, garments, weapons, spices, horses, mules) every year. We may pause to note the neat phrasing of 9:23: Solomon's wisdom is *his* (*khokmato*), yet he possesses it only because Elohim has given (*natan*) it in his heart. So it is with all human possession and achievement—genuinely *ours*, yet always and everywhere ours in the mode of gift.

The center of the first section is a description of Solomon's great throne, the symbol of his rule as Yahweh's prince on earth. His throne resembles Yahweh's, with its gold footstool made after the pattern of the ark's cover (9:18). The throne is a holy mountain, a cosmic model, with six steps leading to the platform on the seventh level. Each step is flanked by two lions, and, again like Yahweh's throne, Solomon's has cherubic lions on each arm of the throne itself (9:18). The twelve lions on the steps (9:19) represent Israel, a ferocious kingdom founded by the Lion of Judah, tamed by Solomon's wisdom. Yahweh sets Solomon on his ivory throne (9:17), which is Yahweh's own throne (9:8). Solomon, the greater Joshua, brings rest to the land, completing the labors of his Mosaic father, David.

Solomon's kingdom reaches the ideal boundaries of the Abrahamic covenant (Gen. 15), stretching from river to river, west to the sea and east to Arabia. But he does not realize this ideal through war. Gentile kings *voluntarily* offer themselves and their treasure to Solomon. He has six hundred large shields and three hundred smaller ones in the house of the forest of Lebanon (9:15–16), but these are not battle shields. Gold is too pliable, not to mention too precious, to take into battle. These are ceremonial shields, a sign that Solomon's *wealth* protects Israel. He has horses and chariots, but they "rest" (9:25 uses the hiphil of *nuakh*, root of "Noah") in chariot cities and Jerusalem. Solomon rules an empire, but not because he breaks eggs. Solomon's imperialism is sapiential. He rules (*mashal*, 9:26) because of his ability to tell and unravel riddles (*mashal*, which means "proverb" or "wise saying").

Solomon's reign prefigures the church's vocation. Something greater than Solomon is here, the eternal Wisdom of God in flesh. He is present among us by his Spirit of wisdom. As we keep step with the Spirit, we expect kings to start knocking on our doors, bearing gifts and looking for help. Solomon's evangelism is a model for the sapiential imperialism that is the church's mission.

7

AFTER THE DEATH OF SOLOMON

2 Chronicles 10–13

First Chronicles begins with the name Adam. The first nine chapters trace the genealogy of Israel, drawing on the genealogies and narratives of Genesis. David is a new Moses who leads Israel from bondage, pitches a tent for the ark, organizes Levites, prepares for his successor's conquest, and dies on the edge of completion. Solomon is a new Joshua who takes his father's counsel to "be strong and coura-geous" and establishes an empire that stretches out to the boundaries promised to Abraham. At the end of Solomon's life, the land is at rest; Israel is devoted to service of Yahweh in the house of prayer.

But then Solomon dies. Joshua ends, and we enter a long period that resembles the time of the judges. Judges 2:11–19 provides an apt summary of the cycles of Judah's history during the divided kingdom. After Joshua died,

the sons of Israel did evil in the sight of the LORD and served the Baals, and they forsook the LORD, the God of their fathers, who had brought them out of the land of Egypt, and followed other gods from among the gods of the peoples who were around them, and bowed themselves down to them; thus they provoked the LORD to anger. So they forsook the LORD and served Baal and the Ashtaroth. The anger of the LORD burned against Israel, and He gave them into the hands of plunderers who plundered them; and He sold them into the hands of their enemies around them, so that they could no longer stand before their enemies. Wherever they went, the hand of the LORD was against them for evil, as the LORD had spoken and as the LORD had sworn to them, so that they were severely distressed.

Then the LORD raised up judges who delivered them from the hands of those who plundered them. Yet they did not listen to their judges, for they played the harlot after other gods and bowed themselves down to them. They turned aside quickly from the way in which their fathers had walked in obeying the commandments of the LORD; they did not do as their fathers. When the LORD raised up judges for them, the LORD was with the judge and delivered them from the hand of their enemies all the days of the judge; for the LORD was moved to pity by their groaning because of those who oppressed and afflicted them. But it came about when the judge died, that they would turn back and act more corruptly than their fathers, in following other gods to serve them and bow down to them; they did not abandon their practices or their stubborn ways.

The passage shares a number of key phrases and terms with 2 Chronicles: "evil in the eyes of Yahweh" (Judg. 2:11; 2 Chr. 21:6; 22:4; 29:6; 33:2, 6, 22; 36:5, 9); "forsake" (Judg. 2:12–13; 2 Chr. 12:1, 5; 13:11; 15:2, etc.); "God of their fathers" (Judg. 2:12; 2 Chr. 20:33; 24:24; 28:6; 30:7; a rare phrase apart from 2 Chronicles); "play the harlot" (*zanah*; Judg. 2:17; 2 Chr. 21:11, 13).

Apart from these verbal echoes, the repetitive story line of Judges is the story of Judah. When Israel does evil and forsakes Yahweh to follow other gods, Yahweh is provoked to anger and gives Israel to its enemies (Judg. 2:11–14). Yahweh raises up faithful judges to deliver them and destroy the idols (Judg. 2:16, 18), but the people refuse to listen and quickly fall back into idolatry (Judg. 2:17, 19). Again and again, Israel is enslaved by Gentiles and delivered by a judge, reenacting the Egyptian sojourn and exodus. A similar cycle recurs throughout 2 Chronicles. Faithful kings are followed by idolaters; idolaters lose battles, and Judah comes under the control of their enemies; Yahweh raises up a faithful king to bring them back from "Egypt" and restore the kingdom. Finally, the kingdom is swept away, and the Davidic kings are replaced by Cyrus as the judges were finally replaced by kings.

Rehoboam's Folly (2 Chronicles 10)

The cycle begins with the death of Solomon and the folly of his son Rehoboam. Second Chronicles 10 is a fall story.

The Chronicler's long account of the reigns of David and Solomon (1 Chr. 11 to 2 Chr. 9) portrays an ideal. David and Solomon form a joint new Adam, overseeing the Levites who stand to serve in the garden-temple, guarding Yah-weh's bride, Israel.[1] All Israel, the chosen people (1 Chr. 16:13) under the rule of Yahweh's chosen king (1 Chr. 28:4–6), who lives in Yahweh's chosen city (2 Chr. 6:6, 34, 38) and reigns from Yahweh's throne near the place Yahweh has chosen (2 Chr. 7:11, 16)—all this is an effective sign of Yahweh's kingdom to the nations.

Rehoboam spoils all that, and does so from the get-go. He heads down from Jerusalem to Shechem so all Israel can make him king (10:1). Shechem is a vener-able place, where Yahweh appeared to Abraham and first promised him the land (Gen. 12:6–7), an Ephraimite city of refuge belonging to the Kohathites (1 Chr. 6:67). With regard to kingship, it has a scandalous past, being the place where Abimelech seized kingship (Judg. 9; Boda 2010: 290). The link with Abimelech, a serpent who ended life with his head crushed beneath a millstone, is not auspi-cious. In his folly, Rehoboam becomes an Abimelech. Acting foolishly, Rehoboam becomes another Saul (McConville 1984: 157–58).

Shechem is not the city Yahweh has chosen, not the city of Yahweh's ark-throne, not the city where Solomon built Yahweh's house of sacrifice, song, and prayer. To hold a coronation at Shechem, Israel has to make Rehoboam king without a sacrificial feast in Yahweh's presence. Making Rehoboam king at Shechem de-taches Rehoboam's throne from Yahweh's. By moving the coronation ceremony to Shechem, Israel "secularizes" the Davidic kingship. As Pratt (2006: 269) notes, the Chronicler subtly hints that something is off-kilter by not including a for-mulaic introduction. Rehoboam does not get introduced until near the end of his reign (12:13). His kingdom is "established" (12:1), and the king himself is "strengthened" (12:13) only after he settles in to reign in *Jerusalem*. Only then does his reign really begin.

By the Chronicler's lights, Rehoboam's fall is a *decisive* turning point in the history of Israel (Pratt [2006: 265] considers 10:1–21:3 a unit of text). Solomon sat on Yahweh's throne (2 Chr. 9:8), as David had (1 Chr. 29:23). Rehoboam sits on his *own* throne. No king after Solomon sits on Yahweh's throne. The Davidic ideal is shattered. The scene with Rehoboam is full of references to a "third day,"

---

1. Johnstone (1998b: 9) describes it this way: "The status of the king of the house of David has been expounded in sacramental terms. He sits on no merely human throne, but on the throne of the LORD: he is the visible expression in physical terms of the cosmic sovereignty of God (e.g. 1 Chr. 28.5). Likewise, the people of Israel are the LORD's host on earth, the counterpart in the physical sphere of the hosts of the LORD in the cosmic (e.g. 1 Chr. 11.9). The ark is the physical representation of the dynamic intervention of God on the field of battle; its resting in the Temple in Jerusalem is the symbol of victory attained (2 Chr. 6.41). Through David and Solomon, the ideal has been achieved: the kings of the earth pay their homage (1 Chr. 29.30; 2 Chr. 9.22–24)."

but it is not a third-day resurrection (cf. 10:5, 12). It is a third-day crucifixion. All Israel will remain on that cross until they are thrown into the grave of exile, from which Yahweh will recall them to life through Cyrus the Persian.

Second Chronicles 10 is a fall scene, but it is not exactly an Adamic fall scene. Rehoboam does not seize forbidden fruit. The structure of the passage highlights a different sin (on the structure, cf. Japhet 1993: 651):

A   Rehoboam goes to Shechem (10:1)
   B   Jeroboam, who fled to Egypt, returns (10:2–3a)
      C   Israel asks for relief, departs (10:3b–5)
         D   Rehoboam consults with and forsakes elders (10:6–8a)
            E   Rehoboam consults young men (10:8b–11)
               F   Second assembly: Rehoboam answers harshly
                  (10:12–13a)
         D' Rehoboam forsakes elders (10:13b)
            E' Rehoboam answers with young men's advice (10:14–15)
      C' King does not hear; Israel departs (10:15–16)
   B' Hadoram stoned; Rehoboam flees (10:17–19)
A' Rehoboam initiates campaign, returns to Jerusalem (11:1–4)

At the center of the structure is Rehoboam's harsh answer to Israel's request. He is not an Adam but a Cain who assaults his brothers (cf. 11:4).

Jeroboam leads a delegation to request relief from the heavy burdens of Solomon's reign. Jeroboam positions himself as a liberating Moses to Rehoboam's Pharaoh (Hahn 2012: 146). Whatever the merits of the request, the fact that it is brought up at Rehoboam's coronation indicates that it is part of a negotiation: if you give us what we want, Jeroboam implies, we will be your subjects. This is already a strike at the roots of Davidic theology. Israel is not supposed to bargain with Yahweh's choices. Jeroboam must have scented vulnerability. If Rehoboam were secure, he would never have come down from the heights of Jerusalem in the first place. The elders who stood before Solomon recognize Rehoboam's peril but also see that the best option is to return good for evil, *not* to return insult for insult.

Rehoboam chooses instead to follow the advice of the lads, those who had risen with him (*gadal* may be "grow up" or "become great," 10:8). The elders become wise by "standing before" Solomon. The lads remain in their macho adolescence because they "stood before" Rehoboam (10:6, 8). We take on the qualities of those we serve. Companions of the wise become wise. Companions of fools become fools. In this fall scene, the voice of the lads is the voice of the tempter, the voice of Satan.

In rejecting the wisdom of the elders, Rehoboam rejects his father's wisdom, and so rejects his father's kingdom. It is another strike at the Davidic theology of kingship. David and Solomon are surrounded by elders (1 Chr. 11:3; 15:25; 21:16; 2 Chr. 5:2, 4). After Rehoboam turns away from them, elders disappear from the Chronicler's narrative until the reign of Josiah (2 Chr. 34:29). Rehoboam's response to the people's request is a display of weakness disguised as strength. Like Hanun of Ammon (1 Chr. 19), Rehoboam and his lads think that bravado is the best policy, that the best way to prove strength is to humiliate others.

The result is a divorce. When Benjamites join David at Ziklag, Amasai speaks in the Spirit: "We are yours, O David, and with you, O son of Jesse! Peace, peace to you. And peace to him who helps you!" (1 Chr. 12:18 AT). Amasai expresses the depth of the union of Israel with its king. Kingship is not merely a political arrangement. The covenant of kings is a wedding vow, a declaration that the tribes are one flesh with David, joined by a covenant of mutual possession. When Rehoboam returns his harsh answer, all Israel answers with a poem that echoes Amasai's vow (2 Chr. 10:16; Pratt [2006: 272] notes the connection). Like Amasai's declaration, the people speak of "David" and "the son of Jesse." In place of a compact of mutual possession, though, they declare a dispossession: "What portion in David, what portion in the son of Jesse?" (AT). The answer is none, and so Israel goes to their tents and leaves the Davidic king to return to his own house. Rehoboam's name means "the people are enlarged." During his reign, the opposite happens.

As we will see throughout the remainder of 2 Chronicles, the people of the north remain Yahweh's people, but they do not have a properly constituted polity (Boda 2010: 285, 291). David's house is supposed to *be* Israel's house. David and Israel now live in separate houses. One can only ask, in Pauline horror, Is David divided?

All this shows why we have to read the Chronicler's final judgment about Rehoboam as a double entendre. "So Israel has been in rebellion against the house of David to this day," he writes (10:19). But who is "Israel"? One is tempted to think the term now applies only to the northern tribes, but a few verses later the prophet Shemaiah speaks of "all Israel in Judah and Benjamin" (11:3). *All* Israel is in rebellion against the house of David. Rehoboam rejects the Davidic theology and institutions of kingship almost as thoroughly as Jeroboam and the northern tribes. (The one redeeming outcome for Rehoboam is that he retains, and gains, Levites [11:13–14].)

God is not mentioned until the very end of the account (10:15b; Japhet 1993: 656). The political division is a "turn" from Yahweh to establish his word through the prophet Ahijah the Shilonite, who prophesied that Jeroboam would receive ten pieces of the robe of Israel (1 Kgs. 11). This is one of several instances in chapter 10 of one of the Chronicler's stylistic tics: he refers to events that he has not recounted (cf. Japhet 1993: 652, 657, 668). He does not relay the encounter between Ahijah and Jeroboam (1 Kgs. 11), just as he has not mentioned the hard labor that provoked the complaint from the northern tribes. He makes only a passing reference to Jeroboam's idolatry and his reorganization of the priesthood (11:14–15). At the least, this indicates that the Chronicler expected his readers to have access to the fuller account in Kings (and, by implication, in 1–2 Samuel).

Judah in Rebellion (2 Chronicles 11)

After the northern tribes abandon the house of David (2 Chr. 10), Rehoboam settles in Jerusalem (11:5). He builds cities for defense and for storage (11:5–12), receives the Levites and priests who flee from idolatrous Israel (11:13–17), and marries and has children (11:18–23). Given the political clout and kinship bonds of the tribe of Levi, Jeroboam's reshuffling of the priesthood is politically astute. He needs to break his rivals and marginalize those who have close attachments to Jerusalem's temple (Japhet 1993: 669).

Chapter 11 moves from land to temple to royal house. It also has hints of a chiastic structure. Verses 5 and 11 refer to fortress cities and food stores, and verses 22–23 return to this theme, noting that Rehoboam distributed "fortress cities" and "food in abundance" to his sons. Between these bookends are some surprising chiastic correlations:

A   Fortress cities and food storage (11:5–12)
   B   Levites, priests, and others who seek Yahweh (11:13–16)
      C   Kingdom strengthened, Rehoboam walked in the way of David
         for three years (11:17)
   B'   Wives, concubines, and sons (11:18–21)
A'   Fortress cities and food storage to sons (11:21–22)

Rehoboam's building projects form a double ring of protection around Jerusalem, stretching into Philistine territory in the west (Gath, 11:8). At the end of the chapter, Rehoboam appoints his son Abijah as his successor and "wisely" distributes power and goods to his other sons. In this way, he hopes to protect the peace of his kingdom, to head off fraternal strife after his death.

The notice that Rehoboam walked in the way of David makes sense as the center of the text. For a brief period, he is a good king. Second Chronicles 11:17 also picks up the notion of "strength" from the beginning and end of the section (11:11; 12:1). B informs us of Jeroboam's satyrs and golden calves (11:15) and his decision to exclude Levites and Aaronic priests from service. They head south to Judah, and those who want to seek Yahweh follow them. With the combination of Judah, Benjamin, and Levi, the southern kingdom replicates the basic structure of the ideal Israel of the genealogies (→ 1 Chr. 1–9; see Johnstone 1998a). Judah begins the genealogies, Benjamin comes at the end, and Levites are at the center. Under Rehoboam, Judah is much reduced, but the skeleton of the original Israel is still apparent.

The surprise in the structure is the parallel of Levites and priests with members of Rehoboam's household. At a certain level of abstraction, the sense is obvious: as Yahweh has his own house with his own Levitical servants, so Rehoboam the king has his household. Perhaps, though, the connection is stronger: priests and Levites are seen not only as members of Yahweh's household but as part of the *king's* entourage. These migrants from the north, after all, "strengthen" the kingdom (11:17). More speculatively, perhaps there is a husband-wife or father-son relationship between king and Levites. The king is the Adam of Jerusalem, and the Levites are his Eve-like helpers. The king is father Adam, and the Levites are among his sons.

The Chronicler does not criticize Rehoboam's polygamy directly (eighteen wives, sixty concubines, 11:21; on the identity of Maacah, see Japhet 1993: 670–71 and → 2 Chr. 15:16), but there are hints of disapproval. The Judges typology noted above is relevant, connecting Rehoboam's polygamy to that of Gideon (Judg. 8:30). Rehoboam's named wives are all relatives, cousins of one variety or another. This endogamy resembles the practices of Egypt and is perhaps a hint that Rehoboam is inverting the exodus even before Shishak shows up to plunder Jerusalem.

The sequence between chapters 11 and 12 also hints that Rehoboam's polygamy is dangerous policy. Chapter 11 ends with the comment that Rehoboam "asked" (*sha'al*) for wives. The term is more pregnant than it might appear. A king with sixty concubines is clearly making a lot of alliances; in asking for wives, he is seeking protection from potential rivals or adversaries. But protection does not lie in that direction. Good kings *sha'al* God in the temple (2 Chr. 1:7, 11). The verb links Rehoboam to Israel's first king, Saul (*sha'ul*), who sought help from a medium rather than from God (1 Chr. 10:13–14). It is not entirely a surprise when we learn (in 12:2) that Rehoboam commits a sacrilege, a *ma'al*, the first king to be charged with this crime since Saul (→ 1 Chr. 10).

If we ignore the break between chapters 11 and 12, we move immediately from Rehoboam "asking" for wives to Rehoboam forsaking the Torah and committing a *ma'al* (12:1–2). The juxtaposition hints at cause and effect. As Johnstone (1998b: 40) suggests, Rehoboam's geopolitical play might have a role in Shishak's invasion of Judah. It is possible that Shishak was alarmed that his neighbor to the north was building alliances with other kings. To forestall the creation of a block of powers, he invades and weakens Judah. Rehoboam's efforts to strengthen his kingdom by "asking" wives backfire: it makes his kingdom weaker, vulnerable to Egyptian invasion.

Into the Hands of Enemies (2 Chronicles 12)

The second portion of Rehoboam's reign is also structured chiastically:

> A Rehoboam becomes strong, forsakes the Torah (12:1)
> > B Shishak invades, captures cities, threatens Jerusalem (12:2–4)
> > > C Prophecy of Shemiah (12:5)
> > > > D Rehoboam and princes humble themselves (12:6)
> > > C' Second prophecy of Shemiah (12:7–8)
> > B' Shishak plunders storehouses (12:9–11)
> A' Rehoboam's humility cools Yahweh's burning nose; Rehoboam becomes strong (12:12–13)

The links between A and A' are verbal: Rehoboam strengthened himself in the early part of his reign, and after Shishak's invasion and his repentance, he again strengthens the kingdom (12:13). B and B' are about Shishak's invasion, perhaps, as noted, provoked by Rehoboam's efforts to establish what may have been an anti-Egyptian network of alliances. Shemiah's two prophecies occupy the C and C' positions, the first a warning to Rehoboam and the second an assurance that the Lord has taken note of Rehoboam's humility. Second Chronicles 12:6 is the hinge of the narrative, the turning point in Rehoboam's fortunes, highlighting the key concept of humility (cf. 7:14). Rehoboam is the first of a series of threatened kings who find safety by responding with humility to the word of Yahweh's prophets.

After three years of faithfulness (11:17), Rehoboam goes astray, perhaps led by foreign wives. He "forsook the Torah of Yahweh" (12:1 AT). "Forsake" is a key word in Chronicles, but kings or the people usually forsake Yahweh himself rather than his law. We are not informed of the nature of the defection. The Chronicler sometimes uses Torah with reference specifically to the cultic law (1 Chr. 16:40; 22:12; 2 Chr. 23:18), and it is possible that this is the meaning here. That would fit with the use of *maʿal* in 12:2, often used to denote a failure with regard to the Lord's house and the worship of the Levites.

Whatever the specifics, Rehoboam's *maʿal* is punished by the ascent (*ʿalah*) of Pharaoh Shishak. Shishak ascends as from Sheol itself, with an innumerable multitude of exotic warriors from Libya, Cush, Sikkim, and Egypt (cf. Boda 2010: 296 regarding Egyptian evidence for the invasion). The fourfold army represents the nations from the four points of the compass, organized against Israel, forming a counterfeit Israel numbered by multiples of twelve: Shishak has 1,200 chariots and 60,000 (5 × 12,000) horsemen. Those fortress cities that Rehoboam built and supplied so carefully are no help. Shishak takes the cities and advances all the way to Jerusalem. Yahweh can keep the land. He is Israel's guardian. But Rehoboam has forsaken him and his law, and Rehoboam's defenses become impotent.

Shemaiah reappears (cf. 11:2–4), calling Israel to faithfulness to the Shema. His message is a *lex talionis*: eye for eye, tooth for tooth, burn for burn, forsake for forsake. Rehoboam has forsaken Yahweh's Torah, tantamount to forsaking Yahweh (12:5). So Yahweh forsakes Judah. The symmetry of the prophetic poem reinforces the symmetry of Yahweh's justice: You / forsake / me // I / forsake / you. Rehoboam's strength has made him complacent and led him to abandon the law (Japhet 1993: 676).

Remarkably, Rehoboam responds. It is not what we expect. He has proven himself a foolish lad, listening to his posse rather than the elders who stood before his father. We do not expect him to hear the prophet whose name means "Yah hears" or to return to Torah. But he hears and humbles himself, and together with the princes (the lads of chapter 10? his sons?) confesses that Yahweh is just. They put themselves on the Lord's good side by agreeing with the judgment he brings. As he promised Solomon, the Lord hears and sees (12:7). He responds to humility and sends Shemaiah with another message. Shemaiah's name carries a threatening overtone when he first arrives: love the Lord your God with all your heart, or he will send Shishak to invade. Now his name carries reassurance: the Lord hears and responds. Whether in judgment or grace, Yahweh is always the God of *shema*, the God who hears and calls Israel to do the same.

Yahweh does not promise a complete deliverance from Shishak. He wants to teach Rehoboam and Judah a lesson in lord-slave dynamics. Not all lords are the same. Service to Yahweh is not the same as service to the nations. To show the difference, Yahweh gives Rehoboam over to Shishak in a measured way. Yahweh preserves Jerusalem, but he allows Shishak to take and plunder the cities of Judah. It is a reverse exodus. An Egyptian Pharaoh becomes lord over Judah. Instead of Judah plundering Egypt, Egypt plunders Judah, as Shishak takes, takes, takes (the verb is used three times in 12:9). Yahweh gives them a taste of exile and divine abandonment. Shishak leaves Judah diminished. He removes the gold shields of Solomon, and Rehoboam has to replace them with shields of bronze, which his guards carry as he moves from the palace to the temple. The king moves in shining replica of Yahweh's glory cloud, but now the glory is tarnished.

Solomon's gold is not merely a sign of Yahweh's favor. The temple storehouses contain the people's tribute to Yahweh, and the storehouses of the king represent the people's tribute to Yahweh's prince, Rehoboam. When they are plundered, it is a sign of the breach between Yahweh and his people. Avoiding Yahweh's yoke leads to a yoke of slavery (Japhet 1993: 680). It always leads back to Egypt. Still, the Chronicler's account of Rehoboam is mixed. He does evil, but also shows humility. He is typical of the kings of Judah until the time of Ahaz, when kings become strictly good or evil.

Marks of the True Israel (2 Chronicles 13)

In the generation after Israel split into the northern and southern kingdoms, Abijah, the son of Rehoboam, grandson of Solomon, and great-grandson of David, goes to war with Jeroboam, son of Nebat and king of the north. It seems an unequal contest. Abijah initiates the war with his 400,000 valiant warriors. But Jeroboam gathers twice as many chosen men who are also strong warriors (*khayil gibborim*). The army of Judah is badly outgunned.

That does not prevent Abijah from taking the high ground—literally. He ascends to Mount Zemaraim in the hill country of Ephraim and launches into theological trash-talk. The place itself is a provocation. The name means "twin peaks," and it is in the vicinity of Bethel (Johnstone 1998b: 52; Josh. 18:22). Bethel is one of the places where Jeroboam has set up his golden calves (1 Kgs.

12). Abijah stands on a mountain opposite Bethel and tells Jeroboam, Israel, and the calves themselves that they are "not-gods" (*lo' 'elohim*, 2 Chr. 13:9).

The speech is the high point of Abijah's reign. We are told about the battle in eight verses; the speech takes nine verses. Rehoboam's son may not seem the ideal spokesman for the Davidic dynasty, and trash-talk before a battle seems an unlikely occasion for theological insight. But Abijah provides one of the most complete statements of Davidic kingdom theology in 1–2 Chronicles.

Abijah focuses on the two main institutions of the Davidic kingdom: the monarchy and the Levitical priests who serve in the temple. He begins with "Hear!" Speaking from a mountain, calling Israel to "hear," Abijah reminds us of Sinai and of Moses's call to Israel, "Hear, O Israel! Yahweh is our God. Yahweh is one" (Deut. 6:4 AT). It is a meaningful opening. The northern kingdom has forsaken Yahweh. They have not kept the first word. They have not loved the Lord with all their heart, soul, and strength or worshiped him as the one God of heaven and earth. They do not have the right to call themselves Israel, the people of Yahweh, the people of the Shema, the one people who serves the one God with a single heart.

Abijah's speech is a modified chiasm (cf. Pratt [2006: 286] on the structure of Abijah's reign):

Hear, Jeroboam and Israel (13:4)

  A Yahweh gave rule to David (13:5)
    B Jeroboam rebelled (13:6–7)
      C Do you come with force and golden calves? (13:8)
        D You drove out priests (13:9)
        D' Our priests minister (13:10–11a)
      C' You have forsaken Yahweh (13:11b)
  A' Yahweh is with us (13:12)

The structure of the speech replicates the political order of Israel. Yahweh is the ultimate guarantor and guardian of the Davidic kingdom. He stands "with us" at the boundary of the land as the God who gave rule to David. The absence of a B' is notable. Jeroboam is not a legitimate king; his kingdom is founded on rebellion (Boda 2010: 148). At the center of the speech is the contrast of priesthoods. The order replicates the arrangement of the genealogy, with Judah at the beginning, Benjamin (another royal tribe) at the end, and the Levites at the center. The Chronicler is once again drawing pictures with words.

Abijah moves from past to present and predicts the future (Japhet 1993: 690). The northern kingdom has forsaken Yahweh by abandoning the house of David. Abijah claims that the sons of David have the right to rule all Israel. All Israel united under a son of David—that is the way the world ought to be. Yet by addressing the northern tribes with this appeal, Abijah treats them as part of the "all Israel" called to worship Yahweh (Japhet 1993: 693).

Abijah himself has the credentials to press this Davidic claim. His mother is Micaiah ("Who is like Yah?"), daughter of Uriel ("God is light") from the Benjamite town of Gibeah, Saul's hometown (Johnstone 1998b: 51), possibly a princess from the fallen house of Saul. In his own person, Abijah combines two royal houses, Saul and David, and two royal tribes, Benjamin and Judah. Like Huram-abi, he is a united kingdom in person, and an advocate for the united kingdom. His own name is a sign of faith in the Davidic promise. Abijah (*'abiyah*) means "Yah is my Father," the heart of the Davidic promise: I will be a Father to him, and he will be a son to me, Yahweh says (2 Sam. 7). The Davidic kings have the right to rule all Israel because they represent in their own person "son Israel" (Exod. 4:23). David did not seize the kingdom by superior strength or political cunning. The kingdom is a gift from Yahweh (13:5). Yahweh has granted this authority to David and his descendants by covenant. He has sworn that David and his sons will be on the throne, committing himself to maintaining the house of David just as surely as he committed himself to maintaining the house of Aaron (see Num. 18 on the priests' "covenant of salt"; Japhet 1993: 691).

David's is not just another human dynasty. The kingdom Yahweh granted by covenant to David's family is Yahweh's own kingdom (13:8). Resisting the Davidic kingdom amounts to resisting Yahweh, since David and his sons are the Lord's princes, his sons who carry out his rule in the world. The northern kingdom, by contrast, is founded on rebellion against David's house, which is rebellion against Yahweh. Abijah does not blame Rehoboam or the hotheads in his court for the division of the kingdom. The kingdom is divided because Jeroboam, a servant of Solomon, rebelled against his lord (*'adon*). Rehoboam is a victim of "sons of Belial," whether in his own court or in the group around Jeroboam. Abijah sees Jeroboam as a counterfeit David. David also gathered men around him ($\rightarrow$ 1 Chr. 11:1; Johnstone 1998b: 54), but David gathered honorable and valiant warriors. Jeroboam's company is full of sons of Belial who take advantage of Rehoboam's youth and timidity to wrest the kingdom from him. David had a lord, Saul, but did not rebel against him. Jeroboam has not learned his lesson. By making war on Abijah, he continues the rebellion against David and against Yahweh. This is not an accidental or inadvertent sin. Abijah claims that Jeroboam and Israel *know* all this (13:5). It is high-handed rebellion: Israel forsakes Yahweh by forsaking David's house. "Hear, O Israel," Abijah says. Return to Yahweh by returning to the house of David.

As important as the monarchy is, the Chronicler considers the ministry of the Levitical priests just as essential to the Davidic order. Israel exists to be an effective sign of Yahweh's kingdom on earth. The armies of the Davidic kings are the earthly hosts of Yahweh of hosts; the wars of David are Yahweh's wars. David's kingdom is an effective sign of Yahweh's kingdom because Yahweh is enthroned in Jerusalem, the chosen city, in his house, the temple, attended by the Levitical priests. Jeroboam has his shrines and his priests, but they do not qualify. Jeroboam allows anyone who comes with a bull and seven rams to "fill his hand" for priesthood (13:9 AT; cf. Exod. 29:29). We are back in the time of the judges, when anyone will fill his hand to serve as priest, so long as someone "filled his hand" with money (Judg. 17:10). Jeroboam's priests serve *made* gods (13:8), and a *made* god is a *no*-god. Abijah is darkly sarcastic: men scramble to Bethel with a bull and seven rams, a hefty payment, for the privilege of serving . . . *nothing at all*! They are priests to the void. No wonder Abijah can speak so boldly from a mountain overlooking Bethel. He can insult the golden calves and their priests to his heart's content. After all, what are they going to do? They are no-things!

Judah is in a very different situation. Yahweh is Judah's God (13:10), since they have not forsaken him. The sign of Yahweh's continuing presence among the people of Judah is the continuing round of temple service. In seven clauses, Abijah summarizes the work of the temple:

A   We have not forsaken Yahweh
   B   Priests and Levites at work serving Yahweh
      C   Ascensions morning by morning to Yahweh
      C^1 Incense
      C^2 Bread
      C^3 Lampstand
      C^4 Lamps evening by evening
   B′ We do guard duty of Yahweh
A′ You have forsaken

And the God whom the priests serve in the temple is mobile. He goes out with the troops of Judah, as the head of the army. The priests go out with the troops, with their trumpets that will call God to draw near.

Abijah's message to Jeroboam is stark: He does not have a legitimate claim to kingship. He is a rebel against David's house, does not have a legitimate priesthood, and does not serve real gods. All he has is an army of 800,000, but it will not help. Give it up, Abijah warns. Do not fight against Yahweh. You cannot win. He is right. Jeroboam cannot win. Like many a rebellious king, he tries to avoid Yahweh by subterfuge and stratagem. He sets an ambush, hiding some of his men. When Judah advances to face Israel, the ambush comes out behind them, and the warriors of Judah are stuck in the middle, surrounded by armies of Israel. It is the kind of strategy that worked at Ai and in other battles. But it does not work here. The people of Judah cry out, like the Israelites in Egypt or at the Red Sea (→ 1 Chr. 5). The priests sound those trumpets, summoning God to draw near to rescue them. Yahweh routs Jeroboam and gives Israel into the hand of Abijah, and Abijah's army kills 500,000 of the men of Israel. They trust in Yahweh and win a great victory. They defeat Jeroboam with cries and trumpets.

Rehoboam fought Jeroboam throughout his reign (12:15). That way of putting it subtly tells us that Rehoboam was not able to close the deal, to finish Jeroboam off, and to end hostilities between north and south (Johnstone 1998b: 51). Abijah finishes the war and pursues his advantage by capturing several cities, including Bethel. Abijah captures Jeshanah, Ephron, and their "daughter villages," but Bethel is the big prize. Judah's boundary moves north a significant distance (Japhet 1993: 698). Bethel is never named again in 2 Chronicles. These portions of Israel come "into the hand" of Abijah (13:16), which means that they come under the hand of the Davidic kingdom (13:8), where they ought to be. This is a theological victory, demonstrating that Yahweh the Warrior is stronger than the no-gods of Bethel. It is another exodus, another humiliation of the gods of the nations. Abijah is like one of the judges, leading Judah to victory over impossible odds.

The chapter ends by contrasting the "strength" of Abijah (13:21; cf. 13:18) with Jeroboam's loss of strength (13:20). As is typical in Chronicles, the difference is trust. Trusting Yahweh leads to strength; relying on golden calves is a prescription for weakness. Abijah's victory is a major blow to Jeroboam's kingdom. The battle takes place in the twenty-first year of Jeroboam's reign (13:1–2), and Jeroboam lasts only twenty-two years. His son reigns only two years before Baasha overthrows the dynasty.

We can read between the lines: Baasha takes advantage of widespread discontent with Jeroboam, who spent his reign in an ineffectual war with Rehoboam and then lost a decisive battle to Rehoboam's son. This battle is the effective end of Jeroboam's reign and the effective end of his dynasty. He goes the way of

Saul. The north's instability continues after Jeroboam passes from the scene, as several dynasties come and go during the reign of Abijah's son Asa. Though the Davidic kings do not rule the northern kingdom, their actions are decisive for the north's political future.

I worked on this commentary as Protestants and some Catholics were commemorating the five hundredth anniversary of the Reformation. Abijah's speech, I think, highlights some neglected dimensions of that historical conflict. The issue in the Reformation was not simply the question of right doctrine, not simply about making sure Christians knew how to be justified before God. The overriding question was, Who is the bearer of Jesus's kingdom? And, to put it in the Chronicler's terms, that question included the question, Who maintains true worship? Who worships God alone? Who listens to the Shema? Who keeps the ascensions ascending and the lampstands burning? The *public* form of the church was being contested, and the Reformers believed they were the true heirs of the apostolic church.

The Reformers were not indifferent to liturgical concerns or the shape of Christian ministry. Luther, Calvin, Zwingli, Bucer, Knox, and all the rest charged that Roman Catholics had corrupted the worship of God by introducing relics and venerations, denying the cup to the laity, enslaving the Mass to their false teaching about eucharistic sacrifice and real presence. Luther and Calvin could stand on the Twin Peaks as Abijah did and trash-talk the Catholics: Who has the true ministry? Your priests cannot teach the word of God, do not provide pastoral guidance, and are morally dissolute. The Reformers asked, Who has true ministers of God? And they insisted that they did.

At the same time, the Chronicler does not allow Judah to be complacent. Abijah charges that Jeroboam is a rebel against Yahweh, but soon enough Judah will rebel against the Lord's chosen king, Nebuchadnezzar. Judah has the rightful king for a time, and they submit to the house of David, but that is no guarantee that their status is permanent. Judah has the right priesthood and the right form of worship. But over and over Judah will abandon the Lord's house. Ahaziah lives in a Jerusalem that has a temple to Baal. Ahaz copies the worship of the Arameans. Manasseh places idols before the face of God in the temple. Even good kings abuse the temple. Asa takes gold from the temple to pay off invaders. Uzziah tries to offer incense in the temple. The fact that Judah has the true priesthood and true worship is no guarantee that it will please Yahweh forever.

Nor does Abijah's speech imply that the northern kingdom is hopeless. After the Assyrians conquer the north, Hezekiah invites people from the north to join a great Passover. When Josiah discovers the law in the temple, he purges Judah and Jerusalem of idols—and then carries out a purge of the northern kingdom. The counterfeit, rebellious kingdom of Israel is eventually reincorporated into Judah. They recover true worship and the true priesthood.

Abijah's speech allows us to adopt the right balance in our celebration of the Reformation. Protestants affirm the rightness of the Reformation: it was not a rebellion; the Catholic Church was in rebellion. His speech calls attention to the liturgical scope of the Reformation, its concern for the right order of the visible church. Yet we ought not be complacent. Judah's history is a warning and also gives us hope that someday, albeit in the grave of exile, Judah and Israel will be reunited to worship the true God.

8

SELF-INFLICTED WOUNDS

2 Chronicles 14–16

First Kings covers the reign of Asa in sixteen verses (1 Kgs. 15:9–24). Chronicles gives him three chapters. During his reign, four dynasties rule the north: Jeroboam, Baasha, Zimri, and Omri (1 Kgs. 15:9, 33; 16:15, 29). The last, Omri, finally brings an end to Israel's political turmoil. Asa's reign marks an interim stage in the history of relations between Israel and Judah. Rehoboam and Abijah fight Jeroboam directly. Asa hires Arameans to attack Israel, and his son Jehoshaphat will ally with Omri's son, Ahab. Throughout this period, the northern kingdom is a test of Judah's faithfulness, and neither Asa nor his son passes the test. After the resolute opposition of Rehoboam and Abijah, Judah begins to contract the infection of idolatry that has sickened the north.

Land Undisturbed (2 Chronicles 14:1–8)

The Chronicler's account of Asa's reign is organized around two military threats, the first from Zerah and the second from Baasha, king of Israel. Within the frame of a formulaic opening and closing (14:1; 16:11–14), the Chronicler juxtaposes the two wars in a parallel structure that highlights Asa's contrasting responses:

A Asa purges the land of idolatry (14:2–8)
    B War with Zerah the Cushite (14:9–15)

        C Oracle from prophet Oded (15:1–7)

          D Asa hears (15:8a)

    A′ Asa leads Judah in covenant renewal (15:8b–19)

       B′ War with Baasha of Israel (16:1–6)

          C′ Oracle from prophet Hanani (16:7–9)

             D′ Asa imprisons prophet, dies of foot disease (16:10–14)

The opening summary is organized in a neat chiasm:

    A   Land undisturbed (*shaqat*) (14:1b)

       B Asa removes altars, high places, pillars, and Asherim (14:2–3)

          C Asa commands Judah to seek Yahweh and Torah (14:4)

       B′ Asa removes high places and incense altars from cities (14:5a)

    A′ Kingdom undisturbed (*shaqat*) (14:5b)

Second Chronicles 14:6 reinforces the theme of 14:1b and 14:5b: after Asa builds fortified cities in Judah, the land is again said to be "undisturbed" (*shaqat* for a third time). The verb is used repeatedly in Judges (3:11, 30; 5:31; 8:28) and typically refers to the tranquility that descends on a land during the lifetime of a judge. It has a similar connotation in Chronicles. After the wars of David, Solomon brings rest to the land. After Jehoshaphat sings off an invasion of Moabites and Ammonites, the land is undisturbed for a time (2 Chr. 20:3). After Athaliah is killed, Jerusalem is at rest (2 Chr. 23:21). Here in chapter 14, after the tumult of the division of the kingdom under Rehoboam and the war between Israel and Judah under Abijah, the land is undisturbed during the early part of Asa's reign. Enjoying peace after the decisive victory of his Davidic father, Abijah, Asa becomes a Solomonic builder. But it will not last. As in Judges, the land is undisturbed only while Judah remains faithful to Yahweh.

The source of safety and peace is not military or political. The Chronicler explains that the land was undisturbed because Yahweh gives rest (*nuakh*). Asa acknowledges the connection. While he exhorts Judah to build walls, towers, gates, and bars around the cities, he reminds Judah that the land is "before us" (AT), and he acknowledges the theological source of this peace and opportunity (14:7):

    A The land is before us

       B because we have sought Yahweh our Elohim;

       B′ we have sought him,

    A′ and he has given us rest on every side.

Land is not merely a possession but an opportunity. It lies "before" Israel to glorify and make fruitful, stretching out as unlimited opportunity because there is rest on every side, a four-cornered Sabbath. At the heart of the land's peace and opportunity, though, is the practice of seeking Yahweh. As long as the people of Judah worship Yahweh, maintain his house, renounce idols, and keep his commandments, the land remains both gift and opportunity.

In the larger chiasm of 14:1-5, "seeking Yahweh" again takes center stage, but it is described in a negative fashion. Asa encourages obedience to the laws and commandments of Yahweh (14:4), but that obedience mainly takes the form of destroying the tools and sites of idolatry. Second Chronicles 14:3 is an eight-word clause describing the purge. Three verbs are used—remove, tear, cut—terms that have some resonance with the actions of sacrifice. Four objects are destroyed—altars, high places, pillars, and Asherim—and "altar" is modified by *nekar*, "foreign." Second Chronicles 14:5 adds that Asa also removed incense altars.

This is the first explicit indication that Judah has followed the northern kingdom into idolatry, and Asa is the first king of Judah to embark on a reformation. It is another example of the Chronicler's habit of mentioning events and institutions whose background he has not explained (Japhet 1993: 706). Asa anticipates the later, more extensive reforms of Hezekiah and Josiah. Only Asa and Hezekiah are described as kings who do what is "good and right" in the eyes of Yahweh (cf. 2 Chr. 31:20). Asa is one of the few kings of Judah who removes high places (cf. 15:17; 28:4, 25; 33:17). High places (*bamah*) are shrines that compete with the central sanctuary in Jerusalem. Though the worshipers at high places may claim to worship Yahweh, their worship is illegitimate. Judah is to worship the one God at his one house, the house of prayer for the nations.

Asa's first speech is, as noted, a speech about building. Like Solomon and Rehoboam (2 Chr. 11:5-6), he aims to be king of construction. His combination of destruction and construction has positive associations in Chronicles. All the great kings of Judah destroy as well as build. But the specifics of his building plans ring a disquieting note. He wants cities with "walls and towers, gates and bars" (14:7). Few cities of Israel are so defended. The combination of terms is, however, typically used to describe the cities of the Canaanites (Deut. 3:5), the supposedly impregnable cities that Yahweh overthrew (though cf. 2 Chr. 8:5). Is Asa attempting to re-Canaanitize the cities of Judah? The disquiet intensifies when we discover that Asa gathers an army of over a half million *gibborim* from Judah and Benjamin, equipped with shields and spears (14:8). He confesses that the land is undisturbed because Judah seeks Yahweh and keeps his commandments. Is he now trying to preserve that rest by arms and fortifications?

We suspect that Asa is not going to maintain his status of "good and right," that the period of peace is coming to an end. The Chronicler has already told us that the Sabbath period lasted only "ten years during [Asa's] days" (14:1). As soon as we learn that Asa has fortified cities and gathered an army, a ginormous opposing army takes the stage, led by a "Cushite" named Zerah. Is Asa being punished for trusting in gates and shields? Has he stopped seeking Yahweh and become a devotee of Mars?

War with Cush (2 Chronicles 14:9–15:19)

Cush is the father of Nimrod, "the first warrior to spread chaos through the world of nations" (Johnstone 1998b: 62; cf. 1 Chr. 1:10). Zerah's rise represents a "primordial threat to the order that God conceived for relations between himself and human society" (Johnstone 1998b: 62). Zerah bears a Hebrew name, "one who springs up," which may indicate that he "sprang up" from within Judah. Though surrounded by a Cushite army, Zerah may be an "insurrectionist" rather than an invader (Johnstone 1998b: 62; on possible links with Egypt, see Pratt 2006: 301; Japhet 1993: 709–10). Perhaps we are looking at a repetition of the reign of Rehoboam, who was opposed by a domestic enemy who had sojourned in Egypt. The original Zerah is one of the sons of Judah (1 Chr. 2:4–6), the putative firstborn who was displaced by the "breakthrough" of Judah's younger son Perez (cf. Gen. 38). The Chronicler has played on the genealogical link between David and Perez (→ 1 Chr. 15–16), and perhaps he is highlighting the same here. Zerah may be a Judahite pretender who wants to seize the kingship back from the upstart Perizzite, Asa.

Given what we have learned about Asa in 14:6–8, we have low expectations of his response. As he faces a million-man army with three hundred chariots, we expect him to turn from Yahweh to rely on military prowess and weaponry. Those expectations are, happily, subverted. Asa fights like a true son of David, like one of the heroic judges who seeks help from Yahweh. The account of the battle uses the name Yahweh seven times (14:11 [4×], 12, 13, 14), and the chiastic arrangement indicates that Yahweh's action is the turning point in Asa's fortunes:

A Zerah comes out (14:9)

   B Asa meets him (14:10)

    C Asa calls on Yahweh (14:11)
    C′ Yahweh routs Zerah (14:12)
  B′ Asa plunders Ethiopians (14:13–15a)
A′ Asa returns to Jerusalem (14:15b)

The chiastic arrangement of the final verses (14:13–15) reinforces the Lord's role in the victory:

A Asa pursues Cushites, who are shattered before Yahweh (14:13a)
  B Judah carries away much plunder (14:13b)
    C Asa destroys cities around Gerar (14:14a)
      D The dread of Yahweh falls on Cush (14:14b)
    C′ Judah despoils cities (14:14c)
  B′ Judah takes livestock, sheep, and camels (14:15a)
A′ Asa returns to Jerusalem (14:15b)

Yahweh wins the battle, but Asa ensures victory by invoking Yahweh. His prayer (14:11) has three sections, each of which begins with the name Yahweh. "Help" (*'azar*) is one of the key terms that binds the prayer together. The first clause is a proposition that grounds the petition that follows. When the powerful meet those who have no strength, only Yahweh can "help." He comes to the aid of the powerless who trust in him, whether they are powerless in battle, in court, or in any dispute. Asa classifies Judah as those who "have no strength." Despite the large size of Asa's army, it is nothing compared to the force that has sprung up with Zerah. The second and third clauses provide several lines of argument in support of the petition. Yahweh should help because Judah trusts in him and has entered the battle against Zerah in Yahweh's name. By entrusting the outcome to Yahweh, Asa has staked not his own but Yahweh's reputation on the outcome: "in Your name [we] have come against this multitude." With Yahweh's name in the balance, Asa is confident that Yahweh will not allow "man [to] prevail against [Him]." Embedded within the petition is a more specific covenantal formula: "You are our God." Yahweh has determined to be the God of Israel. He has taken its name into his, for he is God of Abraham, Isaac, and Jacob, the God of Israel. The sheer fact that *Judah* is on the battlefield puts Yahweh's name in play, whether that name is invoked or not.

Solomon's prayer (2 Chr. 6) is programmatic for the history of Judah's kings. The solution to every social and political crisis is found in the temple, if only the kings will pray to the God of heaven by praying toward Yahweh's house, where his name dwells. Asa does what Solomon prescribes, and Yahweh responds as promised, by striking and scattering the Cushites. Yahweh the divine Warrior has a "camp" (*makhaneh*, 14:13), Judah, and *together* Yahweh and his army "shatter" the Cushite invaders. That this is a repeat of Passover and exodus is signaled by the emphasis on plunder (14:13, 14, 15). In Egypt, Yahweh unilaterally defeated Pharaoh and Egypt's gods, and he alone received the plunder; in the conquest, Yahweh fought with and through Joshua, so that Israel shared, at times, in the spoils. Here, Yahweh fights along with his hosts, and he shares spoils with those who fight alongside him. It is a repetition of the conquest, as Asa pursues the Cushites to Gerar and destroys the surrounding cities. Like one of the judges, Asa recovers the land.

Asa's reign begins in Sabbath. That peace is shattered by the rise of Zerah, whose name means "uprising." Zerah's invasion is a test of Asa's faith. Will he be good and upright in a crisis? Will he seek Yahweh when he is weak, when the land is disturbed? He passes the test, is enriched, and returns to his capital, which is again a place of rest.

Upon his return, Asa is met by the aptly named prophet Azariah, "Yah helps." Azariah's speech is a pastiche of earlier prophetic oracles (15:3 parallels Hos. 3:4; 15:4 parallels Hos. 5:15; Japhet 1993: 716–17). Yah has helped, and now his Spirit inspires an oracle to encourage Asa to continue to trust the trustworthy God (the other Spirit-inspired prophets are Amasiah, Jahaziel, and Zechariah; Japhet 1993: 717).

The oracle is a densely composed poem. When we pay attention to the pronominal suffixes, 15:2 is a chiasm, with two phrases ending with -*kem* at the center ("with you"; "in your being"). In substance, the verse is organized in parallel fashion:

A Yahweh (name based on verb *hayah*)
  B with you
A' in your being (*hayah*)
  B' with him

Two lex-talionic conditional statements follow, each organized chiastically. First:

If
  A you (second-person verb form)
    B seek
      C him (pronominal suffix),

C′ he (third-person singular of niphal)
   B′ is found
A′ to you.

More straightforwardly, in the structure "If / seek // is found / to you," the dynamic of seeking and finding lies at the center. The second is like unto it:

If

   A you (second-person verb form)
      B forsake
         C him (pronominal suffix),
      B′ he forsakes
   A′ you.

Here is the negative corollary of the first statement: those who seek find; those who forsake are abandoned.

Second Chronicles 15:3–4 provides a historical illustration of the first conditional promise. Israel was bereft "for many days" of the three gifts that make Israel Israel: the God of truth ('emet), a priest who is capable of teaching (yarah), and the written Torah. The three deprivations correspond to the gifts in the ark. Yahweh himself is the heavenly life of his people, like the manna stored in the ark; the teaching priest is the rod that leads and directs the flock of Yahweh; the Torah is summed up on the tables of the Ten Words that are in the ark. Israel was deprived of the threefold foundation of Yahweh's throne, his royal presence. Such deprivation necessarily leads to distress, but in distress Israel turned to Yahweh, as Asa has turned to Yahweh in the midst of a battle, kicking off the seek-find movement.

Azariah expands the scope of his oracle in 15:5–6. The initial historical review focuses on the condition of Israel (or Judah). The following verses are not so narrowly construed. During the time when Israel was without Yahweh, priest, and Torah, the "lands" were in turmoil (15:5). Disturbances were on all the inhabitants, nation fought nation, and city against city, in apocalyptic confusion (cf. Matt. 24). "Go out and come in" is military language; when there is no peace for "those who went out or came in," it means that their wars were inconclusive— unwinnable and unlosable. God "troubled" the nations with distress because Israel was without God, priest, and Torah. The stability of Israel depends on seeking and finding the Lord of the covenant, and the stability of Israel's world depends on the same thing.

Azariah ends by repeating words that David spoke to Solomon, words that Moses earlier spoke to Joshua: "Be strong and do not lose courage." He backs up the exhortation with a promise of reward (15:7). The Hebrew contains two words for reward: *pe'ullah*, often translated as "work" but which means "wages" in Lev. 19:13, and *sakar*, "reward," which also means "wages" (e.g., Gen. 30:18, 28, 32–33; 31:8). Thus: "Be strong, and do not let your hands drop, for there is wage for your wage." Yahweh speaks a double promise of wages, promising a double wage.

Asa takes the speech as encouragement to continue and extend his purge of the land (note the repetition of "took courage" in 15:8, though the verb is different). Azariah began the prophecy with "Hear," a call to return to the demands of single devotion to Yahweh articulated in the Shema (Deut. 6, "Hear, O Israel"). Asa *shema*-ed Yahweh's call to hear. He heard and took courage, and took action to make Judah's commitment to the Shema take public form.

Asa's postwar program is described in a carefully constructed passage:

A He removes abominations from the land (15:8a)
  B He restores the altar to its place in the temple (15:8b)
    C He leads Israel in covenant renewal (15:9–15)
A' He removes Maacah, his mother, from her position (15:16–17)
  B' He brings the dedicated implements back into the temple (15:18)
    C' There is no more war (15:19)

Several details of this reform movement stand out. First, Asa purges "detestables" (*shiqquts*) from the land (15:8). The term has a similar range of meaning to *to'evah* (abomination), which describes acts that pollute the land, sicken the land, and eventually cause the land to vomit out the inhabitants. Removing the detestable things is necessary to preserve Judah's residence in the land and their care for the Lord's house. And this, as noted, is necessary for the preservation or establishment of international peace.

Second, Asa's reform efforts are not confined to his own kingdom of Judah, which includes Benjamin. He removes idols not only from Judah and Benjamin but from the "cities which he had captured in the hill country of Ephraim" (15:8), that is, cities that lie within the boundaries of the northern kingdom. When he gathers the people to Jerusalem to renew covenant, the assembly includes the people of Judah and Benjamin along with people from northern tribes—Ephraim, Manasseh, and Simeon—who fled from Jeroboam's Israel to the south. Abijah's victory over Jeroboam destabilized Jeroboam's kingdom, and many are migrating from north to south. They see that Yahweh is with Asa, and they want to be with the king who is with Yahweh (15:9). The covenant is a covenant with "all Israel" (Boda 2010: 309), albeit a somewhat shadowy Israel. In this, Asa anticipates the greater covenant renewals of Hezekiah and Josiah, both of whom carry out reforms in northern territories and include Israelites from all the tribes in their Passover celebrations and covenant renewals.

Asa assembles a covenant ceremony in the third month, the month of Pentecost, which celebrates, among other things, the cutting of the covenant at Sinai. Chronicles moves through the annual calendar in reverse, from Solomon's seventh-month dedication ceremony through Asa's third-month covenant renewal toward Hezekiah's second-month Passover and Josiah's climactic Passover of the first month. Time moves in reverse toward new year.

Asa does not "cut" a covenant but "enters" one, suggesting that the covenant is a preexisting arrangement Judah needs to reenter. The link between Asa's response and the Shema becomes explicit in 15:12, where the content of the covenant is stated in terms of Deut. 6: "They entered into the covenant to seek Yahweh God of their fathers with all their heart and soul." Covenant cutting is an act of worship, like the dedication of the temple in the days of Solomon, embedded in feasts of peace offerings (*zavakh*, "slaughter," refers to the peace offering, Lev. 3). Plunder from the Cushite army provides seven hundred oxen and seven thousand sheep. Queen Sheba brought tribute to Solomon voluntarily; Zerah's contribution is involuntary. Either way, Gentile wealth is stored up for Israel and devoted to Yahweh. The repetition of the number seven is significant, especially as we are heading to the conclusion that Yahweh gave "rest" (*nuakh*, 15:15). This is linked to the repetition of "oath" (15:14–15), since the Hebrew *shava* (swear an oath) puns on the word for "seven." It is a sabbatical moment, as Israel acknowledges Yahweh's kingship and swears whole-souled fealty to him. The combination of three (month) and sevens (numbers of animals) hints at the realized eschatology of the moment: in the third month, they party like it's the end of history.

Asa backs up the covenant renewal with the threat of force. The people of Judah are not left to decide whether to seek Yahweh or not. Those who refuse to seek him are put to death (15:13). As we have noted, "seeking Yahweh" is to be a wholehearted, whole-souled affair, but Asa is not trying to enforce attitudes. "Seeking Yahweh" is also a public program, involving support for the temple and the priesthood, and renouncing the worship of idols. Idolaters will be executed.

The oath is accompanied by a fourfold sound: a loud voice, shouting, trumpets, and horns (15:14). Once again, the Chronicler highlights the role of music in Israel's worship. But this is an oath taking, surrounded by a cloud of sound that expresses and also elicits joy (15:15). Judah rejoices in their own oath taking and God seeking, in the fact that God allows himself to be found. Yet 15:14 indicates a more intimate link between music and the covenant oath. The people of Judah swear to Yahweh with a fourfold sound: voice, shouting, trumpets, and horns. It is a *musical* covenant making.

Covenants are made by sacrifice (Ps. 50). "Sacrifice" implies not only slaughter and burning but also a meal. When Israel cuts or enters covenant, they seal it with a meal in the presence of Yahweh. In Chronicles, music takes up much of the work of sacrifice. Song accompanies ascension offerings. Song is, like sacrifice, a memorial presented to God. Levites do the "work" (*'avodah*) of music, and music is the new "burden" (*massa*) they bear, replacing the physical burdens of transporting the tabernacle. Now, with Asa, we see another sacrificial function of music: like offering an animal, music is a covenant-making or covenant-entering act. Song is a means of seeking Yahweh; song is also a commitment to seek him.

This is a Sinai event, and the removal of Maacah and the destruction of her Asherah fit into that typological paradigm. At Sinai, Aaron constructed a calf and led the people in idolatrous worship (Exod. 32). Moses ground the calf to powder, scattered it on the water, and made Israel drink the water. He deployed Levites to slaughter those who were worshiping at the calf. Asa is a new Moses here. Like a true Levite, he "hates" his mother and removes her from her position as queen mother. He destroys her image, crushes it (*daqaq*, cf. Exod. 32:20; Deut. 9:21), and burns it at the wadi Kidron, which runs between the Temple Mount and the Mount of Olives. The defiling idols flow away in the waters of the Kidron.

Asa pays little attention to the temple, but there are two indications that he restores the proper order of worship there. First, he "restores" the altar of Yahweh in front of the *ulam* of the temple. "Restore" means "restore to use" and involves purging and rededication after the altar has been put to abominable uses. Second, he brings the dedicated things into the temple. They had been removed and put to use in idolatrous worship, and Asa makes sure they are rededicated, like the people themselves, to the service of Yahweh.

Though Asa does not remove the high places (15:17), the Chronicler commends him: his heart was *shalem* (whole) all his days (15:17b). The word evokes the memory of Solomon, the king of peace, who also had a *shalem* heart (1 Chr.

28:9). Asa is the last king who resembles Solomon in this way. He is the last king who acts fully like a true son of David.

Sin Makes You Stupid (2 Chronicles 16:1–14)

Zerah's invasion takes place in the tenth year of Asa's reign (14:1, 9). Asa leads the covenant renewal five years later (15:10), and for the next twenty years Asa does not experience disruption or war. His heart is *shalem*, and he enjoys *shalom*. The peace does not last until the end, though. In the thirty-sixth year of his reign, another threat appears, and Asa fails the test. From his thirty-fifth year to the forty-first year, when his reign ends, Asa is plagued by war and eventually suffers a humiliating disease.

Things start to go badly with another war. When Zerah attacked with his overwhelming force earlier in Asa's reign, Asa prays, presumably toward the temple, and Yahweh hears (14:11–12). But when Baasha of Israel fortifies Ramah, near the border of Israel and Judah, Asa's response is very different. Asa was faithful in his battle with the Cushite stranger, but he abandons the Lord when threatened by the Israelite brother. The Chronicler organizes the opening of the war (16:1–6) in a neat chiasm:

A   Baasha invades
   B   Asa sends silver and gold to Damascus
      C   Asa's speech
   B′   Ben-hadad listens and attacks Baasha
A′   Baasha withdraws, Ramah dismantled

The war with Baasha has a back story (on the difficulties of harmonizing the chronology of Kings and Chronicles, see Pratt 2006: 311). In the previous generation, Asa's father, Abijah, fought with Jeroboam. Abijah won the war and in the process captured cities from the north—Bethel, where the golden calf was, Jeshanah, and Ephron, along with the daughter villages associated with each city (2 Chr. 13:19). Now, in the time of Asa, Baasha, who overthrew the dynasty of Jeroboam, tries to recover that lost territory and makes Ramah his base of operation. The Chronicler tells us explicitly that Baasha is attempting to stanch the flow of people from the northern to the southern kingdom. Asa is a David character, picking up the refugees from the kingdom of Baasha, another Saul.

Asa does not pray. He does not seek the Lord. He *does* go to the temple, not to worship or sing, but to strip the storage rooms of silver and gold so that, along with treasure from his own house, he can offer a bribe to the Arameans. The Arameans have been allied with Baasha, but Asa hopes that his treasure will entice the king of Aram to break that covenant and switch sides (16:3). It works. Ben-hadad breaks his treaty with Baasha and enters into a military alliance with Asa. He attacks Baasha from the north, in the territory of Ijon, Dan, Abel-maim, and other cities of Naphtali. Rushing to defend his northern flank, Baasha abandons his fortifications and Ramah, and Asa and Judah move in to seize the materials for their own building projects.

It is a clever move, and a successful one. It is the kind of political manipulation by which the world runs. It is also one of the stupidest things that a king of Judah ever does, and sets a pattern for the folly of Asa's son Jehoshaphat (Boda 2010: 311). How is it stupid? Let me count the ways.

For starters, Asa uses the treasures of the temple to buy off Ben-hadad. These are the *same* treasures he has just devoted to Yahweh as part of the covenant renewal between Judah and Yahweh (2 Chr. 15:18). Even if Asa does not believe that Yahweh is real, it is foolish for him to devote treasure to the temple only to remove it. But Asa *is* a Yahweh-worshiper, and taking Yahweh's stuff is extremely stupid. Asa consecrates silver and gold to Yahweh, making it holy, Yahweh's possession. Twenty years later, he *takes* the silver and gold away from Yahweh. The treasure is not his to use. He steals from God, committing sacrilege in order to secure a victory. He commits a *ma'al*. The Chronicler does not explicitly charge Asa with *ma'al*, but Asa all but confesses it. When he sends the money to Ben-hadad, Asa says that he wants Baasha to "ascend from over me" (16:3 AT). The Hebrew is *ya'aleh me'alay*, a pun on *ma'al*.

Asa does not seem to realize the implications of what he does. Ben-hadad has been in an alliance with Baasha to attack Judah. Asa pays him off to break his covenant and attack Israel. How clever is it to cut covenant with a partner who is willing to abandon a covenant when a better offer comes along? How reliable can Ben-hadad be?

Besides that, Asa inflicts a wound on his own realm. Asa funds an Aramean attack on the northern kingdom, his own brothers. But it is worse: As a descendant of David, Asa is the legitimate king of the *whole* territory of Israel. The towns in the north that Ben-hadad attacks are as much a part of Asa's realm as the cities that Baasha is trying to recover. Asa funds an Aramean attack *on his own territory*. He effectively renounces his own standing as Davidic king by acting as if the northern territories rightly belong to Baasha.

The seriousness of his folly comes clear in the following generation when Aramean soldiers, supported by gold from Jerusalem's temple, nearly kill Asa's son Jehoshaphat (18:28–34). The ultimate result is a complete reversal of the relations between Judah and Aram. After David defeated Aram, they paid him tribute (1 Chr. 18:5–6). Now Asa pays up to Aram.

Asa's disloyalty makes him stupid. Worse, it makes him virtually an idolater. The prophet Azariah met Asa as he returned from his war with Zerah (2 Chr. 15:1–7) with an encouraging message: "Be strong and do not lose courage, for there is a reward for your work." In response, Asa reinitiated his efforts to reform Judah's worship. After the war with Baasha, another prophet, Hanani, meets the king. He brings not a message of encouragement but one of rebuke.

The issue, Hanani says, is one of trust (16:7–8; some form of the word "trust" appears three times). Faith is not a private set of beliefs. Faith is a political factor, and the political and military fortunes of Judah depend on the direction of the king's faith—toward Yahweh or toward Aram. Ben-hadad's name highlights the contrast. Ben-hadad means "son of hadad," and Hadad is the proper name of the god usually known as Baal. Ben-hadad is in the same position in Aram as Asa is in Judah—a son of Aram's god. Supporting Ben-hadad is not merely a political matter of relying on a Gentile power; it amounts to a confession that Hadad is stronger than Yahweh. Asa's political action is a breach of faith with Yahweh and virtually a confession of faith in Hadad.

Hanani reminds Asa that the Lord delivered Judah from an immense army of Ethiopians and Libyans. The same could have happened in the war with Baasha. Asa could have trusted God to deliver him from Baasha, and Aram itself could have been brought under his power (16:7). Instead, Asa enables Aram to become a regional power that will threaten the northern kingdom for several generations. Aram's rise depends on Asa's gold and silver, *Yahweh's* gold and silver.

Yahweh supports those who rely on him. Asa knows this. Yahweh's eyes, which are directed toward the temple (2 Chr. 7:16), also keep surveillance over the earth, going to and fro to support those who have a *shalem* heart. Asa's heart was once *shalem*, but no longer. And because he is no longer *shalem* with Yahweh, he wastes Yahweh's gift of *shalom*. Asa is faithless in war, and Hanani warns that he will have war for the remainder of his reign. When he sought Yahweh, he had rest. When he gave treasure to Yahweh, the land was at peace. When he steals from Yahweh and allies with the son of Baal, his borders become porous and he has to fight throughout the remainder of his life.

Azariah son of Oded called on Asa to "hear," and Asa heard (15:1–8). Hanani also brings the word of Yahweh to the king, but Asa's ears are no longer open. Instead of receiving the message, he imprisons the messenger (16:10), becoming the first king to attack Yahweh's prophet (→2 Chr. 18:26; →2 Chr. 24:19–22). Even when he contracts a foot disease (perhaps a euphemism for a genital disease; Schipper 2009), Asa refuses to seek Yahweh (16:12). He does not turn to the one Lord who heals (2 Chr. 7:14) but to other healers. Resentful at Yahweh's word, he forsakes Yahweh, and Yahweh forsakes him.

Asa begins well, but his breach of faith leads to defeat, disease, and an ignominious death. Asa's life and death is a cautionary tale, both personal and political.[1] It is a tale that will be repeated with other kings, a tale that is the tale of the Davidic dynasty as a whole.

---

1. Johnstone (1998b: 75) suggests that the spices used at Asa's funeral are another sign of his apostasy: These spices are mentioned in other contexts as luxury items brought to Solomon as tokens of homage by the monarchs of the earth (2 Chr. 9.1, 9, 24; so also for Hezekiah, 2 Chr. 32.27). If that is the significance here, then it expresses the status that Asa enjoyed among the nations of the world and thus the claim that he has discharged successfully, at least for the most part, the responsibilities attached to the Davidic throne. But it is difficult not to detect a note of disapproval in [the Chronicler] that this king, who had promised so well but had ended in such failure, should have arrogated to himself such tokens of significance. These spices are otherwise used in the cult (cf. 1 Chr. 9.29–30); it was surely scarcely appropriate for a compromised Davidic king so to infringe the sphere of the holy. It may be all part of the presumptuousness that precipitated illness in the last years of his reign (cf. Uzziah in 2 Chr. 26.16–23).

9

LOVING YAHWEH'S ENEMIES

2 Chronicles 17–20

Renewing Judah (2 Chronicles 17–18)

Like the reign of Asa before him, Jehoshaphat's reign is organized around two wars that contrast with one another:

A Jehoshaphat fortifies cities and seeks Yahweh (17:1–6)
   B Jehoshaphat appoints teachers and receives tribute (17:7–11)
      C Jehoshaphat joins Ahab in war with Aram (17:11–18:34)
A' Message from Hanani: Do not help the wicked; seek Yahweh (19:1–3)
   B' Jehoshaphat appoints judges (19:4–11)
      C' War with Moab and Ammon (20:1–30)
A" Message from Eliezer: Yahweh destroys ships because Jehoshaphat allies with Ahab's son (20:31–21:3)

Jehoshaphat spends the early part of his reign breaking things. He tears down the high places and Asherim (17:6). Breaking things is as much part of the king's job description as building things. Jehoshaphat refuses to seek the Baals and instead walks in the way of his father David (17:3). All this is a sign of the fact that his "heart was high" in the ways of the Lord (17:6). Elsewhere in Chronicles, an elevated heart is a dangerous thing. Uzziah's heart becomes high, and he tries to seize a priestly privilege, ending up with leprosy as a result. Jehoshaphat's heart, however, is high on the law of Yahweh, and so he does the right thing and purges the land of idols.

Not content with a purge, he takes steps to ensure that Judah continues to walk in the ways of the Lord. In the third year of his reign—the "third" being the time of resurrection and revival—he sends teachers throughout the land, equipped with the book of the Torah, an authoritative written source for their instruction (Boda 2010: 315). Sixteen teachers, Levites, and priests are listed, with names like "Servant of Yah," "Yah Remembers," "Who Is Like Yah," "Gift of Yah," and "God Gives." Levites with names like "Yah Hears" and "Gift of Yah," names like "Yah Is Lord," "Yah Is Good," and "Yah Is Good Lord."

As a result, the "dread of Yahweh" falls on the Gentile peoples nearby. The teachers "surround" (*savav*) Judah, and the "surrounding" (*saviv*) nations are too frightened to attack Jehoshaphat, as they were too frightened to attack David (1 Chr. 14:17). Later, Yahweh strikes dread into the nations again when he defeats the combined forces of Moab, Ammon, and Edom through Levites armed with harps, lyres, trumpets, and voices (2 Chr. 20:28–29).

It is a remarkable thing: not horses or chariots or fortifications but *teaching* and *music* are key to Judah's national security. If Judah knows and guards Yahweh's commandments, he will provide all the security they need. When they lift Yahweh up on their praises, he goes to war with their enemies. Jehoshaphat later follows up with a judicial circuit. He appoints judges who spread out throughout the land to resolve disputes and bring justice. Attentive to the law, Jehoshaphat instructs them to fear God, to judge without partiality, to remember that they represent Yahweh himself in their judicial actions, and to refuse bribes (19:1–7). He makes sure that the law of Yahweh is taught and enforced, and he becomes, Martin Bucer says, a model for Christian kings, who are called to promote the spiritual welfare of their subjects (*De Regno Christi*, in Cooper and Lohrmann 2016: 625). More immediately, he becomes a model for Persian kings like Artaxerxes, who appoints teachers for the restoration community, like Ezra (Japhet 1993: 749).

Nations bring tribute to Judah—Philistines from the west and Arabs from the east. The Chronicler describes the tribute in liturgical language (17:11). Gentiles bring gifts of silver as "tribute" (*massa'*), also their flocks and herds, and the Chronicler uses terms that often refer to the Levitical task of bearing the furniture of the tabernacle and, in Chronicles, the "burden" of musico-prophetic ministry (1 Chr. 15:22, 27). The number seven is used four times in 17:11, as the Chronicler enumerates the numbers of rams and male goats brought to honor Jehoshaphat, which gives Jehoshaphat's reign an aura of "new creation." It is not evil for Yahweh's king to receive such praise. Yahweh is high king and deserves all praise and tribute; his prince, the Davidic king, should also be acknowledged by the nations with quasi-liturgical gestures. Jehoshaphat is not guilty of sacrilege, *ma'al*. On the contrary, like David and Solomon, he becomes greater and greater, lifted up (*ma'alah*). Yahweh becomes great by greatening; he enhances his glory by glorifying his royal son.

Jehoshaphat is one of the heroes of Chronicles, and the Chronicler devotes a lot of admiring attention to his reign. But virtually no king in Chronicles is perfect. David is near perfect, failing only in his decision to take a census of the people. Solomon is the model king. Other kings are good, but flawed in one way or another. Jehoshaphat's flaw is massive, marking a new stage in Judah's relationship with Israel to the north. Abijah knew that Judah's superiority depended on faithful worship (→ 2 Chr. 13). Asa forgot and sought help from Gentiles in his war with the north. Jehoshaphat does something worse: he allies with the idolatrous King Ahab.

Even before Jehoshaphat enters that alliance, the Chronicler hints that things may be turning around. As he grows "greater and greater," he builds fortresses and storage cities and gathers *gibborim*, valiant men, to Jerusalem (17:12–13). We had the same disquiet when Asa gathered an army of over 500,000, equipped with shields and bows (14:8). We began to wonder if he was trusting in his military strength. Jehoshaphat's military buildup raises similar questions. He stations troops in fortified cities throughout Judah and then adds an enormous number of troops in the capital city, listed in five groups (five being the number of military organization) according to their father's house, three from Judah and two from Benjamin:

1. Adnah of Judah, 300,000
2. Johanan of Judah, 280,000
3. Amasiah of Judah, 200,000
4. Eliada of Benjamin, 200,000
5. Jehozabad (of Benjamin), 180,000

It is a total of 1.16 million men, to defend a country that was similar to the size of New Jersey (which currently has about 7,500 active-duty US military personnel).

Ahab pops into Chronicles for the first time in 2 Chr. 18. The Chronicler expects his readers to know the background that 1–2 Kings provides—about Ahab's father, Omri; about Baal worship and the temple of Baal in Samaria;

about Ahab's marriage to Jezebel (1 Kgs. 16). Even within Chronicles, we know enough about Israel's kings to be worried. When Jeroboam leads ten tribes out of the kingdom of David, the Chronicler records that Israel went into "rebellion against the house of David" (2 Chr. 10:19). Jeroboam expels the sons of Aaron and Levites from serving as priests (11:13–14) and makes golden calves for Israel to worship (13:8). Jehoshaphat ignores all this and "in-laws" himself to Ahab (18:1) by arranging for his son Jehoram to marry Ahab's daughter Athaliah (21:6). The marriage establishes a de facto union of the two dynasties (Japhet 1993: 758), with Ahab's Omride house in the dominant position. Jehoshaphat wants to re-unite Israel and Judah. Perhaps he wants to bring an end to generations of war. As worthy as his aims may be, union in Baal worship is evil. Judah and Israel can be rightly reunited only if all Israel serves Yahweh and submits to the house of David. Jehoshaphat's form of all-Israel ecumenism is wicked.

Some years after Jehoram marries Athaliah, Jehoshaphat "goes down" to Samaria, descending from Jerusalem to the capital of the north (18:2). As Johnstone (1998b: 83) points out, things never go well in Chronicles when Davidic kings leave home. Rehoboam goes to Shechem (→ 2 Chr. 10:1), and there the ten tribes rebel. At the end of Chronicles, Josiah marches out to confront Pharaoh Neco and is killed in battle at Megiddo (→ 2 Chr. 35:20). The chosen Davidic kings belong in the chosen city, where the temple has been erected on the place Yahweh has chosen. Jehoshaphat is overconfident in his ability to stay faithful and strong while subordinating himself to Ahab's agenda. He provides another illustration of the danger of strength and prosperity (Japhet 1993: 747–48, 758).

In Samaria, Ahab prepares a huge feast. It might be no more than an elaborate state dinner (like Queen Sheba's with Solomon; → 2 Chr. 9), but the verb *zavakh* (slaughter) is part of the Old Testament's liturgical vocabulary. "Ahab slaughtered many sheep and oxen" sounds like a sacrifice on the scale of Solomon's temple dedication. The setting confirms that this is a religious feast: Ahab is preparing to go to war, and he wants his gods on his side. As the narrative unfolds, we become more and more aware that Ahab's gods are not Yahweh. Jehoshaphat's marriage alliance becomes a religious alliance. Jehoshaphat goes to Samaria to feast at a table of demons.

And that marital-religious covenant becomes a military alliance. Jehoshaphat works on the commonsensical assumption, What good is an army if you never use it? The feast is part of Ahab's effort to "induce" or "entice" Jehoshaphat to join his quest to conquer the city of Ramoth-gilead. The verb "induce" is, significantly, the same used to describe Satan's enticement of David (→ 1 Chr. 21).

That suggests an analogy: Satan : David :: Ahab : Jehoshaphat. The analogy is a strong one. David was tempted to muster and count the hosts of Israel as if they were his own rather than the hosts of Yahweh. David prepares to deploy Yahweh's armies for his own purposes. Jehoshaphat does the same. "Will you go with me?" Ahab asks, and Jehoshaphat answers, "I as you, my people as your people" (18:3 AT). The chiastic structure of Jehoshaphat's response (following the structure of the Hebrew sentence) symbolizes the entanglement of the two kings and their peoples:

A As I
   B as you;
   B′ as your people
A′ my people;
   B″ and with you in battle.

But the soldiers of Judah *are not* Jehoshaphat's people, and he has no right to send the Lord's armies to fight for the idolater Ahab.

If nothing else, Jehoshaphat's decision to join Ahab is strategically inept. The Arameans captured Ramoth-gilead and other cities of the north with the help of Asa, Jehoshaphat's father (→ 2 Chr. 16:1–6). Because of Asa's bribe, the Aram-Israel alliance turned into an Aram-Judah alliance, and now it is morphing again into a Judah-Israel alliance against Aram. Ahab wants to recover some of the territory that the Arameans seized *with Judah's help*. Jehoshaphat, whose father helped the Arameans take Ramoth-gilead, is now helping Israel take it back! Jehoshaphat's eagerness for peaceful relations with Israel blinds him.

Ahab takes the lead in this alliance. It is *his* war, and Jehoshaphat promises to throw his weight behind Ahab. The Chronicler highlights Jehoshaphat's theological error with subtle uses of names and titles. Ahab is not called "king of Israel" until he has seduced Jehoshaphat into joining the military expedition (18:3). From that point, there is a "king of Israel" and a "king of Judah." Ironically, the effort at united action reinforces the division of the two kingdoms. Thereafter, "king of Israel" is used more often than the proper name "Ahab." As a descendant of David, *Jehoshaphat* is the one with a right to the title "king of Israel."[1] Jehoshaphat's alliance with Ahab upends that balance, so that the northern king becomes "king of Israel." Jehoshaphat treats Ahab as a legitimate king and thus undermines his

---

1. The Chronicler treats the northern kingdom as an illegitimate rebel state, and Asa's kingdom included territories in the north (15:8–9) so that he could be called king of "Israel" (15:17).

own legitimacy and the unity of his own kingdom. Like Asa, who enlisted Aram to attack his own kingdom, Jehoshaphat is alienated from his Davidic vocation. His foolish covenant alienates him from himself.

Twice, prophets met Jehoshaphat's father, Asa. First Azariah came with a message of encouragement, then Hanani with a message of rebuke. Jehoshaphat also encounters prophets twice, but in the reverse order. First he hears the warning prophecy of Micaiah, which he ignores, and later, when Jerusalem is threatened by an invasion of Moabites and Ammonites, Jahaziel ben Zechariah, a Levite descended from Asaph, assures him that the battle belongs to Yahweh (2 Chr. 20:14–19). The Chronicler arranges the episode chiastically:

A Jehoshaphat and Ahab feast to seal their alliance (18:1–3)
   B At Jehoshaphat's request, prophets assemble before the kings (18:4–7)
      C At Jehoshaphat's request, Micaiah is brought out (18:8–13)
         D Micaiah and Ahab: sheep without a shepherd (18:14–17)
      C′ Micaiah tells his vision of Yahweh and the spirits (18:18–22)
   B′ Zedekiah strikes Micaiah (18:23–27)
A′ Kings go to war, where Ahab is killed (18:28–34)

A number of these sub-scenes are arranged in back-and-forth dialogues between different sets of characters. In A and A′, Ahab and Jehoshaphat speak to one another. The central D section moves from Ahab to Micaiah to Ahab to Micaiah and back to Ahab. Micaiah's vision of Yahweh enthroned among his spirits (18:18–22) might be seen as the conclusion to that dialogue, and it serves as a "second witness" against Ahab. In C′ the order is more complex: Zedekiah to Micaiah to Ahab to Micaiah. Micaiah speaks again to close out the dialogue, calling out, "*Shema*, all you people" (18:27). Importantly, Zedekiah does not get a second word in this dialogue; Micaiah speaks again in the place where symmetry would lead us to expect Zedekiah. As before, Micaiah closes a dialogue with a double speech, a double witness to the false prophet to follow the double witness to the idolatrous king. Yahweh's prophet speaks the *final* word.

Even before Micaiah appears, we have reason to suspect the prophets. "Shall we go up against Ramoth-gilead, or shall I refrain?" Ahab asks. And the prophets answer, "Ascend! For God will give into the hand of the king" (18:5 AT). Give *what*? Into the hand of *which* king? The prophets do not specify. It could mean "God will give Ramoth into the hand of King Ahab." With equal plausibility, it could mean "God will give Ahab (or Israel) into the hand of the king of Aram." Ambiguous as it is, it is an irrefutable prophecy, because at the end of a war someone or something will have been given into the hand of someone. Like the witches in *Macbeth*, the prophets speak equivocation. Ahab hears what he wants to hear and falls into the trap. As we will see, it is a divine trap.

Jehoshaphat recognizes that the prophecy lacks the probative value of the word of Yahweh and asks for a true prophet. In the interlude, while a messenger fetches Micaiah ("Who is like Yah?"), the Chronicler describes the scene of the kings (18:9). The two kings are enthroned at the threshing floor at the gate of Samaria. Gates are often associated with judgment in the Bible, naturally so, since judgment gives access or excludes; the king is a guardian of the gates of the land, deciding who is admitted and who is not. The temple was built on a threshing floor (→ 2 Chr. 3:1), the one purchased by David after the plague (→ 1 Chr. 21). A threshing floor is a space for separating wheat and chaff and so a symbol of the Lord's sifting judgments. It is an appropriate place for kings to set up court, since they "winnow with their eyes" by passing judgments in court cases. Here, though, the accent is not on the kings' authority to judge but on the fact that they are themselves subject to judgment. Micaiah's apocalyptic prophecy will pull back the curtain to show that there is another king on a heavenly throne, also surrounded by servants, a high king who threshes kings. Uzza touched the ark on a threshing floor and was killed (1 Chr. 13:9). Ahab, who defies the messengers from the throne of King Yahweh, should take warning.

The messenger who brings Micaiah wants the prophet to join the chorus. Ahab's court prophets speak with a single voice. Their words are "as one mouth" in speaking good to the king, and Micaiah should speak "like one of them" (18:12). Micaiah's chiastic response indicates that he speaks only the words he receives. Swearing by the life of Yahweh, he says, "What says / Elohim // him / I speak" (18:13 AT, following Hebrew word order). This is the difference between Micaiah and the court prophets: they speak words that arise from within them, or bend their ear to hear the words of the king, whereas a true prophet has his ears open to Yahweh's word, and that received word alone looses his tongue to speak. A true prophet thus cannot speak "as one" with other prophets. His voice will always be discordant. Court prophets form a mimetic mob to enforce politically correct speech. Yahweh's prophets break the consensus, and suffer for it.

When Ahab asks Micaiah whether he should attack Ramoth, Micaiah repeats the prophecy of Ahab's court prophets almost verbatim: "Go up and succeed, for they will be given into your hand" (18:14). Micaiah's prophecy differs slightly from that of the other prophets (Boda 2010: 319). It is, in fact, *more* favorable to Ahab than that of his own prophets, but Ahab rejects it. When it comes from the false prophets, he accepts it; but Ahab hates Micaiah and refuses to accept even the *same* words from the mouth of Yahweh's spokesman.[2]

Ahab somehow knows that Micaiah's initial prophecy is insincere. Perhaps it is the simple fact that Micaiah speaks "as one" with the rest of the prophets, something that he never does, or perhaps it is the fact that Micaiah speaks in Ahab's favor. In any case, Micaiah's further oracle to Ahab is a prophetic rejection of Ahab's kingship or a prediction of Ahab's death. Israel will be scattered either because Ahab does not fulfill the function of shepherd or because he soon will cease to be the shepherd (18:16).

But the expansion of the prophecy is the key indication that Micaiah is a true prophet of Yahweh (18:18–22). He begins with an exhortation to "hear" (18:18). Prophets foretell the future, but that is not the primary mark of prophetic ministry. Rather, a prophet is a man or woman who has been granted access to the divine court. Court prophets may cluster around kings who are arrayed in their robes on the threshing floor at the gate of Samaria, but true prophets are admitted to the court of another king, a heavenly one, and stand among the spirits who attend, priestlike, at Yahweh's throne (Pratt 2006: 341). Admitted to Yahweh's throne room, the prophet listens to the deliberations of the court and reports them to the king or people. At times, the prophet is even given the privilege of the floor, to add his own counsel to the council of spirits.

The Chronicler depicts a layered conflict. The sole prophet of Yahweh stands against the many prophets of Ahab. Micaiah's throne vision sets Yahweh against the kings of Israel and Judah. These two conflicts are reinforced by the structure of Micaiah's speech and its aftermath:

A Micaiah: Hear Yahweh (18:18)
   B Micaiah's vision of Yahweh and spirits; Yahweh's decree (18:19–22)
      C Zedekiah strikes Micaiah (18:23–24)
   B′ The king's decree: Thus says the king (18:25–26)
A′ Micaiah's last words: Hear (18:27)

---

2. Micaiah has said he can speak only what Yahweh gives him to speak. Is his initial response from Yahweh? It seems not. But then he describes the scene in the heavenly court, in which Yahweh sends a spirit to be a deceiving spirit in the mouths of Ahab's prophets. This hints that Micaiah's initial speech is also from Yahweh. Micaiah speaks only what he receives, because even the *deceptive* prophecy comes from Yahweh.

Micaiah's "Shema" surrounds the passage. Within the frame (B/B'), the text draws out a contrast between Yahweh's decision and Ahab's. The main prophecy ends with *ra'ah*, the "evil" that will fall on the house of Ahab (18:22; Japhet 1993: 765). At the center is the direct confrontation between Zedekiah and Micaiah concerning possession of the Spirit. Zedekiah's name means "Yah is righteous," and he is the son of Chenaanah, whose name resembles the word "Canaanite." Ahab and his prophets represent a reversal of the conquest, a re-Canaanitization of the land, appropriately led by a prophet who (symbolically) traces his ancestry to the Canaanites. But Zedekiah's given name will trump his ancestry. Yahweh will prove himself just by leading Ahab into the trap that he sets; he will show his justice when Zedekiah seeks refuge in an inner room (18:24). With the two kingdoms now united by marriage, the division shifts to another key: it is no longer king versus king but prophet versus prophet.

In Micaiah's vision, Yahweh is looking for someone to "seduce" Ahab to attack Ramoth-gilead. The verb can refer to sexual seduction (Exod. 22:16) or to entice-ment to serve other gods (Deut. 11:16), to spiritual infidelity. Yahweh wants a volunteer to turn Ahab away from Yahweh, to catch his ear so that he listens to the word of false prophets rather than submitting to the Shema of the God of Israel. Micaiah gives us a frightful insight into the stern ways of God. As with Pharaoh in the time of Moses, Yahweh hardens a king's heart and leads him astray in order to pulverize him. Yahweh sets a trap so that Ahab will fall into it. We can, and must, say that Pharaoh and Ahab harden themselves and that Yahweh turns them over to their own desires. That does not alter the fact that he actively works to destroy these kings.

That point may be reinforced by the fact that the spirit (*ruakh*) who answers Yahweh's call is called "*the* spirit" rather than "*a* spirit" (18:20). *Ruakh* is used four times in the chapter: of the volunteering spirit, twice of the "deceiving spirit" put into the mouths of Ahab's prophets, and finally in Zedekiah's taunt to Micaiah, "How did the Spirit of Yahweh pass from me to speak to you?" (18:23). If the spirit who stirs the prophets of Ahab to deceive is the Spirit of Yahweh, then Zedekiah's taunt is accurate: the same Spirit who leads the prophets of Ahab to seduce inspires Micaiah to tell the truth. As we have seen, the words of the prophets are not so much false as ambiguous. In fact, they come true: Yahweh *does* give something into the hand of some king—Ahab into the hand of the king of Aram.

Micaiah joins Hanani in the role of suffering prophet. Zedekiah strikes him on the cheek (cf. Isa. 53; Matt. 5), and Ahab turns him over to the prison guard with orders to feed him only bread and water. Ahab believes he will return from battle in peace (18:26). Micaiah picks up on the term and provides an empirical test of the truth of his prophecy: if Ahab does return in peace, then Micaiah is not a mouthpiece of Yahweh (18:27). We never see Micaiah again. Perhaps he was released after Ahab fell; perhaps he was executed as a dangerous rebel. We are left with the word with which he began: "Hear, O King. Hear the word of King Yahweh." It rings down the decades that follow, because the kings of Israel and Judah will both be judged by how well they respond to that Shema.

Ahab is confident that he will return in peace, because he has a scheme up his sleeve.[3] He believes he can outwit the decree of Yahweh; he believes that his decree will weigh more heavily than that of the King of spirits. Perhaps he is putting the prophecy to the test (Japhet 1993: 767). Second Chronicles 18:29 lays out the plan and its execution in parallel:

> A The king of Israel speaks to Jehoshaphat:
> > B I will disguise myself
> > > C and enter into battle
> > > > D but you put on royal robes.
> A' The king of Israel
> > B' disguised himself
> > > C' and entered into battle.

Ahab intends this as a disguise, but it is a striking demotion. Earlier in the passage (18:9), both kings were robed, indistinguishable royal figures. As they go to the battle, only Jehoshaphat dresses like a king. Ahab has been called "king of Israel" throughout the battle, but the Arameans are more discerning. When they see Jehoshaphat, they recognize him as "the king of Israel" (18:30–31), their assigned target. This is not a misidentification, for Jehoshaphat, despite his folly, is truly the king of Israel.

The Chronicler makes subtle changes to the account in 1 Kgs. 22 to bring out his own distinctive themes. In Kings, Jehoshaphat "cries out" and the Arameans turn back; but the Chronicler writes that when the king cries out, Yahweh "helps" (*'azar*) and "diverts" (*sut*) the Arameans (18:31). Prayer is the

---

3. The battle scene is organized chiastically:
> A Ahab to Jehoshaphat: Disguise yourself (18:28–29)
> > B King of Aram to charioteers: Seek king of Israel (18:30–31a)
> > > C Jehoshaphat cries out to Yahweh (18:31b)
> > B' Chariots abandon pursuit of Jehoshaphat (18:32)
> A' A random arrow pierces Ahab's armor and kills him (18:33–34)

primary tactic of war throughout Chronicles ($\rightarrow$ 1 Chr. 5:20; $\rightarrow$ 2 Chr. 20:9; $\rightarrow$ 2 Chr. 32:20), the main means of access to the help of Yahweh. Yahweh, the God who diverted Ahab through his lying prophets, now intervenes to divert the Arameans from destroying the Davidic king. At the last moment, Yahweh opens the eyes of the Arameans. Initially, they look at Jehoshaphat and see the king of Israel; after he cries out, the captains of the chariots look again and see that he is not the king of Israel. Instead of turning after him to fight, they turn away from him (18:32).

Ahab plots, and so does the king of Aram. Both have plans for the battle, but neither plan comes to fruition. Instead of targeting the king of Israel, the Arameans find that they are targeting the king of Judah. Ahab intends to save himself to return in peace by hiding in the armor of a common soldier, but instead he is killed. Kings plan, but Yahweh's decrees overrule their plots and bring the outcome Yahweh determined in the heavenly council. An arrow pierces the soldering at one of the joints of Ahab's armor, wounding him. He dies like Saul, an ominous note for the future of his dynasty, which will end as Saul's did. He dies at sunset, a fitting symbol of the declining fortunes of the house of Ahab.

Jehoshaphat returns to Jerusalem, barely saved from death. But his covenant with Ahab reverberates through several generations. His son Jehoram proves to be an Abimelech, killing his brothers and spending his life walking in the ways of Ahab, that is, serving Baal and Asherah. In another allusion to Judg. 2, he makes Judah "play the harlot" with other gods and leads Judah astray. Of course he would: he was the son whom Jehoshaphat married off to the daughter of Ahab. His wife is Athaliah, daughter of Ahab.

His son Ahaziah also walks in the way of Ahab, being the son of Athaliah, the daughter of Ahab and Jezebel. Jehu kills Ahaziah, and then Athaliah wipes out all the remaining descendants of Jehoshaphat. The Davidic dynasty is hanging by a thread. The Lord gives a new birth to the Davidic dynasty by preserving Joash alive, but Joash, too, falls under the spell of courtiers from the days of Athaliah ($\rightarrow$ 2 Chr. 24:17). Only in the reign of Joash's son Amaziah is the influence of the house of Ahab finally put to rest.

Generation after generation of idolatry (Boda 2010: 318). A near destruction of the Davidic dynasty. The kingdom of Judah teetering on the edge of extinction. The Davidic dynasty is wrecked and unfaithful for generations. And why? Because Jehoshaphat made a covenant with Ahab. He "in-lawed himself to Ahab." Jehoshaphat's betrayal of Yahweh, and of his own status as Davidic king, nearly destroys his own family.

"What partnership does righteousness have with lawlessness?" Paul asks (2 Cor. 6:14 AT). What communion does light have with darkness? Is there *symphonia* between Christ and Baal? Does the temple of God have any room for idols? It is absurd. Light wants to accommodate a bit of darkness rather than dispel it? God lets us leave a little room for idolatry on the side? Paul poses a stark choice, as does Jesus: You are either with me or against me. You either gather with me or scatter abroad. It is a stark choice that shapes our most important relationships. Whom will you marry? Are you going to become in-lawed to idolaters? Is compromise going to be infused into your family? When we come to the Lord's table as the bride of Christ to enjoy the marriage feast of the Lamb, we renew our marital covenant with Jesus our Husband and renounce all other husbands, all other tables. "You cannot drink the cup of the Lord and the cup of demons; you cannot partake of the table of the Lord and the table of demons. Or do we provoke the Lord to jealousy?" (1 Cor. 10:21–22). We are wed to Christ and are forbidden to ally ourselves to any other.

Jesus calls his church to unity. He prays that his church will be one, and we *will* be. But the church cannot be unified by idols. Jehoshaphat is a cautionary tale: trying to build unity on the basis of idolatry, trying to ally with idolaters, is disastrous. It is not going to produce unity but destruction. A war of utter destruction against idols is not divisive. It is the only possible path to unity.

The Lord is merciful. Despite his folly, Jehoshaphat returns in *shalom* to Jerusalem (19:1). Micaiah had spoken of each Israelite returning in peace (18:16), pointedly excluding Ahab, who would not return in peace to Samaria (18:26). The prophet Hanani confronted Jehoshaphat's father, Asa, for his folly; as Jehoshaphat returns to the capital, the prophet's son confronts the king's son. Jehoshaphat's alliance with a "wicked" king who "hates Yahweh" manifests a disorder in Jehoshaphat's loves. Ahab hates Yahweh because he "hates" Yahweh's word that comes through the prophet Micaiah. Jehu warns Jehoshaphat that he should not help the ones who hate God or show loving loyalty to the wicked (19:2). Help should be extended, but help must be discriminating. Helping the wicked risks wrath, which Jehoshaphat has only narrowly escaped. Like Jesus's messages to the churches of Asia (Rev. 2–3), Jehu's message is both rebuke and assurance: to the "I have this against you," he adds an "in this you do well." Jehoshaphat is judged "good" because he has removed Asheroth from the land and has set his heart to seek Yahweh (19:3). Yahweh's eyes see everything, and they "find" good things in Jehoshaphat. "Good" is a creation term; by burning away the idols, the king has restored the Edenic quality of the land as a place where Yahweh and his people can meet on peaceful terms.

Judges and War (2 Chronicles 19–20)

The sequence of chapter 19 suggests that Jehoshaphat hears the rebuke. He remains in Jerusalem; that is, he does not venture out again to form an alliance with Ahab's house. When he does go out, he goes to call the people back to worship Yahweh, God of their fathers. His evangelistic campaign goes south to Beersheba and north into the hill country of Ephraim, territory normally controlled by the kings of Israel (19:4). Like Asa, he chips away at the divided kingdom and brings some of the people of the north back into the sphere of the Davidic house and temple worship. He turns to Jerusalem and turns the people toward Jerusalem, too, the place that the Lord has chosen to set his name.

Earlier, the king sent teachers and priests on a circuit to instruct Judah in Torah (17:7–10). After his near disaster with Ahab, he reinforces that program by establishing judges in the fortified cities of Judah. Jehoshaphat's judicial reform picks up on the language of Jehu's warning: Jehu warns him of guilt and wrath, and Jehoshaphat exhorts the judges to judge rightly to avoid "wrath" (*qetseph*, 19:10). The court system is set up in two phases. First Jehoshaphat appoints judges in "all the fortified cities" of Judah (19:5–7), then in the capital city of Jerusalem (19:8–11). Under the monarchy, judicial process is centralized (Boda 2010: 324; Japhet [1993: 777] cites Deut. 17:8–13), so that local judges pass judgment on local cases, while the Jerusalem court functions as an appeals court that handles "any dispute [that] comes to you from your brethren who live in their cities" (19:10), whether it is a matter of sacred or civil law (Amariah the priest handles "matters of Yahweh," while Zebadiah is over "the king's matters," 19:11 AT). To each group, Jehoshaphat delivers an exhortation that resembles Moses's exhortations to the judges over hundreds and thousands (Exod. 18; Deut. 1). Though both king and priests are called to promote the kingship of Yahweh over Israel and the nations, they have distinct roles and distinct jurisdictions (Japhet 1993: 773). That complex legal and political space is the space of freedom.

The first exhortation (19:6–7) is arranged in a fairly neat chiasm:

A See what you do.
    B You do not judge for man but for Yahweh
        C who is with you in judgment.
        C' Let the dread of Yahweh be upon you
    B' and guard what you do
A' for there is not for Yahweh unrighteousness, partiality, bribe.

Second Chronicles 19:6 uses some form of *mishpat* three times, twice to refer to judges and once as a verb, "to judge":

A To the judges
   B See what you do
      C for not for man
A' you judge
      C' but for Yahweh
   B' And with you he is
A" in the word of judgment

Judges stand in a multiple relationship to Yahweh, whose name is invoked repeatedly (Japhet 1993: 779). They judge "for" Yahweh, are to judge in the "dread" of Yahweh, and are to imitate the impartiality of Yahweh, who is "with" them in judgment. Josiah's circuit teachers bring "dread" on the surrounding nations, but the judges are themselves to live and judge under the "dread" of God—fear of his anger if they judge unjustly, fear that the High Judge will take up cases that they judge wrongly. Judges can incur wrath as readily as litigants (Boda 2010: 325). When they fear Yahweh and judge impartially, they become agents for establishing Yahweh's justice. Under Jehoshaphat, whose name means "Yah judges," justice spreads from Jerusalem throughout the land of Judah. Jehoshaphat urges the local judges to "guard" (*shamar*) what they do, specifically to guard against injustice, partiality, or bribes (19:7). *Shamar* has its natural home in priestly texts, describing the priestly task of controlling access to the sanctuary. Judges, too, are guardians of a house, standing sentry at the gates of the house of Judah, where Yahweh dwells.

In the exhortation to the judges of Jerusalem, the king brings out another facet of their work. Judges "warn" their brothers (19:10), a term that suggests a pedagogical or prophetic dimension to the work of a judge. Perhaps the judges are expected to instruct Judah in Torah, as the teachers had done earlier. But it appears that a *mishpat* is itself a warning: when judges judge with and for and in the dread of Yahweh, their judicial decisions encourage certain paths of action and discourage others. Law needs to be taught, but law itself teaches. Law opens and closes possibilities of behavior. It cannot be morally neutral. The fact that litigants are described as "brothers" suggests a familial dimension to their work. Judges are not a separated class but are charged with maintaining order in the family of Judah.

Both exhortations use the verb *'asah*, "make" or "do" (19:6, 7, 9, 10, 11), a creation word. Yahweh "makes" the creation by verbal decrees that distinguish this and that, waters above and below, water and land. Judah is Yahweh's new creation, formed by his own promise, but the task of maintaining Judah's boundaries and order is delegated to Jehoshaphat and then to the judges. Misjudgment incurs *'asham* (guilt), which provokes Yahweh's wrath (19:10). By doing their *mishpat*, judges maintain the new-creation order that is Judah.

After Jehoshaphat sent out teachers, he allied with Ahab to go to war at Ramoth-gilead. After he sends out judges, he engages in another war, a defensive war against the invading forces of the Moabites, Ammonites, Meunites, and Edomites. David subdued the Moabites and Ammonites, making them tributary states of Israel (1 Chr. 18:2, 11; 19). Ahab lost control of the Moabites, and, since Jehoshaphat is allied with Ahab, he becomes a target for the Moabite backlash (Boda 2010: 330; Japhet 1993: 786). In some Hebrew texts, these nations are accompanied by Arameans (2 Chr. 20:2). If that is accurate, it is a further ironic twist. Jehoshaphat's father, Asa, paid the Arameans to attack Baasha's Israel, and now, fortified with gold from the temple and Judah's royal treasury, they turn back to attacking Judah. The entire crisis is the result of Jehoshaphat's alliance with the northern kingdom. The nations come from "beyond the sea" (20:2), the sea that represents the chaos of the Gentile world, the sea from which monsters come. These nations *are* the sea, a foaming flood threatening to overwhelm Judah.

The Chronicler's account has a roughly chiastic structure:

A Invasion and assembly at the house of Yahweh: Jehoshaphat's prayer (20:1–12)
   B Prophecy of Jahaziel: no need to fight (20:13–17)
      C Worship, prostration, and song (20:18–19)
         D Morning: Jehoshaphat speaks (20:20–21)
      C' Song and confusion of enemies (20:22–23)
   B' No fight: see corpses (20:24–25)
A' Assembly at Berakah and return to Jerusalem (20:26–30)

Jehoshaphat is afraid, but instead of scheming to avoid the invasion, he turns to seek Yahweh (20:3). He fears, gives (his face), and calls Judah to assemble, not as a military regiment, but for a fast. "Seek Yahweh" occurs three times in 20:2–3: Jehoshaphat "seeks Yahweh," Judah assembles to "seek help from Yahweh," and all the cities of Judah come to "seek Yahweh." Jehoshaphat earlier helped the king of

Israel who hated Yahweh. But in a crisis he still knows where help comes from. The people also fear, and they respond by forming a spontaneous *qahal*, a sacred assembly (20:5, 13; Japhet [1993: 787] notes that Jehoshaphat does not *qabats* [gather] the people). It is the first *qahal* since the time of Solomon. The term is used seven times in Solomon's reign, as it is in the account of David's reign (1 Chr. 13:2, 4; 28:8; 29:1, 10, 20 [2×]). After Jehoshaphat, the word disappears again until Hezekiah renews covenant (*qahal* is used fourteen times in the Hezekiah narratives). These are crucial junctures of the Chronicler's history: David assembles the people to prepare for the temple; Solomon to dedicate the temple; Jehoshaphat to pray toward the temple, as Solomon prescribed; Hezekiah to restore the temple and the covenant. All Israel's good—communion with Yahweh, joy and festive meals, victory over enemies, the coronation of kings—comes at and through assemblies. The Chronicler anticipates the letter to the Hebrews (10:25): do not forsake the assembling of yourselves together.

The king addresses his prayer to "Yahweh, Elohim of the fathers":

A Yahweh, our Elohim (20:6)
    B You drove out nations and gave land (20:7)
        C They dwelled and built (20:8)
            D Summary of Solomon's prayer of dedication (20:9)
        C′ Nations we did not drive out are trying to drive us out
            (20:10–11)
A′ Our Elohim (20:12a)
    B′ Execute judgment on them (20:12b)

Yahweh is "ruler" of all nations before whom "no one can stand" (20:6). Like Asa before him (→2 Chr. 14:10), the king confesses Judah's helplessness before the invaders; they are "powerless" to repel Moab and Ammon (20:12). The structural and substantive heart of his prayer is an appeal to the covenant commitment of Yahweh, full of allusions to Solomon's prayer of dedication. Jehoshaphat calls on God to remember his covenant with Abraham (20:7, 11; see Gen. 15:18), and he offers a verbal memorial of the conquest under Joshua. He reminds the Lord of his promise to deliver Israel when they turn to him at his house (20:8–9; →2 Chr. 6:24–25, 34–35). Under the fivefold threat of evil, sword, judgment, pestilence, and famine, Judah will stand and cry out before the house where Yahweh's name dwells. The summary of Solomon's prayer closes with an alliterative flourish. "Hear and save" is *vetishma' vetoshia'*, a punning poetic hint that, for Yahweh, to hear is to save, that he is the saving God because he is the hearing God. There is no deeper ground of hope for Israel than this: Does he who planted the ear not hear?

Before the divine King and Judge, Jehoshaphat brings a case against the nations: These are the very nations that Israel treated with compassion on their way out of Egypt. Israel did not invade and conquer Moab, Ammon, or Edom, and now these nations are rewarding that kindness by trying to reverse the conquest, driving Israel out of the land as Israel once drove out the Canaanites. They show their ingratitude (Japhet 1993: 791) by trying to drive out (*garash*) Israel from its inheritance (a form of *yarash*; 20:11). Israel spared these peoples because they are related to Israel. Moab and Ammon are descendants of Abram's nephew Lot, and Edom is Esau, Jacob's brother. This is not a conflict with distant, faceless Gentiles. It is a conflict between brothers; these nations are Cain to Judah's Abel. Jehoshaphat wants Yahweh to punish the cruelty of nations that attack the Israel that spared them.

Jehoshaphat stands before Yahweh to offer prayer; now the people stand before Yahweh awaiting a response, which comes through the prophet Jahaziel ("He sees God"; Boda 2010: 330). The Chronicler informs us that the assembly includes not only the men of Judah but "little ones, wives, and children" (20:13 AT). This is a priesthood of all Israel, Judah standing to serve. The inclusion of infants is notable. Hezekiah, too, includes infants in his covenant renewal (→ 2 Chr. 31:18). In part, this continues a series of allusions to the exodus, in which Israel's infants were very much at stake: Pharaoh attacked Israel's infants; Moses refused to leave Egypt without infants; Yahweh took vengeance by destroying the firstborn sons of Egypt (Exod. 10:10, 24; 12:37). It is also a hint that the assembly of Judah not only includes the present generation but stretches out to the future. This is a liturgico-military assembly, and infants are included because God ordains praise through them to still the enemy and avenger (Ps. 8). One is left to ponder what kind of power churches give up when they shuffle the kids off to the nursery or children's church.

The Lord responds with a word of promise through Jahaziel the prophet, who is filled with the Spirit (20:15–17). It is a more favorable message than Jehoshaphat received through the prophet Jehu:

  A Hear, Judah, Jerusalem, king
      B Do not fear or be dismayed, for the battle is God's
          C Tomorrow go down, they will come up
             D No fight
             D' Station, stand, see salvation

A' Judah and Jerusalem

    B' Do not fear or be dismayed

        C' Tomorrow go out, for Yahweh is with you

Israel should take heart because "the battle is not yours but God's" (20:15). Jahaziel's prophecy corresponds exactly to Jehoshaphat's prayer. Jehoshaphat confesses Yahweh as the almighty Sovereign of all nations and admits Judah's impotence. In response, the Lord says in effect, "Yes, I know you are powerless, and so I am not going to ask you to do anything. Just stand there and see the great wonders that I do." Jahaziel's instructions to "stand and see the salvation of the Lord" (20:17) are reminiscent of Moses's words at the Red Sea (Exod. 14:13; Boda 2010: 330; cf. the comparative chart of Exod. 14:13–14 with 2 Chr. 20:17 in Japhet 1993: 795). It is a new exodus from an Egypt-like threat, complete with plunder.

Jehoshaphat and Judah respond to the word of the prophet with humility. The people bow low (20:18), and the Levites praise God (20:19, 21). Jehoshaphat reacts to a political and military threat by calling the people together for worship, and the passage presents an order of worship: prayer, preaching, praise. Worship is the first line of defense against the invaders.

The next morning, Jehoshaphat finally leads the people out to the battlefield, but their advance is less a military maneuver than a continuation of the temple liturgy. The king gives another speech at a time when a general might be expected to rouse the bloody-mindedness of his soldiers. Instead, Jehoshaphat urges them to "believe" (20:20):

A Hear (*shama*), Judah and Jerusalem,

    B trust (*'aman*) Yahweh your God

        C and be established (*'aman*).

    B' Trust (*'aman*) his prophets

        C' and succeed.

Like the prophet, Jehoshaphat begins with a *shema*, a call to the people to remember the one God, Yahweh, and to devote their whole heart, soul, and strength to him. Trusting Yahweh means trusting the prophets who deliver Yahweh's word (B/B'), and when Judah trusts, the Lord proves himself trustworthy by establishing them (C) and granting success (C').

At the end of the worship assembly, the Levites, praising with a loud voice, lead the people out of the city (20:20–22), still praising. Jehoshaphat does not put his crack troops in front, but rather singers armed with musical instruments and song. They are not wearing armor but "holy attire," the priestly attire of worship. While they sing and praise the Lord, the Lord "sets ambushes" for the Ammonites and Moabites, turning them to fight among themselves (20:22–23). When Judah goes to find out what has happened, they discover a valley of corpses and so much scattered plunder that it takes three days to gather it all (20:24–26). Moab and Ammon come to plunder Judah, but the plunderers end up plundered. The battle of the Valley of Berakah (which means "Valley of Blessing") reverberates throughout the remainder of Jehoshaphat's reign. Just as the Canaanites in Joshua's day were fearful of Israel because of the rumors they heard coming up from Egypt, so this "new exodus" terrorizes surrounding nations (20:29). They leave Jehoshaphat alone, and his kingdom returns to peace.

Though 2 Chr. 20 is one of the clearest biblical examples of liturgical warfare, it is by no means the only one. Israel commonly wins victories by calling on the Lord in prayer and exalting him in praise. Yahweh began his war against Egypt in response to the cries of Israel (Exod. 3:7). At Jericho, Israel won by processing around the city with the ark of the covenant, blowing trumpets and shouting (Josh. 6). Samuel led Israel to victory at the battle of Ebenezer by offering sacrifices and crying out to the Lord (1 Sam. 7). In the New Testament, Revelation describes the progress of a heavenly liturgy: the book is opened, the trumpets proclaim the word of God, and the angels pour out blood from sacramental bowls. As the heavenly worship progresses, the Lord pours out his judgments on "the great city."

The liturgy's power does not lie in the liturgy itself. There is nothing automatic or magical about a worship service. Liturgical warfare is effective only as it expresses the worshiper's reliance on the Lord of Hosts, the God of Battles. When he is exalted in our praises, he becomes a terror to our enemies, leaves the field strewn with corpses, and makes the valley of battle into a Valley of Berakah.

This would be a good place to end the account of Jehoshaphat's reign. The crescendo of victory would make a neat counterpoint to his foolish covenant with Ahab. It would make a neat inversion of Asa, who began with a great, trusting victory over Zerah, is encouraged by a prophet, but then muffs Baasha's invasion. Jehoshaphat begins with an ungodly alliance with Ahab, is rebuked by a prophet, and trusts Yahweh in the next war. Asa's reign begins with undisturbed rest; Jehoshaphat's reign ends with it.

Yet the battle is not the last episode in the Chronicler's account. He includes a "file-closing" coda, indicating the length of Jehoshaphat's reign, his uprightness in the way of Asa, and his failure to remove high places, and then cites a source for additional details (20:31–34). The comparison to Asa is double-sided: like his father, he is a faithful king whose reign is tainted by political folly (Japhet 1993: 800).

But there is an extension after the "The End." Jehoshaphat does one last thing, which leads to one last meeting with a prophet. One would think he learned his lesson from his disastrous alliance with Ahab, but he again enters into an alliance with a king of Israel, Ahab's son Ahaziah. He attempts a quest of Solomonic daring, building ships that will trade on the sea (→2 Chr. 8:18; 9:21). A ship is a portion of land that takes dominion over the threatening sea; it is a symbol of Israel, tossed but intact, riding the sea of nations. Solomon's ships were a fitting symbol of the extent of his dominion and the spread of his international reputation. That Solomon allies with Huram of Tyre for his trading ventures italicizes the political ramifications of the fleet.

Jehoshaphat's efforts are not so successful. He allies with the northern kingdom and "act[s] wickedly" (20:35). The prophet Eliezer ("My God helps") rebukes and warns him: a union with Ahaziah will end in destruction, as did Jehoshaphat's union with Ahab. Solomon allied with a Yahweh-worshiping Gentile; Jehoshaphat allies with an idolatrous Israelite. His ships wreck and fail to make it to Tarshish (cf. 1 Chr. 1:7, where Tarshish is linked with Javan). And here, finally, the Chronicler ends his long account of Jehoshaphat's reign—with a scene of wreckage floating on the sea. It is a sign of things to come, as Jehoshaphat's folly leaves a wake into the following generations.

10

JUDAH BECOMES ISRAEL

2 Chronicles 21–24

Jehoshaphat is a good king, upright before Yahweh. Yet his alliance with Ahab nearly kills him and throws Judah into a tailspin for several generations (Boda 2010: 334). As in the book of Judges, the death of a ruler is quickly followed by a return to idolatry and political upheaval. We enter another cycle of idolatry, slavery, and distress that will be (partially) relieved in the reign of Joash. Second Chronicles 21–25 is largely devoted to describing the progress of the Omride infection in the southern kingdom.[1]

Jehoram (2 Chronicles 21)

Jehoshaphat takes pains to ensure a smooth transition to his son Jehoram. With seven sons (listed in 21:2), Jehoshaphat knows that there is potential for rivalry over the crown. He attempts to satisfy all parties. To six of his sons he gives "many gifts of silver, gold and precious things" (21:3), along with cities to manage and rule throughout Judah. Preoccupied with those grants, so Jehoshaphat hopes,

---

1. As Johnstone notes, the Chronicler's "purpose is to show how the poison introduced into the system by Jehoshaphat's alliance with the royal house of the north, sealed by Jehoram's own marriage to Ahab's daughter, Athaliah, continues its deadly influence. [The Chronicler] has just recounted how the two disasters of Jehoshaphat's reign—the campaign to liberate Ramoth-gilead and the merchant-venture in the Red Sea—were caused by his association with Ahab and with Ahab's son, Athaliah's brother Ahaziah, respectively. The poison now spreads into the heart of the life of Judah itself" (Johnstone 1998b: 108–9).

they will not think of overthrowing their brother Jehoram. It is intended to work in the other direction too: Jehoram has less reason to fear his brothers if they are wealthy governors of their own cities. Jehoshaphat arranges his succession to avoid bloodshed.

It does not work. Once Jehoram establishes his kingdom, he slaughters his brothers and other rulers of Israel (21:4). He proves to be a king on the model of Abimelech (Judg. 9). Perhaps he fears that his brothers will use their fortress cities as bases from which to launch coup attempts. Behind the specific motivation, the Chronicler explains Jehoram's conduct by pointing to his connection with the house of Ahab: he walks in the "ways of the kings of Israel, just as the house of Ahab did (for Ahab's daughter was his wife)" (21:6). Ahab is not only an idolater but also an oppressive king who arranges for Naboth's death and seizes his ancestral vineyard. Jehoram's wife Athaliah, daughter of Ahab, takes cues from her father and husband: when she takes the throne, she wipes out the whole royal seed to ensure the stability of her kingdom. In the house of Ahab, violence and idolatry go together.

Yet the "evil" that Jehoram does in the eyes of Yahweh (21:6) does not cause Yahweh to abandon his commitment to David. The structure of 21:7 highlights Yahweh's covenant:

A   Yahweh was not willing to destroy
   B   the house of David
      C   because of the covenant
   B'   which he cut to David
A'   and said to give to him and his sons a lamp.

Yahweh's commitment in a previous generation determines the ultimate fate of future generations. Though Jehoram tries to snuff out most of the lights in the Davidic firmament, Yahweh leaves David a lamp (Boda 2010: 336). "Lamp" may be a reference to Jehoram himself. Despite his wickedness and despite the fact that he walks in the ways of Ahab, he is a son of David and bearer of the Davidic promise. In any case, Yahweh's covenant puts a constraint on his discipline of Judah. He ensures that the house of David will stand, even when it stops looking anything like the house of David, even when Jehoram reverses all the gains of his fathers Asa and Jehoshaphat (Boda 2010: 337).

Though the Lord preserves the dynasty, he disciplines Jehoram by chipping away territory from his kingdom. Edom revolts and establishes a separate dynasty (21:8).

Jehoram assembles his commanders and chariots and attempts a surprise attack on Edom at night. A nighttime raid might be a Passover, when the Lord sends his angel to eliminate his enemies. But it is an ineffective Passover. Jehoram strikes the Edomites, but he does not put an end to the revolt. Edom remains independent of Judah, as Esau throws off the yoke of Jacob. For the moment, the elder does *not* serve the younger. Perhaps emboldened by Edom's revolt, Libnah also revolts.

As in Judges, political turmoil is a result of religious infidelity. Because Jehoram forsakes Yahweh, the Lord forsakes him and distributes his land to other nations (21:10). That is the message of the prophet Elijah, who sends a letter to Jehoram, rebuking him for leading Judah into Baal worship (Japhet 1993: 808). As in 1 Kgs. 17, Elijah appears out of nowhere, unintroduced and unexpected. He always shows up when Israel falls into Baal worship (Japhet 1993: 812; cf. Mal. 3–4). The letter is organized to stress the unfaithful "walk" of Jehoram, which leads him to "prostitute" Judah:

A You have not walked
   B in the ways of Jehoshaphat and Asa;
A′ you have walked
   B′ in the way of Israel.
      C You caused-prostitution
         D to Judah and Jerusalem
      C′ as caused-prostitution
         D′ the house of Ahab.

The verb *zanah* ("play the whore") is used three times in two verses, once from the narrator (21:11) and twice in the letter (21:13). Elijah holds up Asa and Jehoshaphat as standards. They are not standards of perfection but standards of faithfulness. Yahweh grades on a curve, but Jehoram does not live up even to that modified standard. Allusions to exodus run through Elijah's letter, but it is an upside-down exodus: Jehoram and his land will suffer plagues, his own sons will be destroyed because Jehoram killed his brothers, and he himself, the firstborn, will die an agonizing death (21:14–15; Johnstone 1998b: 113).

As in the case of Asa (→ 2 Chr. 16:12), the sickness of the king embodies the sickness of the land. Jehoram's disease is worse, striking him in the bowels instead of on the feet. The infection is spreading, and the king and his kingdom are nearing their deathbeds. In Exod. 15:26 the Lord promises not to let any of the *makhaleh* of Egypt fall on Israel (cf. Exod. 23:35). Now that the house of David is abandoning the Lord and turning to false gods, the diseases of the nations infect them. There is a solution: Jehoram could turn to the Lord in his house and cry out for healing. The Lord has promised to hear and heal, hear and save (→ 2 Chr. 6:30; 7:14, which uses the verb "cure," *rapha'*). Jehoram clings too closely to the gods of Ahab to do that. He is sickened by his idolatries and bloodshed, as is the land itself.

The structure of Jehoram's reign highlights the rebellions from various sides (Pratt 2006: 350). Edom rebels from the south, Libneh from the north. After Elijah's letter arrives, Jehoram is squeezed by Arabs from the east and by Philistines on the west. These rebellions are not accidental. Nations have spirits, which Yahweh, the Spirit of all, stirs up to invade Judah (21:16; Boda 2010: 338). Arabs plunder the king's house and take away all of the king's sons and daughters except Jehoahaz, Jehoram's youngest son (21:17). Jehoram is given a preview of what will happen when Israel and Judah again play the harlot: Assyria will invade and plunder, and then Babylon. It is a reverse conquest that follows an inversion of the exodus. The Davidic dynasty is being reduced, partly by invading Gentiles, mostly because of the unfaithfulness of David's own descendants.

It is a humiliating defeat. Like the Moabites and others who plagued Israel during the period of judges, Arabs come with a mere "raiding party" but are able to penetrate to the capital city. Cushites are behind the Arab invasion (21:16), an ominous note. Asa defeated a gigantic Cushite army, but only because he cried to Yahweh. Because Jehoram refuses to turn to Yahweh, he will be overwhelmed by this power from the deep south (Johnstone 1998b: 113). Philistines are related to Egyptians (Gen. 10); subjection to Philistia is yet another inverted exodus. Philistines were among David's main enemies, whom he subdued before Solomon took the throne. Now Philistines are back, a sign of the deep reversal of the history of the Davidic dynasty.

Elijah's prophecy comes true. Yahweh strikes Jehoram in the bowels until the bowels come out. The king is turned inside out, like a sacrificial animal, and he dies in agony. No one misses him. No one honors him at death. Yet, as Judah turns into a mirror image of Israel, Yahweh keeps the Davidic dynasty alive, but the lamp is flickering low.

Ahaziah (2 Chronicles 22)

Judah is sick, and so are its kings. Asa dies of a disease of the feet, and Jehoram dies of a painful disease of the bowels. In the north, Ahab dies of wounds he receives in the battle of Ramoth-gilead, and his son Jehoram of Israel will likewise die of his wounds. Sick kings and sick kingdoms are the inevitable results of an alliance between the house of David and the wicked house of Ahab. The Chronicler reserves the category of "wicked" for the house of Ahab, and, as Johnstone puts it, wickedness "is not just the failing of individuals; it becomes systemic, genetic and contagious, militating against the 'righteous' regime of the house of David" (1998b: 117). The infection spreads during the reign of Jehoram of Judah; it spreads further in the reign of Ahaziah his son. It seeps from the head into the whole body.

Ahaziah repeats the sins of his father. He walks in the way of Ahab and takes evil counsel from his mother, Athaliah, and her advisors (22:2, 4). The opening evaluation of his reign (22:3–5) is structured to highlight the fact that he walks in the counsel of the wicked:

A He walked
   B in ways of the house of Ahab
      C because his mother was a counselor to do wickedly.
      C^1 He did evil in the sight of Yahweh
   B^1 like the house of Ahab
      C^2 for they were counselors.
A^1 He walked
      C^3 in their counsel
A^2 and walked
   B^2 with Jehoram of Ahab to wage war.

Rehoboam listened to foolish counselors and split the kingdom. Now the counsel has become evil, as the kingdom is being reunited in the ways of Ahab. Following their counsel, Ahaziah repeats the sin of Jehoshaphat that started the whole disastrous cycle. Jehoram of Israel is still, comically, trying to recover the city of Ramoth-gilead from the Arameans, just as Ahab had done. Ahaziah, not so comically, repeats the folly of Jehoshaphat by joining with his cousin to the north.

Jehoshaphat escaped from the battle by crying out, but Ahaziah cannot escape the Lord's vengeance. He puts himself in harm's way by being faithful to a covenant with a hater of God. When Jehoram retreats to Jezreel to recover from his battle wounds, Ahaziah visits him. It is a replay of Jehoshaphat's original fateful visit to Samaria, but worse. Now Jehu is on the warpath, anointed by Yahweh to hunt down members of the house of Ahab to wipe it from the face of the earth.

On his way to destroy the princes of the house of Ahab, Jehu meets the princes of Judah—the remaining members of the royal house of David—and slaughters them. Ahaziah scuttles off to Samaria and goes into hiding, but he can no more hide from Yahweh's doom than Ahab could elude the Lord's arrow. Jehu's men find him and bring him out for execution (cf. Gen. 3:8–10).

Joash, from the Ashes (2 Chronicles 23–24)

Jehoshaphat's folly has led to the deepest crisis in the history of the southern kingdom. No one is left to protect the house of Ahaziah, and the princes are exposed to the predatory, paranoid violence of Athaliah, daughter of Ahab and Jezebel. A product of intermarriage of an Israelite father and a Sidonian mother, Athaliah is a malicious version of Huram-abi, the half-Danite, half-Tyrian craftsman who helped Solomon make the furnishings of the temple. Athaliah inverts everything that the earlier Israelite-Gentile alliance attempted: she slaughters her own grandsons because they threaten her throne, and she establishes the ways of Ahab as the way of Judah, the way of the house of David. The ideal of the chosen Davidic king ruling in the chosen city, where the chosen people worship Yahweh at the place he chooses, has been teetering since the reign of Rehoboam. Now it is on the verge of extinction.

By every empirical measure, the Davidic dynasty is doomed. It has only *one* thing going for it: "Yahweh has spoken concerning the sons of David" that David's descendants will reign in Jerusalem (23:3). The Davidic dynasty hangs by *this* thread, but it is enough, because the weakness of God is stronger than men. Jehoiada the priest trusts in this promise, but that does not make him complacent and passive. He does not say, "Well, if God wants the Davidic king restored, he will do it." Rather, *because* the Lord has spoken, "this is the thing which you shall do" (23:4). The Lord's promises do not excuse inaction but motivate action. Trustful Jehoiada is swept up into the promise of Yahweh and so becomes a means for its fulfillment. Readers may wish to pause a moment to contemplate the relation of faith and works.

Joash's father, Ahaziah, tried unsuccessfully to hide from the vengeance of Jehu. Jehosheba ("Yah's oath") hides Joash in an inner room. Jehosheba's plot works. Yahweh's eyes run to and fro through the earth. He sees hidden things. But he also provides cover for those who seek the shelter of his wings. No one can hide from the Lord, but he is himself the only safe haven, the only rock of refuge. The word for "inner" is *mittah*, which typically means a bed and can refer to a bier (2 Sam. 3:31). At the end of his life, Joash is killed in his *mittah*, having spurned the Lord's prophet. But he begins by rising from his "bier." He is a true son of Judah, the tribe of royal resurrection (→ 1 Chr. 2–4). It is a contest of mothers, the protective mother versus the cannibal mother (Boda 2010: 347). Jehosheba places the infant prince, like Moses (Exod. 2:7, 9), in the care of the nurse. Athaliah is a pharaoh, slaughtering infants of the royal family of Israel, and Joash is a new Moses who will be the agent of a renewal of the covenant (Johnstone 1998a: 122).

In the seventh year of Athaliah's reign, Jehoiada the priest plots to restore the Davidic kingdom. It looks like a coup, but in reality it is a countercoup. The covenant renewal is actually a double or triple covenant cutting. The first covenant involves Jehoiada and five captains of hundreds who enter a covenant to gather Levites to restore the Davidic monarchy (23:1). Then the high priest, these five chiefs, and the Levites covenant with the king in the temple (23:3). They commit themselves to put the king on the throne. Finally, the whole people commit to keep covenant with Yahweh.

It is significant that the covenant making is organized by a priest and that he gathers Levites from all the cities of Judah to assist him (23:2). Levites are at the center of the Chronicler's vision of Israel. He records the history of the Davidic kingdom, but the Davidic kingdom only is what it is called to be, and does what it is called to do, when the king is surrounded by Levitical priests who carry on the ministry of the temple. Their presence highlights the fact that this restoration is not merely a political act. It is a liturgical act.

The Levites gather to protect the king, each with his "weapons" in his hand (23:7), specifically spears and shields. Jehoiada wants them to be like Phinehas, who speared a fornicating couple that was defiling the holy camp (Num. 25). Levites have killed before, and not just Phinehas. They received priestly status because of their zeal in slaughtering calf-worshipers at the foot of Mount Sinai. They "filled their hands" with swords, and so Yahweh "filled their hands" to carry out priestly duties. Here again, they "fill their hands" with spears in order to kill. Jehoiada wants to restore the Davidic kingdom, and he knows that it will be a failure if any unauthorized person enters the temple (23:7). The restoration will not be successful if they restore Yahweh's prince but defile Yahweh's house.

The Levites are ready to use those weapons, but they have another responsibility. The Hebrew word for "weapons" (*keli*) also means "temple vessel" and "musical instrument." Levites use musical weapons too: priests trumpet, people rejoice, and the singers lead the praise (23:13). Joash is protected by the Levitical bodyguard, but, like Yahweh, he is carried to his throne on the praises of the Levites.

Gatekeepers are a big part of the plan. Between Solomon and Joash, there are no references to gatekeepers. Their absence from the text symbolizes Judah's neglect of this duty: nobody has been guarding the doorways, and so Ahab and Jezebel and Athaliah have been able to enter Judah with their Baals and Asherah. Putting the kingdom back together requires the establishment and maintenance of boundaries. Throughout Chronicles, renewal of the Davidic kingdom takes the form of a revival of orderly government in the house of God and the kingdom. Chronicles is a vindication of bureaucracy, a biblical endorsement of flowcharts, managers, and duty rosters.

Jehoiada has practical reasons for organizing this restoration on the Sabbath. Extra sacrifices are offered on the Sabbath, and more Levites are present in the temple. He schedules the event at the changing of the temple guard, when some Levites go off duty and others come on duty. The large number of Levites will not rouse suspicion. It is normal Sabbath practice. But Jehoiada arranges for both groups to remain in the temple; those who go out and those who come in will form a great assembly in the temple, none of them dismissed from service (23:8). He deploys one third at the gates of the temple, another third at the king's house, and another third at the gate of the foundation (23:4–5). Every entrance and exit is guarded, so that the coronation can be carried out without interruption.

The choice of a Sabbath day is not merely pragmatic. It is a Sabbath year (the seventh of Athaliah); on a Sabbath day during this Sabbath year, a sabbatical king takes the throne of Yahweh that belongs to the house of David. It is not just a restoration of the Davidic dynasty. It is a restoration of Yahweh's kingdom, but Yahweh's kingdom has a particular shape to it. It is only Yahweh's kingdom when the chosen king reigns in the chosen city and, with the Levites, cares for the chosen place, the temple (→ 2 Chr. 13). This is not merely Joash's coronation. In this Sabbath year, *Yahweh* again takes the throne. This is his parousia.

Judah covenants together "to be Yahweh's people" (23:16). In Hebrew this is a series of three prepositional phrases, each starting with the preposition *l-*. This preposition usually means "to," but it can also mean "as" or "for." This phrase could be translated "to be as the people for Yahweh." Yahweh is the end, goal, and aim of Judah's entire national existence; the people of Judah have abundant life because their life is directed "to Yahweh," and they are called to do all they do "for Yahweh." The initial phrase—"to be"—is a pun on Yahweh's own name, which comes from the Hebrew verb "to be." Yahweh, the God who is, the great

I Am, is the very *substance* of the covenant. For Israel to be at all is to commune with and be directed toward Yahweh. This is what covenant life is: existing/being as a people directed to and for Yahweh.

Embedded within the covenant making is the crowning of the boy king. Everything about the coronation is significant. He is crowned in the court of the temple. Though not a priest, he is a son of Yahweh and so is made king in his Father's house. Armed Levites form a ring around the king, on the right and left side of the temple, by the altar and the house (Boda [2010: 354] and Japhet [1993: 832] note the emphasis on Levites). The king is surrounded by Levites as Yahweh's own throne is surrounded by Levites. Once the ring is set in place, Jehoiada brings Joash out and places him by the pillar, probably the royal "Boaz" pillar at the doorway of the temple. The king is a pillar in the Lord's house, part of the architecture of the human temple, Judah. He is a ladder, linking Judah to the God of heaven.

As Johnstone (1998b: 128) observes, "The word for 'crown' [*nezer*] is related to 'Nazirite,' the individual who is separated from ordinary life by an oath of abstinence and dedication (Num. 6.1–21). The crown is thus the symbol of exclusive dedication to the one to whose service he is set apart (thus it is also used of the high priest's consecration and of the diadem, which is the symbol of that consecration, Exod. 29.6; Lev. 8.9; 21.12)." Joash, in short, wears a crown like Jehoiada the priest's own golden crown. Jehoiada has functioned as surrogate father to the infant Joash; fittingly, the crown of the "son" resembles the crown of the father. More, the usage points to the Melchizedekal priest-kingliness of the Davidic kings, a theme highlighted throughout Chronicles (cf. Pss. 89:38; 132:18). Equally significant is the connection with Num. 6, where *nezer* describes the "separation" on the head of the Nazirite (cf. 6:7). Literally, what is on the Nazirite's head is his uncut hair; but this is described as a "crown" that indicates his separation to a sacral duty. From that we can extrapolate a string of associations: hair is a crown; a crown is glorified hair; oiled, anointed hair is glorified hair, another form of crown; oil on the head also makes the anointed one a lamp, burning with a flame of oiled hair. Kings, crowns, tongues of fire, lampstands, lamps, burning mountains and pillars . . . continue at your leisure.

All this takes place in the midst of an assembly, a *qahal*, that Jehoiada has gathered (*qibbuts*). Jehoiada takes the lead, but the Chronicler emphasizes the role of the people; the restoration of David's house is the result of a "popular uprising" (Japhet 1993: 829). As I have emphasized, David gathers the elders and people to make Solomon king, and then Solomon gathers the people to dedicate the temple.

As David's kingdom is restored, Israel gathers for another *qahal*. But the assembly around Joash reaches further back, to the original assembly in 1 Chronicles, the assembly to bring the ark into Jerusalem. There, too, Levites gathered with musical instruments, shouts and songs of praise, and trumpets blowing. The ark is the ark of "testimony," and Joash is given something called "the testimony" along with his crown (23:11). This is another way of saying that Joash's coronation restores Yahweh's kingship in Judah, with the human ark-throne, Joash, ascending to the chosen city, to the throne of David, which is Yahweh's throne. Joash is the bearer of the Lord's presence, the throne of the Lord in person.

Sabbath is for joy, but Sabbath joy is founded on Yahweh's victory over his enemies. Athaliah hears a commotion in the temple and interrupts the proceedings. She cries "treason" but is seized and removed from the temple. The elimination of Athaliah is the turning point of the series of events.

> A Athaliah killing princes, Joash rescued (22:10–12)
> > B Seventh year: Jehoiada assembles Levites and makes covenant (23:1–11)
> > > C Athaliah enters (23:12–13)
> > > C' Athaliah taken out and killed (23:14–15)
> > B' Covenant to destroy Baal and restore temple (23:16–20)
> A' Quiet, because Athaliah put to death (23:21)

The story arc is notable: Athaliah seizes and kills, Athaliah is seized and killed, peace comes because Athaliah the killer is killed. In a quasi-sacrificial procedure, she is executed at the Horse Gate, reminiscent of the death of Jezebel (Boda 2010: 348). Athaliah is not Yahweh's only enemy. A house for Baal has been erected in Jerusalem, and on this Sabbath day, this day of Yahweh's enthronement as judge in the enthronement of Joash, the house of Baal is dismantled, his altars and images pulverized, and his priest executed. The last descendant of Ahab is eliminated (Japhet 1993: 829), and it appears that Ahab's god has been purged once and for all.

Once Joash is installed on his throne, the Chronicler offers the Lord's assessment of his reign. Like Asa and Jehoshaphat, Joash is commended for doing what is "right" in the eyes of Yahweh, but that commendation is ominously qualified by the phrase "all the days of Jehoiada the priest" (24:2). What, we are left to wonder, will he do once Jehoiada is gone? We will eventually find out.

Initially, Joash does what a Davidic king should. He attends to the temple. His heart is stirred to gather priests and Levites to collect funds for the upkeep of the Lord's house. He is following the model of David and Solomon, who use their authority as kings first to prepare for and then build the Lord's house. The house is in disrepair, neglected by Joab's Ahabite predecessors and plundered by Athaliah's sons, who removed holy things and placed them into service to Baal (24:7).[2] Athaliah has paid for the sacrilege, but the holy things need to be restored. Joash sets himself as the anti-Athaliah, the king who breaks decisively with the ways of Ahab. Instead of serving the Baals, Judah devotes itself to the service of Yahweh, to whom Judah makes ascension offerings ascend *tamid*, "continually" (24:14).

Joash will prove to be a new David in his zeal to organize and maintain Yahweh's house (Japhet 1993: 836). Yahweh answers David's prayer that Israel would remain a generous people (→ 1 Chr. 29:10–19). As in David's time, gifts and tithes to the Lord's house are an index of national health. As in David's time, careful accounting and distribution of gifts is a sign of spiritual renewal. Once again, accountants and bureaucrats are commended as heroes.

Joash is a Torah-keeping king, demanding that the chief priest collect the levy fixed by Moses, apparently a reference to the atonement tax (Exod. 30:12–16) that was collected from Israel's hosts when they prepared for battle. Though the tax is initially collected as a covering for bloodshed in war, it is here transferred to the upkeep of the temple. It is an appropriate application. The temple service is the system of "coverings" that protects Israel from the Lord's anger and restores Israel when they sin. The levy is a *mas'et*, a "lifting up," a burden like the burden of the Levites who carried the furnishings of the tabernacle. The people gladly shoulder the burden (24:10).

To make the levy permanent, Joash constructs a coffer (*'aron*; 24:8, 10, 11, 12 [2×]). The word is also used for the "ark" of the covenant, and the verbal connection brings out the fact that the levy is collected to maintain the house where the Lord has chosen to place his throne. Joash and Jehoiada distribute the funds collected in the coffer to masons and carpenters, workers in iron and bronze, who can repair the house and its furniture (24:12–14). The Levites "complete" (*kalah*) the collection (24:10) so that the carpenters and craftsmen can "complete" (*kalah*)

2. Note the structure of 24:5–10:
    A King commands to collect money (24:5)
      B Joash summons Jehoiada to inquire about levy of Moses (24:6)
        C Sons of Athaliah broke through and plundered (24:7)
        C' Joash commissions a coffer (24:8)
      B' Joash issues a proclamation regarding levy of Moses (24:9)
    A' The people bring the Mosaic levy to the coffer (24:10)

the work (24:14). The Chronicler used the same verb to describe the completion of the temple (→2 Chr. 5:1; 7:1), and it alludes to Yahweh's completion of the creation (Gen. 2:1–4). By maintaining the temple, Joash is engaged in world maintenance, world completion, and world glorification.

Once again, the commendation of Joash's reign is qualified: they offer ascensions "all the days of Jehoiada" (24:14). In the following verse, Jehoiada dies as a "son of" one hundred and thirty years, full of days, satisfied with life. The kingmaker is honored like a king, buried in the city of David (24:15). He surpasses normal priestly achievement. He takes up the royal task by doing "well in Israel and to God and his house" (24:16).

In the following verses, we finally grasp the qualifications of Joash's faithfulness (24:2, 14). As soon as Jehoiada is dead, "officials of Judah" approach Joash (24:17). We do not know where they come from, but we can guess that they are the remnants of the court of Joash's predecessors, protectors of the tradition of counsel that began in the reign of Ahaziah (→22:5). While Jehoiada is alive, Joash turns his ear to him. Now that the priest's voice is silent, the king "hears" (*shama*) the voice of the officials and abandons the house that he has spent his reign repairing and restoring. Forsaking Yahweh, the people serve the Asherim and idols, and their *'asham* (guilt) provokes Yahweh's wrath (24:18). Joash forgets that Yahweh responds to abandonment by abandonment: If you forsake me, I will forsake you ("forsake," *'azav*, is used five times in the passage, 24:18, 20 [2×], 24, 25).

Joash will not hear the voice of Yahweh's prophets either (24:19), even though one of those prophets is Zechariah, son of Jehoiada. He charges Joash with "passing over" the Lord's commands, and his warning is identical to Azariah's (→2 Chr. 15:1–7): You have forsaken the Lord, so he has forsaken you. Joash responds like Asa and Ahab and conspires to silence the prophet. The king who has been careful not to put Athaliah to death in the temple arranges for the prophet to be stoned in the court of the house of Yahweh (24:21; Japhet 1993: 850). Zechariah dies with the martyr's plea on his lips: "May Yahweh see and avenge." His very name—"Yah remembers"—is assurance that the prayer will be heard. Joash's sin is compounded because it is a sin against Jehoiada's *hesed*.

Zechariah's prayer is heard, and the Lord repays Joash, conspiracy for conspiracy (Pratt 2006: 377). Yahweh sends the Arameans to kill the royal officials and capture Jerusalem (the same Arameans that Asa funded!). Joash's own servants conspire and murder him on his bed (*mittah*), forming an ironic conclusion to the story of a king who was originally rescued from a conspiracy by being placed in a *mittah*. The Chronicler tells us that the conspirators acted to avenge the blood of Zechariah, and they refused to bury Joash's body with the other kings. For all his achievements, Joash's end is pathetic because it is rebellious.

Joash's death marks a reversion in the history of Israel. His life story has the same shape as Asa's—faithful early, unfaithful late. Both Joash and Asa close their ears to a prophet. Asa puts Hanani in prison; Joash goes a step further and kills Zechariah. After Asa, Jehoshaphat covenants with Ahab and sends the Davidic dynasty and the kingdom of Judah into a death spiral. Because of Jehoiada, Joash brings David back to life, but his Asa-like end is ominous. We are back in the age of the judges, where Israel swings wildly back and forth between devotion to Yahweh and idolatrous treason. Will Joash's successors repeat Jehoshaphat's folly, or worse? After Asa, it took four generations for Judah to be imperiled (Jehoshaphat, Jehoram, Ahaziah, Athaliah). What can we expect from Joash's successors (Amaziah, Uzziah, Jotham, Ahaz)? Will another Athaliah come on the scene?

11

ISRAEL BECOMES JUDAH

2 Chronicles 25–28

Jehoiada restores the Davidic dynasty, pulling it back from the precipice. By the end of Joash's reign, the malign influence of the house of Ahab is nearly expunged. But it is only in the reign of Amaziah that it is completely exterminated from Judah. Rehoboam, Abijah, and Asa all battled with the northern kingdom. Jehoshaphat brought in an era of détente, which nearly destroyed David's house. Amaziah returns to war with Israel, but from a weakened, compromised position. Abijah could boast that the Lord was with Judah. That is no longer so obvious, as they have turned from the temple and from Yahweh for several generations. The arc of Judah's history does not bend toward faithfulness, and between Joash and Hezekiah we are treated to a grim history of, at best, partial faithfulness and, at worst, apostasy.

Each of the kings who follows Joash has pluses and minuses. Each shows faithfulness in some respects but also follows the example of Joash (and Asa and Jehoshaphat) in committing sins or making political blunders (Boda 2010: 375; McConville 1984: 229–30). But this history is not a holding pattern. As Israel did in the time of the judges, Judah is declining, lurching toward the pure evil of King Ahaz. As it lurches, its relationship with the north changes. Once dominant (under Abijah), then compromised (under Asa and Jehoshaphat), Judah is becoming relatively weaker. By the time of Ahaz, the *northern* kingdom has become a model of Hebrew charity. Under the influence of the house of Ahab, Judah was made over into the image of Israel. Under Joash's successors, Israel becomes the kingdom Judah ought to be.

Amaziah (2 Chronicles 25)

Amaziah takes the throne after his father's assassination. The Chronicler commends him. He does "right in the sight of Yahweh" (25:2), but, as with his father, the commendation is qualified: "yet not with a *shalem* heart." The Lord's eyes move to and fro on the earth, supporting those who are *shalem* in heart ($\rightarrow$ 2 Chr. 16:9), supporting those who show the steadfastness of Solomon. Amaziah does right, but the instability of his heart is a weakness and will cause weakness in his kingdom. Because his heart is not fully *shalem*, he will not be fully supported. Because his heart is not *shalem*, he will not enjoy *shalom*.

He begins well, executing the men who killed his father (25:3). That punishment is somewhat ambiguous. Joash had it coming to him after he conspired to kill the prophet Zechariah; Joash's death was an eye-for-eye punishment from Yahweh. Yet, while Shimeath and Jehozabad carry out Yahweh's justice, they commit a crime, and Amaziah is right to put them to death. He follows Torah to a T, killing only the conspirators themselves, and not their sons, thus fulfilling the rule of justice enunciated in Deut. 24:16. It is a principle of royal justice, but it will haunt his reign. Amaziah himself will not be put to death for his father's sins. But he will have plenty of his own, and he will eventually be on the receiving end of another assassination plot (25:25–27).

After the introductory remarks, the Chronicler recounts the reign of Amaziah in three cycles, each of which has to do with a military expedition:

A Amaziah hires Israelite mercenaries (25:5–6)
   B A man of God warns him to send them home (25:7–9)
      C Amaziah listens to the man of God (25:10)
A¹ Amaziah leads an army to fight and defeat Edom (25:11–13)
      C¹ Amaziah worships the gods of Edom (25:14)
   B¹ A prophet rebukes Amaziah and the king threatens him (25:15–16)
A² Amaziah challenges Joash of Israel to fight (25:17)
   B² Joash of Israel warns him off (25:18–19)
      C² Amaziah does not listen and is captured (25:20–24)

The pattern of his reign resembles that of Asa and Jehoshaphat, each of whom engaged in battles of faith and of unbelief, interacted with the northern kingdom, and was confronted by two prophets.

Amaziah's military exploits get off on the wrong foot when he takes a census of soldiers from Judah and Benjamin (25:5). David was punished for seizing the

Lord's host. Even though Amaziah assembles 300,000 troops who have skill with shield and spear, they are not likely to win. And Amaziah himself is not satisfied with the numbers. He spends one hundred talents of silver to hire an additional 100,000 Israelite troops. It is an ironic foreshadowing of his eventual war with Joash of Israel, who will plunder gold and silver from the temple (25:24). It also comes close to repeating the error of Jehoshaphat, who also fought with a mixed army of soldiers from Israel and Judah.

With an army of nearly half a million, Amaziah seems to be ready for anything, but a man of God warns him not to go out with his army. Success in war depends on the Lord's presence with Judah, and the Lord is not with the men of Israel (25:7). Amaziah should have learned the lesson of Jehoshaphat: cobelligerency with idolaters is not the path of success. The man of God warns that God will bring down even the strongest army. Second Chronicles 25:8 is structured to highlight the contrast between Yahweh's strength and the strength of Amaziah's army:

A If you go, be strong for battle.
  B But brings down
    C Elohim
      D before enemy.
A' For there is strength
    C' in Elohim
  B' to help or bring down.

Amaziah's concerns are petty and misplaced. He worries about losing his sizable investment and lets the mercenaries go only after the man of God assures him that the Lord will provide resources. Amaziah listens and dismisses the troops, who return home with noses burning against Judah. They will have a chance to unleash their wrath.

With his diminished troops, Amaziah goes to the Valley of Salt to fight against the Edomites. The Edomites have been restless for several generations. Originally subdued by David, they gained their independence when Judah began to turn from Yahweh (→ 2 Chr. 21:8–15). Amaziah wins the war. His troops kill ten thousand and then sacrifice another ten thousand by throwing them from cliffs to the rocks below. In one of the strangest twists in Chronicles, Amaziah adopts the gods of the Edomites, whom he has just defeated, setting them in a shrine, bowing before them, burning to them (25:14). A prophet asks him the obvious question: Why would you worship gods who could not deliver their own people, gods who are clearly inferior to Yahweh? Instead of recognizing the contradiction, Amaziah threatens to strike the prophet, joining Asa, Ahab, and Joash in the line of kings who persecute prophets. Amaziah is now doomed—not because he lacks troops but because he has not clung to Yahweh (25:16).

When Amaziah sends away the Israelite troops, they take out their frustrations on cities of Judah, raiding and plundering them while Amaziah is busy fighting Edomites (25:13). Flush with success over Edom, Amaziah challenges Joash the grandson of Jehu to fight (25:17) in an effort to avenge the losses caused by the dismissed Israelite mercenaries (Boda 2010: 363). "Let us face each other" (25:17) could be a challenge to battle or an invitation to conference. In either case, it includes an implicit claim to equality. Equals stand face-to-face, while a subordinate always keeps his face low before a superior. In his parable (25:18–19), Joash denies the symmetry by comparing himself and his kingdom to the mighty, immovable cedar and Amaziah to a useless, dangerous, cursed (cf. Gen. 3:17) thornbush. Amaziah can no more "face" Joash than a thornbush can look a cedar in the eye. Joash is likely alluding to Judg. 9, implying that Amaziah is an Abimelech, violent and doomed, a bramble king.

The reference to marriage in Joash's parable is surprising. Perhaps the king's "daughter" is his capital city or his land. If so, Amaziah challenges Joash to a combat that will determine the "husband" who will "marry" the land. In challenging Joash, Amaziah makes a bid to reunite the kingdom by force. Joash's parable introduces a third party, a beast of the field from Lebanon. In Hebrew animal symbolism, domesticated animals (oxen, sheep, and goats) are analogous to Israel, the people "domesticated" at Yahweh's house and available for sacrifice. Beasts of the field, whether predators or not, represent Gentiles who are not near the house of God. Joash's parable warns that Gentiles will soon come to trample the thornbush of Judah.

Amaziah pays no heed and proudly continues his preparations for battle. At Beth-shemesh ("House of the Sun"), they face off and Israel defeats Judah. It is Israel's first victory over Judah, and it marks a decisive shift in the fortunes of the two kingdoms. Amaziah suffers a complete defeat. Joash captures him, breaks down a portion of the wall of Jerusalem, and plunders gold and silver from the temple and the palace (25:23–24). The broken wall is toward the north, which leaves Jerusalem open to further attack from Israel (Johnstone 1998b: 161). Joash of Israel inflicts a small exile on the king of Judah, a foretaste of what later kings will suffer.

Amaziah's life has the same moral as that of his father Joash. So long as Joash king of Judah listened to Jehoiada, he was good and things went well; when he rejected Zechariah's prophecy, he was killed. Amaziah initially listens to a prophet's warning but then refuses to hear the Lord's word through Joash of Israel. He refuses to follow the Lord, and so he dies, like his father, at the hands of conspirators.

Uzziah (2 Chronicles 26)

Through most of Judah's history, Egypt is barely on the radar. In the latter part of 2 Chronicles, Egypt suddenly becomes prominent. Josiah dies in a battle with Pharaoh Neco (2 Chr. 35); the king of Egypt deposes Jehoahaz, makes Eliakim his brother king, and takes Jehoahaz to Egypt. Then Nebuchadnezzar of Babylon invades, breaks the walls of Jerusalem and burns the temple, and takes away the people of Judah into exile (2 Chr. 36).

When all is said and done, some are back under the hand of Egypt. Judah loses the land, the temple, and all the spoils of Egypt that are plundered by Babylon. The exodus and the conquest have been reversed. All that Israel received and achieved unravels. Judah's history ends where it began, Israel among Gentiles, Josiah at Megiddo dying like Saul, a victim of Egypt as Saul was a victim of the second-tier Egypt of Philistia. Israel is ready for a second exodus, ready for a new Moses and a new David who comes in the surprising shape of Cyrus of Persia.

When God judges people and nations, he throws the clock of the world into reverse and makes time run backward. Achievements unravel. What's done *can* be undone. Under God's judgment, the end is not better than the beginning; the end and the beginning correspond. Sometimes the end is worse than the beginning. On a smaller scale, this is the shape of Uzziah's reign, which includes both exodus *and* reverse exodus, both conquest *and* expulsion. He is, in effect, David and Saul in one person.

Uzziah's reign is a bright spot in a dismal period of Judah's history. His father, Amaziah, is defeated by Joash of Israel and suffers a mini-exile. Uzziah, by contrast, is a victorious warrior. After David subdued the Philistines, Solomon ruled them, and as late as the reign of Jehoshaphat the Philistines brought tribute to Judah (2 Chr. 17:11). Under Jehoram, they raided Judah (21:16–17). Uzziah has to be a new David, pushing the Philistines from Judah and conquering Philistine territory. During his father's reign, Joash of Israel "burst through" the walls of Jerusalem (25:23); under Uzziah, Judah "bursts through" the walls of the Philistine cities of Gath, Jabneh, and Ashdod. His control of Philistine territory is so complete that he builds cities of his own there (26:6–7). He does not even have to fight the Ammonites. They see what he does to the Philistines and pay tribute (26:8).

To secure his victory, Uzziah produces innovative military equipment and technology. No army in Israel's history is as well equipped as Uzziah's. Each soldier has a sevenfold panoply of arms, offensive and defensive—shields, spears, helmets, body armor, bows, slings, and stones (26:14). The battlements of Jerusalem are equipped with cunning "engines of war" (the Hebrew repeats the same term three times—"designed-things designed by designers") that shoot arrows and launch huge stones from the walls (26:15). Uzziah's reputation as a military leader is so great that his name (*shem*) spread as far as the "border of Egypt" (26:8). No king since Solomon has had power that extends so far.

One of the key words in the account of David's early reign is "help," *'ezer*. Yahweh helps David by sending him helpers. It is the word used in Gen. 2 to describe Eve: it is not good for David to be alone, and so Yahweh constructs an army to be a helper suitable to him, a bridal army. That key word appears again in the reign of Uzziah: "God helped him against the Philistines" (26:7). Yahweh gives miraculous victories, victories like those of the exodus and conquest: "He was marvelously helped until he was strong" (26:15).

When Uzziah is not designing military equipment to defend Jerusalem, he embarks on ambitious agricultural projects. The Chronicler has structured the account to nestle the agricultural projects (26:9–10) between accounts of war (26:6–8, 11–15). Uzziah makes war to ensure a fertile peace. He fights in order to plant, build, and grow. There is a cosmological dimension to his building. He builds towers in Jerusalem and in the wilderness, apparently to guard the frontiers of Judah. He builds *up*. He also digs cisterns, building *down* to get water. Uzziah's kingdom reaches to heaven, includes the land, and reaches down to the waters below. He needs the water because he is a keeper of livestock, like one of the patriarchs. He is a shepherd-king, a new Adam, who rules over animals as well as the land. He pays for men to work the fields and the vineyards, growing grain and grapes and olive trees—sacramental plants that, along with the livestock, supply the worship of the temple. He pursues these projects because he is a "lover of the *'adamah*," a unique phrase in the Bible (26:10).

The only other king who devotes such attention to the land is David, who organizes a department of agriculture to take care of the royal lands, the royal animals, and the royal fields and vineyards, and to maintain the storehouses of grain and wine (→ 1 Chr. 27:25–34). In war Uzziah is a David; in peace he is a David.

Uzziah becomes "strong" and prospers, but just at that climax (26:15) things fall apart. The Chronicler repeats the verb "become strong" at the end of 26:15 and the beginning of 26:16: "He was strong. When he became strong, his heart

was lifted up" (AT). His strength lifts his heart high. That might be a good thing
(→ 2 Chr. 17:6), but in this case it is not. Uzziah's strength leads him to act
"corruptly," in a way that brings destruction. The Chronicler uses a pun to reinforce the catastrophe: At his height, when Ammonites brought tribute, Uzziah
was "exalted"; the Hebrew is *ma'alah*. Now he falls because he commits a *ma'al*
(→ 1 Chr. 10:13–14).

What is his fault? He tries to burn incense to Yahweh, a prerogative reserved for
priests. Perhaps he does it out of a distorted sense of piety: God has helped him,
so he wants to serve God. Perhaps he has become so confident that he thinks he
can do anything; the kingdom is all his, including the palace of Yahweh himself.
Exalted as Uzziah is as the Davidic "son of Yahweh," he is a subject of the High
King. The temple is a "sanctuary," consecrated space, God's space, open only to
those who are consecrated, the household servants descended from Aaron. Led
by Azariah (whose name is an alternative name for Uzziah; Japhet 1993: 899),
eighty priests surround Uzziah, "men of valor," probably armed and ready to
cut down the king if he does not turn. They do not have to take action. Uzziah
responds with rage, but just as he begins to offer incense, the Lord "touches"
him with the stroke of leprosy. On his forehead, in the very place where the high
priest's golden crown is placed, leprosy breaks out. The priests hustle him out.
Terrified, he runs from the temple.

Uzziah experiences his own reverse exodus and reverse conquest. Leprosy is
like an Egyptian plague, and Uzziah's life is marked by this plague for the rest
of his life. He is cast out—not from the land but from the temple. Stricken with
leprosy, he cannot even assemble in the temple courts for worship or return to
his own palace. With Uzziah living in a separate house, his son Jotham takes
over royal responsibilities. Even in death Uzziah is excluded: he is buried with
his fathers, not in the city of David, but in the "field of the tomb," since he is a
leper. Uzziah's sin throws his life into reverse. He begins like a David, fighting
and building and organizing and growing and harvesting. Because he acts with
an "exalted heart," he dies like Saul, a king who committed a sacrilege and was
excluded from royal privileges. Uzziah is an Adam, seizing forbidden privilege.
His life limps to the end in a series of Adamic exclusions.

Uzziah may have planned and plotted his assault on the temple for a long time.
From the text, it appears that he ruins his life by one transgression, one *ma'al*. His
clock runs backward because of this single moment in his life. Pride and humility provide the hinges of much of the history of Chronicles. Second Chronicles
7:14—one of the few memory verses people take from this book—is a key text:

"[If] My people who are called by My name humble themselves and pray . . . , then I . . . will heal their land." Rehoboam humbles himself, and the Lord preserves Jerusalem. Even wicked Manasseh humbles himself, and the Lord gives him a reprieve. Uzziah is a counterexample. His strength makes him proud, and his pride comes before his fall. The Chronicler wants us to draw the lesson. Strength comes with its own temptations and dangers. Be strong. Prosper. But stay humble. Be strong, but do not let your heart be exalted. And more frighteningly, *one moment* of pride can ruin your life.

This is a particular challenge in our time, when pride and arrogance are seen as marks of manhood and success. Many assume that success depends on seizing whatever is in front of us, breaking boundaries, forcing ourselves forward. We think that pride is progressive. But the Chronicler shows us otherwise. Pride may get us short-term gains, but in the long run it is not progressive. Pride is *regressive*. Pride turns the clock back to where we started.

We *will* be humbled, one way or another. Some of Judah's kings humble themselves and find mercy. Others are proud, but even proud kings are humbled. Everyone will bow the knee to the Lord Jesus. Better to do it voluntarily.

The Chronicler's cautionary tale about Uzziah's pride is not just a moral lesson. It is a pointer to the gospel. The gospel is about the humility of God the Son, who lowered himself so that we might be exalted with him. The gospel calls us to have that mind in us which is in Christ Jesus, who took the form of a servant and obeyed his Father even to death. The Eucharist incorporates us into the humility of God as we eat and drink. By the Spirit, the Supper keeps us on the path toward a future kingdom of glory. That path is the humble way of Jesus, the way that *is* Jesus, the humble Way who walks the way of humility.

Jotham (2 Chronicles 27)

The Chronicler's brief, undetailed account of the reign of Jotham begins and ends formulaically. "Jotham was twenty-five years old when he became king, and he reigned sixteen years in Jerusalem," we learn in 2 Chr. 27:1. Seven verses later, in case we have forgotten, the same is repeated: "He was twenty-five years old when he became king, and he reigned sixteen years in Jerusalem" (27:8). If nothing else, this sets up a neatly symmetrical structure for the account of his reign:

A Formulaic introduction (27:1)
   B He did right in eyes of Yahweh, like Uzziah (27:2)

C Building projects (27:3–4)
C′ War and tribute (27:5)
B′ He became mighty because he ordered his ways to Yahweh (27:6)
A′ Formulaic conclusion (27:7–9)

Nearly half of the chapter consists of formulaic summaries in which Jotham's name might have been inserted, as into blank spaces on a tax form.

The opening verses do indicate, however, the state of Judah in Jotham's time. Jotham's mother's name, Jerushah, means "dispossessor" and in the context of 27:1 puns on Jerusalem. That note of danger is perhaps mitigated by her ancestry. She is the daughter of Zadok, "righteousness," a common priestly name. Royal and priestly families appear to be intermarrying. That might be a sign of the piety of kings, or it might be a sign that the priests are losing the independence they showed when Uzziah attempted to enter the temple.

Jotham does right (or "makes" right), doing as his father, Uzziah, had done. Uzziah, rather than David or Solomon, is the standard of right kingship. That comparison is qualified by the note that Jotham "did not enter the temple of Yahweh" (27:2). Johnstone (1998b: 171) takes this as a negative statement: Jotham did not frequent the temple for prayer or worship. But the reference is to Uzziah's unauthorized entry into the temple, and so the qualification shows that Jotham is even *more* right than Uzziah.

Despite Jotham's faithfulness, Judah is still in danger. The "people still followed corrupt practices" (27:2 AT). That is an indictment of Jotham, since he could, like Hezekiah or Josiah, undertake reform to purge the land of idolatry. Yet the impetus for "corrupt practices" comes not from the king (as it will with Jotham's son Ahaz) but from the people. Corruption (*shakhat*) is a danger. It is the verb used to describe the evils of the generation prior to the flood. As long as the people of Judah continue in corruption, storm clouds are on the horizon and a flood of Babylonians will soon be surging into Judah. As long as they are corrupt, Judah is stuck in the repetitive cycles of Judges.

The few specifics of Jotham's reign come under two headings: building and war. The note about building is chiastically arranged (27:4):

A Cities
B he built
C in the hill of Judah;
C′ and in the forest

> B′ he built
> A′ fortresses and towers.

He builds in three zones: the upper gate of the temple; the wall of Ophel in Jerusalem; and cities, forts, and towers throughout the land of Judah. He builds in the garden, in the city, and in the land. Alternatively, we could take this as a fourfold list: building at the temple, in the Ophel, in the hill country of Judah, and in the forest. In that case, the Chronicler's list informs us that Jotham builds to the corners of the land. Like other kings of Judah, he builds "towers" (27:4), perhaps an echo of the tower of Babel and another sign of impending crisis, a hint that Judah will soon be scattered among a people of strange tongues. Overall, though, the impression is positive. Like Solomon and other heroic kings, Jotham is a builder. Building is a sign of productivity, fruitfulness, prosperity, and good management.

The hints of Solomonic success continue into the following verses. Jotham's father, Uzziah, did not have to fight the Ammonites, because he overawed all the surrounding nations with his military buildup. Jotham is less intimidating and so has to go to war with Ammon. We learn no details about the war, except that Jotham prevailed. The Chronicler is more interested in the tribute of silver, wheat, and barley (27:5). Neither wheat nor barley has been mentioned in Chronicles since the reign of Solomon (2 Chr. 2:10, 15). Jotham does not bring in wheat and barley on the scale of Solomon, and he receives a tribute of silver rather than gold. Yet he is Solomonic in receiving a tribute offering of grain from a foreign nation. The Ammonites pay homage to Yahweh by paying homage to his king.

Uzziah's battles with the Philistines remind us of David (26:6–7), as does Uzziah's military prowess. Even Uzziah's sin of entering the temple is reminiscent of David's illegitimate census (1 Chr. 21). The Davidic Uzziah is followed by the Solomonic Jotham, a building king acknowledged by Gentiles. That is a hopeful sign, but the rhythms of Chronicles suggest that the trend will not continue into the next generation. After David and Solomon came Rehoboam and Jeroboam, division in the kingdom, and the spread of idolatry. It is poised to happen again: David, Solomon, Rehoboam/Jeroboam is replicated in Uzziah, Jotham, Ahaz.

Ahaz (2 Chronicles 28)

The Chronicler is a generous judge of Judah's kings. King Joash "did what was right" (2 Chr. 24:2), even though he murders Zechariah the prophet, son of Joash's savior, Jehoiada (24:20–21). Amaziah "did right" (25:2), even though he worships Edomite gods for a time (25:14–15). Uzziah "did right" (26:4), although he spends the latter part of his reign as a leper because of his sacrilegious attempt to offer incense (26:16–21).

Alone among the kings of Judah, Ahaz merits the entirely negative judgment "he did *not* do right in the eyes of Yahweh" (28:1 AT). Unlike other kings, Ahaz does not fall from early faithfulness and success. He rebels from the outset, setting up Baals, offering his sons in the fire in the valley of Hinnom (28:2–4). Like Jehoram (→ 2 Chr. 21:6, 13), Ahaz walks in the ways of the kings of Israel (28:2). He makes molten things (*massekah*), similar to the golden calf at Sinai (Exod. 32:4, 8, 17). Second Chronicles 28:3 contains the first of two references to the Valley of Ben-hinnom, where sons pass through the fire (cf. 33:6). Usually, the Chronicler punningly *contrasts* sacrilege (*ma'al*) with exaltation (*ma'alah*). With Ahaz, the latter modifies the former: Ahaz is *superlatively* unfaithful (*ma'ol ma'al*, 28:19); his sacrilege towers to the skies. Ahaz is another Saul, whose unfaithfulness and refusal to seek Yahweh endanger not only himself but his dynasty (Johnstone 1998b: 180). For the first time, the Chronicler uses the ominous term "abomination" (*to'evah*, 28:3; cf. 33:2; 34:33; 36:8, 14) and charges Ahaz with following Canaanite practices that led to their expulsion (cf. 33:2, 9). The threat of exile intensifies (cf. "drive out," *yarash*, 28:3). Ahaz is true to his name, which is identical to that of Ahaziah (22:2), without the suffix that names the God of Judah (Johnstone 1998b: 175). He is as his name, for he is without Yah.

The chapter's structure details the consequences:

A Ahaz does evil, builds high places, provokes Yahweh (28:1–4)
   B Exile in Damascus (28:5)
      C Exile in Samaria (28:6–15)
      C' Ahaz seeks help from Assyria (28:16–21)
   B' Ahaz worships gods of Damascus (28:22–24)
A' Ahaz builds high places, provokes Yahweh (28:25)

Exile is not on the horizon. It has come over the horizon and invaded Judah. It is an immediate danger, doubly so, as the structure of 28:5 emphasizes:

A Yahweh Elohim gave Ahaz into the hand of the king of Aram
   B and they struck and captured captives (*shavah . . . shivyah*) great
      C and made them enter Damascus,

A' and also into the hand of the king of Israel he gave him

B' and he struck on them a striking (*nakah* ... *makkah*) great.

Yahweh delivers Ahaz into the hands of Aram and Israel, so that he suffers a double capture and a double striking, exile in Damascus and then in Samaria.

The Chronicler devotes a sizable chunk of his account of the reign of Ahaz to the war with the northern kingdom of Israel, ruled by Pekah *ben* Remaliah. As usual, he shows little interest in the political dynamics of the situation. We know from Isa. 6–8 that Pekah formed an alliance with Aram as a buffer against Assyrian expansion, and that together they tried to force Judah to cooperate (McConville 1984: 225). As part of this effort, Pekah restored the Omride policy of reuniting the two kingdoms under northern leadership (Johnstone 1998b: 176). As Johnstone observes, when Judah is faithful, they are the undefeatable host of Yahweh; when they turn from him, they no longer function as Yahweh's army. Ahaz's host is *not* Yahweh's, and Pekah scores a massive victory. Out on the battlefield, Israel slaughters 120,000 warriors of Judah (28:6), and Zichri, one of Pekah's mighty men, penetrates far enough into Jerusalem to kill Ahaz's son and high-ranking members of the court (28:7). Pekah heads home with 200,000 women and children, captured captives (the Hebrew uses the verb and the noun), with great spoil (28:8). It is the beginning of an exile for Judah, not in Egypt or Babylon, but enslaved to their brother Israelites (Japhet 1993: 900).

Somehow in the midst of the corrupted northern kingdom is a "prophet of Yahweh," Oded. He meets the host of Pekah at Samaria and delivers an oracle (28:8–14):

Captives carried away (28:8)

    A Oded: Yahweh angry with Judah, so you slaughtered them (28:9)

      B Now you plan to subdue them as slaves (28:10a)

        C This is *'asham* against Yahweh (28:10b)

          D Hear: return captives (28:11a)

            E Yahweh's nose burns (28:11b)

    A' Heads of Ephraim respond (28:12)

          D' Do not bring captives (28:13a)

        C' Proposing to bring guilt, adding to sin and guilt, guilt is great (28:13b)

            E' Yahweh's nose burns (28:13c)

So they left captives (28:14)

Oded interprets Pekah's victory as a sign of Yahweh's burning anger against Judah but then rebukes Israel's army: "You have slain them in a rage that touches heaven" (28:9 AT). The cruelty of Israel and the suffering of Judah rise like prayer in Solomon's temple, like the smoke of incense or sacrifice, and Yahweh responds. "Hear," says the prophet: "return the captured captives" to turn away the Lord's anger from Israel (28:11). Return to the one God of the Shema and treat Judah as "brothers" rather than slaves. The exile in Samaria has been described with a double use of "capture/captive." Oded's speech mimics the alliterative doubling to insist that the captives must be returned (*shuv*; the whole phrase is *hashivu hashivyah 'asher shevitem*). He warns that the anger of Yahweh has moved from Judah to "you" (Japhet 1993: 902).

That a prophet like Oded lives and prophesies in the northern kingdom is a shock. But the bigger shock is what happens next: four of the leading men ("heads," *ro'sh*; a cherubic reference?) from Ephraim/Israel *listen* to the prophet and stop the returning army before they get to Samaria. They confess that their guilt (*'ashmah*, three times in 28:13) has provoked Yahweh's anger, and they convince the army to release the captives and return the spoil. Prophets who confront Davidic kings end up in prison (→ 2 Chr. 16:7–11) or dead (→ 2 Chr. 24:20–22). Oded confronts Pekah and his noblemen, and they have ears to hear.

It is one of the loveliest passages in Chronicles: the Israelite army lays the spoil before the "assembly" (*qahal*) of Israel and they "strengthen" the captives (28:15). From the spoil, they clothe naked women and children, put sandals on their feet, feed and give them water, anoint them with oil, seat the feeble on donkeys, and send them back to Jericho, the oasis "city of palms" (28:15), the first city Israel conquered in the first conquest. Israel treats the captives of Judah not as slaves but as brothers and sisters, generous even to the "least of these." The echoes of this passage in the judgment scene in Matt. 25 are not accidental.

For a brief moment, Israel is what Israel should be, one nation, a brotherhood of generosity, with ears open to the voice of Yahweh through his prophet. For a brief moment, Israel is what *Judah* is supposed to be. While Judah has been turning into a replica of idolatrous Israel, Israel suddenly acts like the true people of God.

Johnstone (1998b: 184) observes, "The magnanimity on the part of the north and their faithful response to the prophetic word merely serves to highlight still further Ahaz's inadequacy on every front." Ahaz walks in the ways of the kings of Israel more than the kings of Israel do. But there is another dimension: soon Judah will be removed from the land for seventy years instead of for a brief time; Babylon will cart away the spoils and enslave their men, women, and children.

But the God who sent Oded to deliver Judah from Pekah of Israel will also stir the heart of Cyrus to let God's people go. And, as in the days of Ahaz, they will come out with much spoil.

For the time being, things will not go so well for Ahaz's Judah. Second Chronicles 28:16–21 lays out the continuing threats:

A   Ahaz seeks help from Assyria (28:16)
   B   Edomites and Philistines invade (28:17–18)
      C   Yahweh humbles Judah because of Ahaz (28:19)
   B'   Tiglath-pilneser afflicts Ahaz (28:20)
A'   Ahaz pays Assyria, but they do not help (28:21)

Ahaz is threatened from all sides. Aram attacks from the east (28:5), Israel from the north (28:6), Edom from the south (28:17), and Philistia from the west (28:18). The Philistines do not send raiding parties but take cities (four of them, signifying the four corners of the land) and settle there. The un-conquest of Judah continues. When Ahaz turns to Assyria for help, things get worse, as the Assyrians besiege Jerusalem and extract a bribe (28:20–21). In a superb piece of understatement, the Chronicler sums up: the Assyrians "did not help him" (28:21).

Ahaz does not turn to Yahweh for help. He abandons ('azav) Yahweh, and so the Lord forsakes Judah (28:6). Even at this late date he could humble himself and seek Yahweh, but he refuses voluntary humility and so suffers the involuntary variety (28:19). Floundering, Ahaz turns to the gods of the Arameans, who have proven themselves powerful by subduing Judah and (apparently) Yahweh (28:23). He closes the temple, and, in place of the one altar in the temple, he builds altars at the corners of Jerusalem (28:24), turning the chosen city of Yahweh into a single altar-platform for the gods of Damascus. Yahweh has an open-door policy, welcoming his people into his house, ready to hear their prayers and receive their sacrifices of smoke and song. Under Ahaz, the temple shuts down and falls silent, and the lamps go dark. It is a sign of things to come.

12

REBUILDING

2 Chronicles 29–32

Yahweh's House Rebuilt (2 Chronicles 29)

Ahaz of Judah did not dismantle the temple, but he might as well have. He cut up the utensils of temple worship, perhaps including the musical instruments used by the Levites (2 Chr. 28:24). He closed the temple doors (28:24), which brought an end to the various rites of the temple—lamps went out (cf. Lev. 6:12–13), incense was not offered, showbread was not replaced, offerings did not ascend in smoke from the altar (2 Chr. 29:7).

When Ahaz's son Hezekiah comes to the throne, the temple system needs a reboot. Hezekiah has to be a David and a Solomon, reorganizing Levites and priests, gathering materials for repair, and dedicating the house all over again. Fortunately, he *is* David and Solomon (McConville 1984: 235; Williamson [1982: 350] notes that Hezekiah gets more space than any king besides David and Solomon). Ahaz was compared to David, but negatively: he did *not* do right as David did (28:1). Hezekiah reverses this. Like Josiah, he is positively compared to David in the introductory formula: "He did right in the sight of Yahweh, according to all that his father David had done" (29:2; →2 Chr. 34:2). His name—the first, emphatic word in the Chronicler's account of his reign (see Johnstone 1998b: 189)—expresses his aims: "May Yahweh establish" (on the variations of his name, cf. Japhet 1993: 915). His family is auspicious on his mother's side, for she is Abijah ("Yah is my father"), daughter of Zechariah

("Yah remembers"). Hezekiah will live up to her name, the name of Rehoboam's son, who so fully laid out the Davidic theology that guides Hezekiah's reign (→ 2 Chr. 13). By acting the role of royal son, he will prove that Yahweh is his father.

Hezekiah's efforts do not end with the restoration of temple worship. The temple is the hub of the world, and a full reformation has to spread from center to periphery. It does. Hezekiah's reform moves out from the temple to the city to the nations (Johnstone 1998b: 188). He reopens and purifies the house of Yahweh (2 Chr. 29), prepares the city for the celebration of Passover (2 Chr. 30), collects and organizes holy gifts from the entire land (2 Chr. 31), and gains a reputation among the nations because of his deliverance from Sennacherib (2 Chr. 32).

Appropriately, his work begins with the priests and the temple, and it begins immediately. His first (*ri'shon*, twice in 29:3) year is the beginning of a new day for Judah. He opens the temple doors, again giving Judah access to the King of heaven, whose eyes and ears are directed toward the house (2 Chr. 6). An open temple means an open heaven, and when heaven is open, Yahweh's gifts rain down. Physically opening the house is not enough. The way into Yahweh's presence has been defiled, and so Hezekiah has to purify the open house. He assembles priests and Levites into the eastern square of the temple to deliver the longest set piece since the days of David and Solomon. He speaks prophetically, with an opening "Hear me" (*shema*), and addresses the leaders as "my sons" (29:11). The speech is chiastically arranged:

A   Consecrate yourselves and the house (29:5)
   B   Our fathers were unfaithful (*ma'al*) and forsook (*'azav*) Yahweh
      (29:6–7)
      C   Therefore Yahweh's wrath is against Judah and Jerusalem (29:8)
   B' Our fathers have fallen by the sword (29:9)
A' Covenant with Yahweh to restore temple service (29:10–11)

Hezekiah uses the Chronicler's own favorite terms, accusing his forebears of sacrilege (*ma'al*) and of forsaking the Lord. He vividly describes it as bodily defiance of Yahweh: the people turn their faces and "give their backs" to their Lord (29:6 AT). That reference to "back" (*'oreph*) recalls the stiff-backed generation of the exodus who erected and worshiped the golden calf at Sinai (Exod. 32:9; 33:3, 5, 9). Because of this defiance, Judah has become an object of fourfold evil:

wrath, terror, horror, and hissing (29:8). The wrath is Yahweh's (cf. 34:18), but the terror is that of the nations who see Judah and Jerusalem in ruins (Deut. 28:25; Isa. 28:19; Jer. 15:4). Hezekiah's use of "hissing" (*shereqah*) becomes a stock description of the nations' surprise and derision toward the ruins of Yahweh's people and city (Jer. 19:8; 25:9, 18; 51:37).

Hezekiah sees a direct link between neglect of temple service and Judah's political turmoil. Alluding to Amaziah's defeat at the hands of Joash of Israel and to the various incursions on the land during the reign of Ahaz, Hezekiah reminds the assembly of the curses that have come on them. The sword devours their men, and their women are captives (29:9). Worse is coming, a more complete destruction and captivity, unless Judah turns back to the Lord and begins to worship him as he prescribes. A fourfold service (stand, serve, be servants, burn) will answer to the fourfold neglect (shut doors, lamps put out, no incense, no ascension offerings) and will turn the Lord's anger from Jerusalem.

In a word, the solution to wrath, terror, horror, and hissing is to cut covenant (29:10), but first the house must be made fit for sacrifice. A double action is required. The priests and Levites need to consecrate (*qadash*) themselves and the house and then remove impurities that defile the temple (29:5). The Hebrew *niddah* (impurity) is typically used in the Torah for menstrual impurity (Lev. 12:2, 5; 15:19, 20, 24, 25, 26, 33; 18:19) or corpse defilement (Num. 19:9, 13, 20, 21). Literally, Ahaz's *ma'al*, his unfaithfulness, consisted of idolatry (2 Chr. 28:25) and neglect of the temple. If we take *niddah* in its original sense, it implies that Hezekiah sees Ahaz's sin as one of spiritual whoredom or as contact with dead idols. Perhaps the usage is also a hint of what is implied elsewhere: the temple is a feminine structure, an "Eve" for Yahweh, so defilements of temple are described in terms of female impurity. Once the impurities are expelled and the house consecrated, the Levites can get back to the work they are chosen to perform, standing to serve as ministers and to burn incense before Yahweh (29:10–11; A').

In response to Hezekiah's speech, a sevenfold grouping of Levites rises to carry out the king's plan. Some are identified by the traditional Levitical subclans (Kohath, Merari, Gershom), while others belong to the clans of musicians that have been so prominent in Chronicles:

1. Kohathites: Mahath and Joel
2. Merarites: Kish and Azariah
3. Gershomites: Joah and Eden

4. Elizaphan: Shimri and Jeiel[1]
5. Asaph: Zechariah and Mattaniah
6. Heman: Jehiel and Shimei
7. Jeduthun: Shemaiah and Uzziel

These priests and Levites assemble, consecrate themselves, and enter the temple to remove impurities (29:15).

Hezekiah preserves the division of labor between priests and Levites, as the structure of 29:16 indicates:

A Priests enter inner room of house to cleanse.
    B They remove all the impurity
        C which they found in the palace of Yahweh
        C′ to the court of the house of Yahweh.
    B′ Levites receive the impure things and remove them
A′ to the Kidron valley.

The structure neatly captures the task. Priests move from the border of the text toward its center, mimicking their movement from the temple court into the inner sanctuary. They bring the unclean things from the inner sanctuary to the court, where Levites are waiting to remove them from the city eastward to the Kidron valley where the wadi can wash away the impurity (29:16; →2 Chr. 15:16, where Asa takes the pulverized Asherah to the Kidron to wash it away).

The purgation begins on the first day of the first month, on new year's day, a new-creation motif. The process takes sixteen days, moving from the inner sanctuary to the porch. The eighth day is the first day of a new week, the day after the Sabbath, the day of entry into new creation. Fittingly, after a double eight-day cleansing, the Levites assure Hezekiah that they have cleansed the altar of ascensions and the table of showbread and all their vessels and tools (29:18). Vessels were dedicated to the service of Ahaz's idols, and they are either destroyed or reconsecrated to Yahweh's service (29:19).

Throughout his account, the Chronicler alludes to the latter chapters of 1 Chronicles, where David prepares for the temple construction, and to the early chapters of 2 Chronicles, where Solomon builds and dedicates the temple.

1. Elizaphan is an outlier. A son of Uzziel, Aaron's uncle, he is Aaron's cousin and is assigned the task of removing the bodies of Nadab and Abihu after they offer strange fire in the tabernacle (Lev. 10). In 1 Chr. 15:8 the subtribe of Elizaphan helps to bring the ark into Jerusalem.

Hezekiah imitates David, organizing the Levites to renew the Levitical ministry and the temple service. Hezekiah gathers Levites by clan (29:12–14) as David had. Seven groups of Levites pitched in to bring the ark into Jerusalem, and Hezekiah speaks to seven clans of Levites. Worshipers "fill their hand" with offerings (*mille'tem yedkem*; 29:31 AT), as they "filled their hand" with silver and gold as votive offerings (→ 1 Chr. 29:5). The worship of the Levites follows the instructions of David—their instruments (2 Chr. 29:25, 27) come from David, as do the very words of the psalms they sing (29:30).

The description of Hezekiah's rededication echoes the original Solomonic ceremony. "Sacrifice" (*zevakh*) is used twice in 1 Chr. 29:21 and six times in the description of the temple dedication (→2 Chr. 7:1, 4, 5, 12; 29:31 [2×]). David calls on the *qahal* to prostrate itself (→ 1 Chr. 29:20); Solomon's dedication ceremony likewise includes several prostrations (→2 Chr. 7:3, 19, 22), and so does Hezekiah's (2 Chr. 29:28–30). In fact, we have more detail about the actual operation of the sacrificial system in 2 Chr. 29 than we do anywhere else in 1–2 Chronicles. Twenty-eight animals are offered, seven each of four types of animals (29:21), an offering that covers the seven days of the week and the four corners of the temple, city, and land. Together these animals provide a triple purification: of the kingdom, the sanctuary, and the people (29:21). Hezekiah seeks to purify the house from the accumulated "sins of the fathers" as well as from the infractions of his own time (McConville 1984: 232). There is no mention of blood at the Solomonic dedication, but 2 Chr. 29:22 says three times that "they slaughtered . . . and took the blood . . . and sprinkled it." Only in 2 Chr. 29 does anyone lean a hand on a sacrificial victim (29:23; cf. Lev. 1:4), and only here does anyone offer a purification offering (*khatta't*, 29:21). Purification offerings cleanse sancta, open doors to heaven, and form a pathway to approach the Lord. Again, opening the physical doors needs to be followed with purgation and purification offerings. Judah requires covering (*kippur*, "atonement," related to the verb *kaphar* found in 29:24). Atonement is the responsibility of the priesthood (→ 1 Chr. 6:49), but Hezekiah's purification of the temple is the only actual "kippuring" that we see in Chronicles (though →2 Chr. 30:18). It is, significantly, the only time we see the *people* offering sacrifice in Chronicles (Japhet 1993: 930).[2]

---

2. Johnstone (1998b: 196) spies an anomaly in the offering of purification offerings: "The application of the law of the sin offering to *deliberate* offences covering the life of the people as a whole . . . represents a radical extension by [the Chronicler] of the legislation of the Pentateuch (it is similar to the way in which he applies the law for the individual guilty of *ma'al* in Lev. 5.14–6.7 to the life of Israel as a whole, 1 Chr. 10.13–14). Its application to a situation unimagined by the legislation represents an equally radical extension of the understanding of divine grace." Johnstone misses an important detail. Four

Following the command of David, Hezekiah stations the Levites to offer musical sacrifice along with the smoke of the animal sacrifices (2 Chr. 29:25–30). Their offerings ascend with song; *they* ascend in song. As Israelites traveled to the temple singing along the way, singing their psalms of ascent, so they ascended singing through their ascension offerings. Mingled with the smoke of the offering, they offer their life breath in song, the ascending auroma[3] of musical instruments.

No song is offered with the purification offering. Music begins with the ascension offering (*'olah*) and continues through the meal. Song appears to displace the animal of the ascension offering. For the purification offering, the Chronicler details the number and types of animals; he repeats key sacrificial terms— blood (four times), kill (four times), sprinkle (three times), altar (five times). In 29:25–28, the description of the ascension offering, only "altar" is repeated. From 29:20–24 we get an idea of how the purification offerings are performed, but we have no details about the rite of the ascension offering. We know only that the ascension offering is accompanied by song. When Hezekiah instructs the Levites to get ready for the burnt offerings, he does not give them slaughter knives, bowls, and instruments for dismembering animals. He tells them to take up their cymbals, harps, and lyres and to sing as the smoke ascends (29:26; *keli* is used for utensils of sacrificial worship and musical instruments). In literal fact, animals were offered as ascension offerings, but the Chronicler's emphasis is on music. As with the original dedication of the temple, the rededication takes place in sacrifice *and* song, song that has become sacrifice. Song has become a mode of ascent, as the Levites "lift up their hearts and voices" to Yahweh.

As in other assemblies in Chronicles (→ 1 Chr. 12:40; → 1 Chr. 15:16, 25; → 1 Chr. 29:17; → 2 Chr. 20:27), the atmosphere is joyful (Boda 2010: 271). The Levites sing "praises with joy" (29:30), a phrase that can be translated as "until there was joy" (Kleinig 2009: 37). The Levites sing in order to *become* joyful. Restoration of Davidic/Solomonic order brings Davidic/Solomonic joy. The people celebrate in astonished joy at their own sudden turnaround: "All the people rejoiced over what God had prepared for the people, because the thing

---

types of animals are brought as "sin offerings": bulls, rams, lambs, and male goats. As Lev. 4 prescribes, nonpriestly leaders offer the male goats (2 Chr. 29:23) in a separate rite. Two of the other animals—bulls and lambs—are required for certain kinds of *khatta't* offerings, the bull for the priests and the lamb for the people. But the ram is not allowed for purification offerings. Instead, the ram is the prescribed animal for the *trespass* offering, which is offered for deliberate, high-handed sins (Lev. 5:14–6:7). The ram is precisely the animal needed to cover *ma'al*, for trespasses. Here as everywhere, Hezekiah does everything according to the words of Yahweh (2 Chr. 29:15).

3. This is a neologism, referring to the "sweet-smelling sound" of the sacrifice of praise.

came about suddenly" (29:36). Joy later characterizes Hezekiah's Passover feast (Williamson [1982: 360–65] discusses its historical plausibility). The sons of Israel keep the Feast of Unleavened Bread with joy (30:21), rejoicing through the seven-day feast (30:23). The Chronicler piles it on: "All the assembly of Judah rejoiced. . . . So there was great joy in Jerusalem, because there was nothing like this in Jerusalem since the days of Solomon the son of David" (30:25–26). Hezekiah marks the high point and the final moment in the Chronicler's history of joy. Ominously, this is the last outburst of joy in Chronicles. After 2 Chr. 30 there is no joy, gladness, or rejoicing in Judah.

As they rejoice, the people bow (*kara'*) before the Lord (29:29). Elsewhere, the verb is used only when the people bow at the pavement during the temple dedication (→2 Chr. 7:3). There, it is a symbol of the living sacrifice of Israel, who offer themselves in song and prayer as the smoke of the offerings ascends. So it is here as well: the priests open the door to heaven with purification offerings, then lead a procession of ascent with ascension offerings. At the completion (*kalah*) of the ascent, the people bow. Through animal sacrifices and song, they have ascended into the throne room and do their obeisance before King Yahweh. Second Chronicles 29:20 captures the theology with the arresting claim that the king and princes "ascend the house of Yahweh" (*wayya'al beth-yhwh*; the preposition "to" is absent). Moriah itself is the "ascent of the house," and we are invited to see the king and princes as the "house of Yahweh" ascending. The temple becomes a conduit enabling the people-house to enter the presence of Yahweh.

Once the way is open, Hezekiah encourages the people to "fill the hand" to bring sacrifices (peace offerings) and *todoth*, thank offerings (29:31). In the Torah, "fill the hand" is a technical phrase for the ordination of priests (Exod. 29; Lev. 8; Hahn 2012: 174). The Chronicler uses it only once in this technical sense (→ 2 Chr. 13:9). The two other uses in Chronicles (→ 1 Chr. 29:5; 2 Chr. 29:31) refer to the commissioning of the *qahal*, the assembly, not of the priests. Judah is a priestly people, and Yahweh fills the hand of the whole congregation to provide for the temple and to carry on its worship. The people fill their hands by generous donations to the Lord and his house. They fill hands by emptying them. As elsewhere in Chronicles, the people's generosity is a vivid indicator of spiritual renewal.

There are so many animals to offer that the priests cannot handle the task. Levites, the recurring heroes of Chronicles, pitch in to do the work, so that the rededication can be completed. The Chronicler specifies that the priests are unable to complete the task of "skinning" (*pashat*) the animals (29:34). He typically uses this verb to describe the "stripping" of slain warriors (→ 1 Chr. 10:8–9) or "raids" that strip the land. Here, the verb draws out the connection between liturgical renewal and political stability. When Judah rededicates the temple with "skinned" sacrifices, raiding parties will stop "skinning" the land and people.

Passover in Jerusalem (2 Chronicles 30)

All of this purging and preparation does nothing unless it restores the temple as a house of festivity, the chosen place where Israel eats and drinks and rejoices before the Lord. A rededicated house is no use unless the *city* celebrates the Lord's feasts. So Hezekiah follows up the dedication with a decree to do the Passover. The first twelve verses of chapter 30 describe the preparations:

A Hezekiah sends invitations to assemble for Passover (30:1–4)
   B Runners take the invitation throughout the land (30:5–6a)
      C Command of the king (30:6b–9)
   B' Runners go from city to city, meet mockery (30:10)
A' Some from Israel come, and Judah responds with one heart (30:11–12)

At the center (30:6b–9) is Hezekiah's letter of invitation to the tribes of Ephraim and Manasseh, the leading tribes of the northern kingdom. It takes the form of a royal decree (Japhet [1993: 937–38] compares it to Persian imperial decrees). It is an intricately structured piece of rhetoric. Overall, it follows a simple chiastic pattern:

A Return to Yahweh that he may return to you.
   B Do not be like fathers and brothers, doing *ma'al*.
   B' Do not stiffen neck but give hand to him
A' so his anger will turn.

Within this overall pattern, the initial command is structured by parallels:

A Return
   B to Yahweh Elohim
      C of Abraham, Isaac, Jacob.
A' He will return
   B' to the survivors and remnant
      C' from the palm of Assyria.

Turning to Yahweh, they will find themselves face-to-face with God turning to them. If they turn, they will be snatched from the palm of Assyria and brought into the fellowship and promise of Abraham, Isaac, and Jacob.

Second Chronicles 30:9 is another chiasm:

A   In your returning to Yahweh
    B   your brothers and sons will find compassion before captors
        C   to return to this land.
    B'   For Yahweh is compassionate
A'   and will not remove his face if you return to him.

The compassion of Israel's captors expresses Yahweh's compassion. In assuring Israel that the Lord will bring them back and accept them, Hezekiah speaks over the heads of his audience to the Chronicler's first readers, who have seen the compassion of Yahweh expressed through the clemency of Cyrus the Persian.

As is evident from the structure, the invitation turns on varied uses of the verb "turn/return" (*shuv*), used twice in 30:6b, once at the end of 30:8, and three times in 30:9. The decree begins with an exhortation to "turn to Yahweh" (30:6b AT) and ends with "if you turn to Him" (30:9 AT). In these framing verses, the word means "repent." In 30:7 it describes the Lord turning from his anger. A synonym (*sur*) is also used in 30:9 ("turn His face"). These two are related: if they turn, Yahweh will turn. Second Chronicles 30:9 promises that Yahweh will "turn" the exiles back home if they turn to the turning God.

This is a remarkable letter. While an invitation to Passover, it is framed as a call to repentance (turn to Yahweh) with attached promises (he will turn to you; his burning nose will turn from you; your captors will return you to the land). Hezekiah invites idolaters to repent by joining a feast and the service (*'avodah*) of the temple. If they come to Passover, they are by that fact turning from the unfaithfulness (*ma'al*, 30:7) of their fathers and turning to Yahweh. Since their sin is idolatry, repentance takes the form of offering worship to the living God. Loyalty to Yahweh is expressed by participation in temple worship (Japhet 1993: 945). Hezekiah commands Israel to turn from the way of their fathers and brothers (30:7). "Fathers" are ancestors and founders, Jeroboam, Baasha, Omri, and others; "brothers" are inhabitants of Israel. To do Passover correctly, the inhabitants of Israel have to hate their fathers and brothers.

The letter circulates throughout Israel, from Dan to Beersheba, and includes Ephraim and Manasseh. Hezekiah claims authority over Israel by issuing a "command"

(30:12) to the northern tribes. In his time, the Assyrians have conquered the north and there is no king in Israel. Only the Davidic dynasty remains, and Hezekiah asserts that Davidic kings have always been the sole legitimate rulers of *all* Israel.

Israel has been officially idolatrous for a couple of centuries. Jeroboam set up golden calf shrines at Dan and Bethel, and they have never been removed. Under Ahab, the northern tribes worshiped Baal and Asherah, and Ahab went so far as to build a temple to Baal in the capital city. Jehu destroyed that but did not get rid of the calf shrines. Despite centuries of idolatry, the northern tribes are invited to share in Hezekiah's Passover. It would have been unfaithful for Hezekiah to share the table of demons in the north, but Judah's northern brothers are welcome to "enter" Jerusalem. Yahweh's *miqdash*—the sanctuary—has been consecrated forever, and the tribes of Israel are welcome to join Judah in worshiping there. The renewal of David's kingdom will not be complete unless all Israel assembles in the chosen city at the Lord's chosen house under the hand of Yahweh's chosen king. A *reunited* Israel must celebrate Passover (Pratt [2006: 416] labels this section of his commentary "Reunited Kingdom").

The invitation is not altogether welcome. As in Jesus's parable of the wedding feast, many of the invitees mock the king's command (30:10). But some *do* come. They accept the invitation and humble themselves (Japhet 1993: 947), performing the act that will bring healing to their land (→2 Chr. 7:14). In Judah, the response is overwhelming: Because the hand of God is on them, they obey the king's command with one heart (30:12; Japhet 1993: 947). The wedding feast is full, and they cannot stop celebrating. After a week of Passover, they add a further period of "rejoicing" (Japhet 1993: 955).

Hezekiah's invitation is a model of royal and eucharistic evangelism, repentance, and covenant renewal. His invitation is a royal command and decree. He invites all Israel to join in Jerusalem's festivity and to become ministers of Yahweh's house. To translate, Jesus the king issues a royal invitation, which has the force of a command. It is an invitation to join in the wedding feast of the Lamb and a command/invitation to be deputized in the liturgy, the work of the people of God. It is a call to radical discipleship, for only those who hate their idolatrous inheritance and their idolatrous brothers are worthy to share in the feast. When people hear the command and turn from idols, Jesus promises to turn his face to them, for he is compassionate and gracious. Accepting the invitation to Eucharist *is* a turn from idols!

There are glitches in Hezekiah's Passover. The people are not ready to celebrate on the fourteenth day of the first month, and so they move it to the second month. That does not violate Torah, though, which provides for a second-month Passover for those who are unclean in the first month (Num. 9; Japhet [1993: 939–40] disputes the connection with Numbers). Hezekiah applies this rule because the entire nation is unclean.

The other glitch is more serious and has more interesting consequences (cf. Japhet 1993: 952–53). Many from Ephraim, Manasseh, Issachar, and Zebulun show up in Jerusalem (30:18). They have been worshiping golden calves and Baals for generations, and they have not purified themselves. Yet they eat the Passover anyway, "otherwise than written" (30:18 AT). It is a *maʿal*, a sacrilege, an intrusion on God's holiness, and in Chronicles a *maʿal* is usually followed by an outbreak of wrath. Hezekiah averts that result by asking "pardon" (*kaphar*, root for *kippur*, "atonement" or "covering"). It is a remarkable circumvention of normal procedure: instead of performing a rite of covering/atonement, Hezekiah simply prays (30:18). As Yahweh promised Solomon (→ 2 Chr. 7:13–14), he hears and answers and "heals" (*rapha'*, 30:20) the people.

Hezekiah asks Yahweh to cover "everyone who prepares his heart to seek God, ... though not according to the purification of the sanctuary" (30:19 AT). "Seek" (*darash*) is a key word throughout Chronicles. Good kings seek God; bad kings do not. Seeking God in prayer and temple worship is just what Israel should be doing, but Hezekiah seems to take heart-seeking as an adequate replacement for following purity regulations. It seems a complete "spiritualization" of temple worship; external rites seem to be transposed into interior preparations of the heart.

That is *not* an accurate inference. Hezekiah prays for forgiveness and covering, treating the people's ritual failure as a violation that needs to be *forgiven*. Yahweh "heals" the people, which suggests that they are already suffering in some way. The whole point of the prayer is to enable the Israelites to participate in the Passover and Feast of Unleavened Bread in a state of impurity. Hezekiah does not suggest that they can keep Passover by "feasting in their hearts."

This is not to minimize the significance of the incident. Royal prayer proves as effective as priestly ritual. Prayer covers sin, allowing the unclean to join the celebration. It is not a "spiritualization" of Israel's worship, but it is a step toward worship in the new-covenant mode, where prayer and praise are the fulfilled forms of sacrifice, where confession is sufficient to cleanse from all unrighteousness.

Purging the Land (2 Chronicles 31)

Hezekiah "completes" a Passover (2 Chr. 31:1a), then starts breaking things. In this, his Passover resembles that of Joshua (Josh. 5:10–11), which immediately precedes the conquest of Jericho. Hezekiah, like Joshua, continues until the destruction is "complete" (*kalah*, 2 Chr. 31:1b). He breaks pillars, cuts down Asherim, and pulls down high places and altars. Hezekiah's purge is described in a single complex verse (31:1):

> A After they completed all this [Passover celebration]
> B all Israel went out
>   C to the cities of Judah
>   D and shattered pillars, cut Asherim, pulled down high places and altars
>   C' in Judah, Benjamin, Ephraim, Manasseh
> A' until they completed.
> B' Then all the sons of Israel
>   C" returned each to his own city.

With this spree of destruction, Hezekiah joins Judah's royal all-stars: good kings in Judah are destroyers of idols. Asa, Joash, Hezekiah, and Josiah are each "new Joshuas" and "new Gideons" who purge the land of false worship. Nebuchadnezzar completes the process as the final Joshua, cleansing the land by destroying Jerusalem's temple, which has become no better than a shrine to Baal. Though led by Hezekiah, this purge is different; it is the work of "all Israel," a popular reform (Japhet 1993: 961).

Though Hezekiah destroys, the Chronicler portrays his actions as creative. The verb *kalah*, which frames 2 Chr. 31:1, provides an initial clue. It is the verb used to describe the "completion" of heaven and earth (Gen. 2:1–2) and the completion of the microcosmic tabernacle (Exod. 40:33) and temple (→ 2 Chr. 7:11). The Chronicler uses three verbs of destruction and describes four objects destroyed, portraying the de-creation in a sentence of seven words (31:1). Solomon was given royal wisdom and skill to build the temple; Hezekiah and the other heroes of destruction exercise royal wisdom in destroying idolatry. Hezekiah's creative destruction is unique. Asa demolishes high places, pillars, Asherim, and altars (→ 2 Chr. 14:3), but Hezekiah surpasses Asa. Carried out by "all Israel," Hezekiah's purge extends into the territory of Ephraim and Manasseh. All Israel is deployed to all Israel to carry out Hezekiah's program of re-creative destruction.

After shattering, cutting, and pulling down, Hezekiah "makes-stand" (hiphil of *'amad*) the priests and Levites, reinstalling them as liturgical leaders at the temple (31:2), establishing offices and allotting tasks like another David (Japhet 1993:

965). He supplies ascension and peace offerings for daily and periodic sacrifices (31:3), and calls the people of Jerusalem and Israel to contribute goods to supply the temple services (31:4–5). The collection begins in the third month and stretches to the seventh month (note the link to other sevens in the passage), when the "heaps" of goods are "founded" and "completed" (31:7; *kalah* again). The sevenfold destruction prepares for the complete reestablishment of temple worship, completed in the seventh month. Creative destruction gives way to creative construction.

The contributions that come into the restored temple must be stored and managed, and Hezekiah appoints faithful Levites to oversee the donations (31:12, 18). The latter portion of chapter 31 harks back to 1 Chr. 23–27. It is another tribute to flowcharts and bureaucratic planning, listing the authority and accountability structure for the management of the temple treasuries:

1. Conaniah and Shimei over tithes and consecrated things (31:12)
   Assisted by ten overseers (31:13a)
2. Azariah, officer of the house of God (31:13b)
3. Kore the Levite over freewill offerings, contributions, most holy things (31:14)
   Assisted by six leaders (31:15)

The first group, consisting of twelve men, receives contributions and consecrated things. Kore, the "keeper of the east," is stationed at the main entrance of the temple to receive freewill offerings and to distribute the most holy things to the priests who are qualified to receive them (31:15; cf. Lev. 6–7). Certain portions are for the priests themselves, others for the priestly families, and Hezekiah's system ensures that all priestly families ("whether great or small") and all the members of the families ("all their little children, their wives, their sons and their daughters"; 31:18) receive their allotment. Priests labor in the temple, performing their daily obligations according to the divisions that David established (31:16). They have no livelihood from the land or from trade but are dependent on the gifts of the people. As in David's reign (→ 1 Chr. 27), Hezekiah's entire kingdom is organized to support temple service. Tithes of the land's produce are given to the temple; other gifts and contributions support the priests who carry out the daily round of temple services. The entire nation is liturgically organized, focused toward Yahweh's house. Hezekiah refounds David's "liturgical empire" (the phrase is from the title of Hahn 2012).

A Name among the Gentiles (2 Chronicles 32)

Chapter 31 ends with an unparalleled commendation: Hezekiah is "good, right, and true before Yahweh." He follows the law and commandment, seeking God in everything. His heart is devoted completely, and so he prospers (31:20–21). Then, suddenly, it all seems to crash. Even after "these things and this faithfulness" (32:1 AT), Sennacherib of Assyria invades Judah all the way to the walls of Jerusalem. Like Zerah (→ 2 Chr. 14), Sennacherib attacks a *faithful* king (McConville 1984: 246). Why do bad things happen to good kings?

Like Zerah's invasion, Sennacherib's is a test of Hezekiah's faith. And he passes the test. He does make practical preparations to head off the siege. Consulting with the princes and warriors (as he had in decreeing Passover, 30:2, 23), Hezekiah cuts off the water supply throughout the region (32:4) and rebuilds the broken wall of Jerusalem (32:5). Like David, Hezekiah receives "help" from the men around him. Israel is a well-watered land that supplies living water to the nations, but in this case that water supply is cut off. To invaders, Israel becomes a desert.

Yet Judah's national defense depends on turning to Yahweh. In a brief speech of encouragement, the king repeats the fourfold command of David to Solomon: be strong, be courageous, do not fear, do not be dismayed. David and Solomon spoke about the building of the temple; Hezekiah gives a pep talk before a battle. David's temple exhortations have military overtones, and Hezekiah's military encouragement is a call to liturgical action. Worship and prayer are Judah's chief tactics of warfare. Hezekiah assures the people that Judah has more power than Sennacherib because Yahweh is once again with Judah. Sennacherib comes with a mere "arm of flesh," but Yahweh is "with us . . . to help us and to fight our battles" (32:8). Judah must rely (*samak*) on Yahweh. The only other use of this verb in Chronicles is 2 Chr. 29:23, where it describes the gesture of leaning a hand on the head of a sacrificial animal. The link is pregnant: At a superficial level, it brings out once again the connection between worship and warfare that is so much a part of the Chronicler's theology. More deeply, it perhaps points to reliance on Yahweh *as* sacrificial victim. Leaning on, slaughtering, and burning an animal "covers" Israel. That rite symbolically enacts the faith of Israel, to lean on the Rock who gives himself for his people.

In this speech, Hezekiah again plays a prophetic role, and the people trust him and so trust the word of Yahweh that comes through him. Remarkably, Sennacherib and Hezekiah see the battle lines the same way. The Assyrian servants who call on Hezekiah to surrender highlight the issue of trust (32:10) and treat the battle as a battle of gods. Second Chronicles 32:13–14 lays out Sennacherib's case:

A   Do you not know what I did
  B   I and my fathers
    C   to all the peoples of the lands
      D   Elohim of the nations?
        E   Who was able to deliver from my hand?
      D'   Who of all the Elohim of the nations
  B'   which my fathers destroyed
        E^1 was able to deliver from my hand
        E^2 that your Elohim is able to deliver from my hand?

Sennacherib places his own power on par with the power of the gods of the nations he has defeated, and he treats the Elohim of Israel as another of the Elohim of the nations. It is a fateful comparison—for Sennacherib, not for Hezekiah. The Chronicler makes the point explicit: Yahweh opposes the Assyrians because "they spoke of the God of Jerusalem as of the gods of the peoples of the earth, the work of men's hands" (32:19). It is not surprising that Sennacherib, with his arm of flesh, can seize the gods of other nations, which are the work of flesh. Seizing the land and city of Yahweh is another thing entirely.

Hezekiah and the prophet Isaiah take care of the threat in short order. Following Solomon's example, they pray (*palal*) and cry out to heaven (32:20). In response the Lord sends an angel to destroy the Assyrians. After Sennacherib's bluster, the Chronicler's account of his defeat is comically compressed. In a single verse (32:21), the angel of death devastates his army and Sennacherib returns shamefaced to Assyria, where his own children kill him in the temple of his god. With a flick of his finger, the Lord dispatches the fiercest army of the ancient world.[4] Sennacherib's rhetoric made him seem formidable, but it was a cover for utter weakness. Hezekiah's prayer exposes the monster for the weakling that he is. By appealing to the God of heaven, Hezekiah shames the principalities and powers and leads those defeated enemies in triumph. Judah's fear is turned to joy, its shame turned to glory; Sennacherib's boasting is turned to *bosheth* (shame).

---

4. "Hand" (*yad*) is used twelve times in chapter 32, mostly of the supposedly powerful hand of Sennacherib (32:11, 13, 14 [2×], 15 [3×], 17 [2×]). Then the Chronicler says that the gods of the nations are gods who originate from human "hands" (32:19), and it is all over. Yahweh easily saves Judah from the "hand" of Sennacherib (32:22 [2×]).

Other kings pray, but Hezekiah is the first king since Solomon who *palal*s (cf. 30:18). "Cry out" is *za'aq*, a pun on the name of Hezekiah. His name connotes strength and stability, but in a moment of weakness we learn the source of his strength. "Crying out" has been an effective strategy throughout Israel's history (→ 1 Chr. 5:20; → 2 Chr. 18:31; → 2 Chr. 20:9). This victory vindicates Hezekiah's policy regarding the temple. The point of the temple dedication is to reopen the communications hub for interchanges between heaven and earth. With Sennacherib's invasion, the effectiveness of Hezekiah's policy is put to the test, and it passes: he and the prophet pray and cry to heaven, and their prayers are heard. Yahweh's eyes and ears are once again attentive to the place he has chosen.

No wonder other nations bring tribute to Hezekiah (32:23). Some marvelous power must be with him if he can survive an Assyrian invasion. The God of Judah must be some God if he delivers from the hand of Sennacherib. As so often in Chronicles, a king's success and elevation is rapidly followed by fall. Hezekiah falls sick (32:24), and he does what kings are supposed to do when they need healing: he prays and Yahweh answers. But his exaltation has made his heart proud, and he does not give Yahweh the recompense he deserves (32:25–26):

A Hezekiah did not return recompense
 B because his heart was lifted.
  C Wrath on him,
   D and on Judah and Jerusalem.
 B' He humbled the pride of his head
   D' with Jerusalem
  C' so wrath did not come.

Wrath breaks out against Judah and Jerusalem, and Hezekiah again responds appropriately, humbling himself before Yahweh's anger (32:26). He rescues himself, but the Chronicler leaves open the possibility that wrath will return: "wrath . . . did not come on them in the days of Hezekiah" (32:26). It is a slight fault, but it is a fault, a reminder that even the greatest of kings sin and rouse the Lord's anger.

Hezekiah has been a worthy heir of David and Solomon throughout his reign, and the Chronicler closes his account by highlighting the riches and glory of his reign. He has great wealth, honor, and riches (32:27), like David (→ 1 Chr. 29:28) and Solomon (→ 2 Chr. 9:22; Japhet 1993: 494–95). After Solomon, only Jehoshaphat (2 Chr. 17:5; 18:1) and Hezekiah enjoy riches. The land prospers, producing the sacramental foods of grain, wine, and oil, as well as sacrificial animals from herd and flock. Hezekiah's reign resembles David's and Solomon's for its prosperity and for the devotion of the whole land to the service of Yahweh in his house. Hezekiah is like a new Adam, subduing and taking dominion over the land.

If we have taken in the rhythms of Chronicles, though, Hezekiah's greatness makes us uneasy. Rehoboam followed David and Solomon; Asa and Jehoshaphat were followed by generations of idolaters; after Joash, Judah descended to the evils of Ahaz's reign. It has become more difficult to sustain reform over generations. Idolatry has become a countertradition within Judah, with political and religious adherents who are always on the ready to set up another image or Asherah pole. The cycle of Judges still haunts the Chronicler's narrative. Samson, one of the most effective and spiritual of the judges, was nearly the last of the judges (Judg. 13–16). Samuel, a contemporary of Samson, led Israel faithfully, but his sons were wicked (cf. 1 Sam. 8). For all his achievements, will Hezekiah be another Samuel?

13

TURNINGS

2 Chronicles 33

Judah's history is punctuated by apostate kings. After David and Solomon, "all Israel" divides into two political entities, one devoted to the service of Yahweh and the other devoted to calves, satyrs, and Baals. Because of Jehoshaphat's alliance with Ahab, idolatry festers in Judah's body politic. Jehoshaphat's son Jehoram and grandson Ahaziah are more children of Ahab than of David. It nearly kills the Davidic line, as Athaliah establishes her throne on the blood of Davidic princes. The Davidic line survives by a hair and revives under Joash. By this time, idolatry has its own tradition and culture in Judah. Within a few generations, Ahaz reintroduces foreign gods, this time without any help from the house of Ahab. Under the influence of Ahab's house, Judah became an Israel; now Judah is idolatrous in its own right, in some respects worse than the northern king. Despite Hezekiah's reforms, idolatry makes a comeback under Manasseh. The Chronicler deletes the comparison with the house of Ahab from his account of Manasseh's reign. It is too late to pass off Judah's idolatry as a foreign element. It has become domesticated in Judah. Back and forth, forth and back, circling and circling in a widening gyre: the history of kings repeats the cyclical history of Judges.

The half-life of faithfulness is decreasing. It takes several generations before Jehoshaphat's foolish alliance nearly topples the kingdom. Between Joash and Ahaz there are only two kings. Hezekiah cannot sustain a reform beyond a single generation. His son and grandson, Manasseh and Amon, promote Baal worship.

Josiah does no better (→ 2 Chr. 35). Despite Hezekiah's dramatic reforms, his sons do evil in the eyes of the Lord, and Judah speeds toward catastrophe.

Forgetful (2 Chronicles 33:1–20)

The Chronicler's account of Manasseh's reign (33:1–20) is organized in a modified chiasm (cf. Pratt 2006: 463; Japhet 1993: 1001):

A Manasseh does evil (33:1–2)
  B He builds high places and altars (33:3–4)
    C He builds altars in the temple (33:5–6)
      D He places a carved image in the temple (33:7–9)
        E He does not hear (33:10)
          F Assyrian host captures him (33:11)
        E′ He turns to Yahweh, prays, and the Lord hears (33:12–13)
    C′ He builds walls to protect Judah (33:14)
      D′ He removes gods, idols, and altars (33:15–16)
  B′ High places remain (33:17)
A′ Acts of Manasseh (33:18–20)

C–D and C′–D′ are inversely parallel to one another. The first describes Manasseh's construction of (a) high places, (b) altars, and (c) images. In the second, Manasseh builds walls instead of altars, and removes (c′) foreign gods and demolishes (b′) altars, replacing them with Yahweh's altar. Yet 33:17 informs us that (a′) high places were not taken away. In E, Manasseh does not pay attention to Yahweh's warnings (33:10). Though the verb is not repeated in 33:12–13 (E′), Yahweh *does* attend to Manasseh's humble prayers. The God who calls Israel to *shama* himself *shama*s King Manasseh.

Within this overall chiasm, 33:2–9 has a complex structure of its own:

A Manasseh did evil in eyes of Yahweh, according to abominations of nations (33:2)
  B^1 Built high places (33:3a)
  B^2 Raised altars (33:3b)
  B^3 Prostrated and served host of heaven (33:3c)
  B^4 Built altars in Yahweh's house (33:4)
  B^5 Built altars for host of heaven (33:5)

B⁶ Made sons pass through fire (33:6a)
B⁷ Practiced witchcraft and divination (33:6b)
A¹ Manasseh did much evil in the eyes of Yahweh (33:6c)
   B⁸ Image of idol in the temple (33:7a)
      (Yahweh's promise to establish Israel, 33:7b–8)
A² Manasseh did more evil than nations Yahweh expelled (33:9)

Second Chronicles 33:2–6 is framed by the phrase "evil in the eyes of Yahweh," but 33:2 and 33:9 also form an *inclusio*: 33:2 speaks of the abominations of the nations that Yahweh dispossessed, and 33:9 again makes reference to the nations that Yahweh destroyed. This double *inclusio* sets up a *"this*, and also *this"* structure, progressing from A to A²: initially Manasseh alone worships idols, but his example misleads the people so that *they* begin to worship. Manasseh does evil like the nations, and he leads the people to "do *more* evil than the nations" (Johnstone 1998b: 226; Japhet 1993: 1008). When Judah surpasses Canaanites in abominations, can expulsion be far behind?

That "this, and also this" pattern is reinforced by the numerical structure of the section. By my reckoning, 33:2–6 lists seven evils done by Manasseh. His evil has a heptamerous fullness; his idolatry makes for a complete de-creation. Just when we think the catalog of idolatry is complete, the Chronicler adds an *eighth*, the worst evil of all, the erection of an idol in the house Yahweh chose for his name (33:7b–8). Just when you think the symphony of horrors has come to its climax, there is a further, dissonant coda. Yahweh's name appears seven times in the first nine verses of the chapter (33:2 [2×], 4 [2×], 5, 6, 9), the last a warning that Yahweh will destroy the sons of Israel. "Evil in the eyes of Yahweh" appears in 33:2 and 33:6 (AT). Yahweh's name is used another ten times in the remainder of the account, for a total of seventeen, the gematria of *kabod*, "glory." The sevenfold name in the early part of the chapter is threatening; the Creator can de-create. In the chapter as a whole, Yahweh's name is associated with glory, the glory of judgment but also of forgiveness and restoration.

Manasseh is a man of sixes. Second Chronicles 33:3 describes his activity with six verbs: turn, build, raise up, make/do, prostrate, serve. "Build" (*banah*) is used six times in chapter 33 (33:3, 4, 5, 14, 15, 19). Manasseh's dalliance with the occult is described with a sixfold list (33:6): his son passes through fire; he does *'anan*, *nikhesh*, and *kishsheph*; he does *'ov* and *yidde'oni* (the list resembles that of Deut. 18:9–11; McConville 1984: 249–50; Japhet 1993: 1005). The terms are rare and difficult to distinguish, but they all refer to various forms of divination and witchcraft. Like Saul (→ 1 Chr. 10:13–14), Manasseh refuses to seek Yahweh and instead turns to other sources of guidance. The parallel with Saul is frightening, because Saul's entire house collapses because he commits a *ma'al* by seeking a medium (→ 1 Chr. 10). Manasseh is a man of sixes, perhaps even a 666, and he threatens the Davidic dynasty with extinction.

When he becomes king at the age of twelve, Manasseh of Judah turns, builds, raises altars, prostrates himself, and engages in liturgical service (33:3). It is a promising sequence of actions, what all the good kings of Judah do. But the quality of Manasseh's reign turns on the direction of his "turn" (*shuv*). The word is often used of repentance, but here it refers to Manasseh's "repentance" from the ways of his father, Hezekiah. He builds high places that his father destroyed. He erects altars, but for Baals and Asherim. Baal makes a comeback, a renewal of the worship of the house of Ahab (→ 2 Chr. 23:17; 24:7). Others made them; we know that because Baals were destroyed and temples of Baal broken. But only Ahaz and Manasseh are caught in the act of making Baals (28:2; 33:3). Manasseh prostrates himself and serves, but his service is devoted to the host of heaven (33:2–3). He reintroduces the abominations (*to'evah*) of Ahaz (28:3), practices that led to the Canaanites' expulsion from the land. The word appears throughout Chronicles but increasingly at the end of 2 Chronicles. Hezekiah had overturned those abominations, but Manasseh hates his father and restores what his father had destroyed. He shows radical, wholehearted devotion—to Baal.

As always, Manasseh's idolatry is profoundly self-alienating. Throughout Chronicles, the "hosts" are the hosts of Yahweh. These are sometimes the angelic hosts who surround Yahweh's throne (→ 2 Chr. 18:18), but more often the "hosts" of Israel's armies. Israel is the earthly "sacrament" of Yahweh's heavenly host (Johnstone 1998b: 223), Yahweh's human army.[1] When Manasseh (whose name means "forgetful") worships the host of heaven, he not only forgets Yahweh and his own people. He forgets himself. Fittingly, he is eventually overcome by a "host" of Assyrians (33:11).

Manasseh's most egregious act is to place a carved image in the house of Yahweh (33:7a). Previous kings worshiped Baal but kept Baal out of Yahweh's house (Japhet 1993: 1006). Ahaz dismantled the temple, but Manasseh puts an Asherah (Baal's consort) in the temple itself, provoking Yahweh's jealousy. The Chronicler underscores the sin by reminding us of the Lord's commitment to his house (33:7b–8). The house and the city of Jerusalem are "chosen," and the house is the

---

1. Perhaps we are to take Baal, Asherah, and hosts as parallel to sun, moon, and stars. Again, this is self-alienating, because Jacob, his wife, and his sons form the heavenly bodies on earth (cf. Gen. 37:9–11).

dwelling place for Yahweh's name. He has taken his rest above the cherubim and placed his feet on the footstool of the ark. He will no longer wander but will place the land under his feet and the feet of the people of Israel (McConville [1984: 250] notes the allusion to Deut. 12). He appointed (a form of *'amad*, "stand," "give standing") his people in the land and planted their feet there. Kings place enemies and lands "under their feet"; as long as Yahweh is enthroned with the ark as his footstool under his feet, Israel will have dominion over the land. All these promises are conditional. Yahweh's name will remain in the temple, and Israel will remain in the land, only if they keep the "law, statutes, and ordinances" of Yahweh. If Judah turns, Yahweh will drive them back to wandering. If Judah turns, Yahweh will rise from his throne, kick away his footstool, and march away from his house (cf. Ezek. 8–11).

Manasseh's history is ultimately a story of hope. Initially he refuses to hear the word of the prophet, so Yahweh sends the Assyrians to capture the king and take him in "thorns" to Babylon.[2] These are perhaps hooks or chains, but the word "thorn" reminds us of the original curse of Eden. Manasseh becomes a king of thorns, suffering exile because of his own idolatries. He bears the curse into the grave of exile but then cries out from Sheol (Ps. 130). In distress, Ahaz hardened himself (2 Chr. 28:20, 22; cf. Japhet 1993: 1009–10). David's distress led to repentance (→ 1 Chr. 21; Bailey 1999: 349–56). Manasseh follows David's example (Boda 2010: 408) and that of his father: he *palals*, prays and humbles himself, following the prescription of 2 Chr. 7:14 (Williamson 1982: 393). Yahweh responds, responds even to Manasseh, and sends him back to Jerusalem.

Both the exile and the return anticipate what later happens to the whole nation of Judah. Jehoiakim and his generation will also be led away in chains to Babylon (→ 2 Chr. 36:6, 10; Johnstone 1998b: 227; Williamson 1982: 393; Boda 2010: 408). Yet Manasseh's example shows that they, too, will be raised if they humble themselves and turn to Yahweh. When earlier kings reject the word of the Lord, their doom is sealed. Manasseh's experience shows that Yahweh can open closed ears. Repentance to life is still possible, even *after* Israel's king has rejected the word of the Lord (McConville 1984: 251; Williamson 1982: 389).

2. On the historicity of this episode, see Japhet 1993: 1002–4, 1009. Boda (2010: 406–7) speculates that Manasseh carried on the alliance with Babylon that began with his father. Merodach-baladan "consistently led revolts against the Assyrians during Hezekiah's period." Boda also suggests that Manasseh's exile fulfills the prophecy of defeat that was delivered to Hezekiah (2 Kgs. 20:12–21; Boda 2010: 409n1). Others have suggested that Manasseh was descended from Arabians or Phoenicians on his mother's side and joined them in an anti-Assyrian alliance.

A number of Judah's kings begin well and sin later (Asa, Joash, Uzziah, Hezekiah, and Josiah). Almost none begin badly and turn toward Yahweh. Rehoboam is the closest analogue to Manasseh (→ 2 Chr. 10–11), but he never did "evil" in the eyes of Yahweh, committed abominations, or promoted idolatry. No one in Judah's history is as evil as Manasseh, and no one turns so dramatically. His repentance is unprecedented in Chronicles, without parallel in the Old Testament.

The consequences of his turn are also unprecedented. Throughout Chronicles, sin turns back the clock. Saul commits *ma'al*, and the Lord sends the Philistines to reconquer the land and subject Israel to another Egyptian slavery. Uzziah's sin throws Judah into a reverse exodus and conquest. Manasseh's turn also turns back the clock; he spends the second part of his reign undoing everything that he did in the first part. He returns to the *status quo ante* of Hezekiah's reign. Because Manasseh's turn is a turn to Yahweh, he also turns the clock *forward*, anticipating the Babylonian exile and the return of the exiles in the Chronicler's own day. Sin is regressive. Only those who turn in repentance hope for a future beyond the grave.

Manasseh continues to foreshadow the future when he returns. Back in Jerusalem, he returns to building, as the exiles will build when they return to the land (Pratt 2006: 468). This time, he builds defenses in the city of David and places commanders in the forts around the land. The outer wall west of Gihon runs from the northern part of the city down the eastern side, protecting the city of David (Johnstone 1998b: 227). "Gihon" (33:14) reaches back to Solomon's anointing (1 Kgs. 1:33, 38, 45), but ultimately to Eden, where the Gihon is one of the rivers that flow from Eden through the garden to the ends of the earth (Gen. 2:13). Work at the Gihon is Eden work, the work of establishing Jerusalem as a paradise, an enclosed garden city.

Idolatry is the main threat to Judah's national security, and to protect Judah Manasseh deconstructs his idolatrous constructions. He removes the idol from the temple, takes down the altars on the Temple Mount, and sets up Yahweh's altar in Yahweh's house. The Chronicler lends Manasseh's restoration of Jerusalem an eschatological overtone when he records that Manasseh removes the altars from "the mountain of the house of Yahweh" (33:15; Johnstone 1998b: 228), the mountain that, Isaiah predicted, would become the chief of the mountains (Isa. 2:1–4). When all is said and done, he offers peace offerings, celebrating reconciliation with Yahweh in feasts at Yahweh's house. Manasseh is a proto-Josiah, carrying out the same reforming work for which his grandson became famous (Japhet 1993: 1011).

The account of Manasseh's reign ends with another small chiasm (33:19):

A His prayer and how Yahweh was entreated
  B His sin (*chatt'at*)
    C His *ma'al*
  B' Places where he built high places, erected Asherim and images
A' Before he humbled himself

This does not add any facts to the story, but the use of *ma'al* at the center of the verse is arresting. Manasseh is expelled because of sacrilege, taken in chains and "thorns" to Assyria. There he prays and Yahweh answers. As Solomon hoped (→2 Chr. 6), Yahweh hears when his people humble themselves and pray, and he restores them to their land. Even *ma'al* can be forgiven; even the enormities of a Manasseh can be atoned for. And even Israel, exiled in Babylon, can hope for release.

Amon (2 Chronicles 33:21–25)

Manasseh initially does not follow his father, though he eventually prays and finds deliverance. Amon follows the lead of Manasseh's early reign but neglects to imitate Manasseh's prayer and repentance (33:22–23). Second Chronicles 33:22 emphasizes the son's mimicry of his father:

A He did evil in the eyes of Yah
  B according to what Manasseh his father had done (*ka'asher 'asah menashsheh 'aviw*).
    C To the graven images
  B' which Manasseh his father did (*'asher 'asah menashsheh 'aviw*)
A' Amon sacrificed and served.

B and B' use identical phrases, highlighting the effect of his father's example. In the Hebrew text, Amon is not named until the end of the verse. Manasseh and his idols dominate. Amon disappears, a mere mirror of his father, overcome by the idols he worships.

Judah tolerated Manasseh for fifty-five years (33:1), but they do not give so much grace to Amon. After two years, his servants conspire and kill him. Judah has become a land of palace intrigue and violence (→2 Chr. 24:21, 25–26; →2 Chr.

25:27), where no king is secure against conspiracy. The people do take action against the conspirators and place Josiah on the throne. Josiah's name—"Yah heals"—is reassuring. But after Manasseh and Amon, it may be too late. Even if Josiah is as great as Hezekiah, the history so far makes us skeptical that reform can be sustained.

14

A NEW AND VERY DIFFERENT KING DAVID

2 Chronicles 34–36

Judah's Last Gasp (2 Chronicles 34:1–35:19)

The Chronicler is a generous judge of the kings of Judah. He does not include some of the sins of David and Solomon—David's adultery and murder, Solomon's multiple marriages and idolatry. David does sin when he takes a census of the people, but he is otherwise flawless. Solomon does not appear to commit any sins. Together, David and Solomon become the standards to measure the other kings of Judah.

Few live up to that standard of perfection, but the Chronicler still evaluates many of them favorably. "Asa did what was good and right in the eyes of Yahweh his God" (2 Chr. 14:2 AT), despite the fact that he plunders his own palace and Yahweh's treasuries to bribe the Arameans into attacking the northern kingdom of Baasha. He is "good and right" despite the fact that he does not seek the Lord when, late in life, his feet are diseased. Jehoshaphat follows the ways of his father, Asa, and "did what was right in the eyes of Yahweh" (20:32 AT), in spite of the fact that he marries his son off to a daughter of Ahab and Jezebel, an intermarriage with the idolatrous north that brings generations of idolatry and turmoil to Judah and nearly snuffs out the Davidic dynasty. Joash "did what was right in the eyes of Yahweh" (24:2 AT). That commendation is qualified: he does right only during the lifetime of Jehoiada the priest. Once Jehoiada dies, Joash begins listening to "officials" who lead him away from the house of Yahweh. In the end, Joash kills the prophet Zechariah, the son of Jehoiada. Still, Joash gets a partial attaboy from the Chronicler. Amaziah also gets a partial commendation. He does what is right in the eyes of Yahweh but "not with a whole heart." Uzziah does what is right but, like Amaziah his father, only partially. Uzziah invades the temple and tries to offer incense, something reserved for priests.

While the Chronicler judges the kings of Judah generously, he also highlights the flaws in all the kings of Judah, apart from Solomon. Hezekiah is virtually flawless, but the Chronicler does record one mysterious incident. Hezekiah got sick and the Lord delivered him. But Hezekiah was proud and did not give any "return for the benefit he received" (→ 2 Chr. 32:25). He failed to show proper gratitude, and so the Lord brought wrath on Jerusalem. Hezekiah immediately humbled himself, and the Lord turned away the threat. All the other kings of Judah have glaring flaws. They forge unwise alliances, or set up Baals and Asherim, or follow the ways of Ahab. Josiah fits this pattern.

Like the Chronicler's accounts of Asa and Jehoshaphat, his record of Josiah is organized by two contrasting sequences (cf. Pratt [2006: 474], who sees a chiasm):

A Reform of worship and repair of the temple (34:1–13)
  B Discovery of the law and interpretation by Huldah (34:14–28)
    C Renewal of covenant (34:29–33)
A' Passover (35:1–19)
  B' Prophetic word of Neco (35:20–21)
    C' Josiah dies because he does not hear (35:22–27)

Josiah is an ideal Davidic king in many ways. He not only "did right," but he "walked in the ways of his father David" and "did not turn aside to the right or to the left" (34:2; cf. 34:33). At the age of sixteen, when he is a mere "lad" (na'ar), he begins to seek (darash) Yahweh (Boda 2010: 413), and four years later he initiates a purge of idolatry from the land of Judah and the city of Jerusalem (34:3–7). He is one of the initiators of Chronicles. Solomon "begins" (khalal) the temple (2 Chr. 3:1–2), Jehoshaphat's singers "begin" (20:22), and Hezekiah "begins" to purify the house (29:17, 27) and to collect contributions from the land (31:10, 21). Josiah is the last to "begin" anything in Chronicles. After Josiah, things are ending rather than beginning.

He does right even though there is no maternal guide. Throughout 2 Chronicles, "he did right in the eyes of Yahweh" is frequently preceded by "his mother was ____" (20:31–32; 25:1–2; 26:3–4; 27:1–2; 29:1–2). Though unstated, the implication is that the king's mother exercised a godly influence on her son. There are counterexamples. Asa has to remove his mother from her position because she makes an Asherah (15:16). Athaliah, wife of Jehoram, influences her husband (21:6) and son (22:2–3) to walk in the way of Ahab, until she is defeated by the bold action of a godly mother, Jehoshabeath (22:11). After Hezekiah, mothers good and bad drop out of the picture. The Chronicler's omission is deliberate, since the mothers' names appear in 2 Kings, his source text. But a woman plays a significant role during Josiah's reign: Huldah the prophetess, who has the longest speaking part of any woman in Chronicles (2 Chr. 34:22–28) and is the last woman in Chronicles. She is a mother in Israel, even if she is not related to Josiah. I smell allegory, given the imagery of "mother Israel" or "mother Jerusalem," as well as the Proverbial figure of Lady Wisdom. The absence of mothers signals the loss of the guiding hand of wisdom.

At the age of twenty, an Israelite is qualified to fight in war and, if he is a Levite, to serve at the temple (cf. Williamson 1982: 398). Josiah does both, embarking on a quasi-sacrificial holy war during which he tears and cuts and pulverizes altars and Asherah poles and incense altars to Baal, sprinkles the dust on graves of idolaters, and burns the bones of the priests on the altars. The Chronicler uses five verbs of destruction—break, cut, pulverize, beat small, sprinkle—to describe Josiah's cleansing of Judah and Jerusalem, the land and the city. Four things are torn down—high places, Asherim, graven images, molten images—in a global, four-cornered purge of Judah. Josiah seems to ignore the temple itself, but 34:8 informs us that he purged the house as well as the land and city.[1]

Josiah does not stop with Judah and Jerusalem. He destroys altars, Asherah poles, and idols in Manasseh, Ephraim, and Naphtali, areas of the northern kingdom.[2] The Chronicler repeatedly emphasizes that Josiah's reform covers the land

1. That suggests that the "Baals in his presence" and perhaps the high altars in 34:4 refer to idols within the temple precincts.
2. Recognizing the different locations disentangles a repetitive text. The purge of Judah and Jerusalem is described in a chiastically arranged account (34:3–5):
    A He began to purge Judah and Jerusalem
      B of high places, Asherim, carved images, and molten images.
        C He tore down altars of Baals and incense altars.
      B' Asherim, carved, molten he broke, ground, scattered; he burned bones
    A' and purged Judah and Jerusalem.
After 34:5 Josiah turns to the northern kingdom, destroying similar cult objects there (altars, Asherim, carved images, incense altars) before returning to Jerusalem (34:7). Johnstone (1998b: 234) notes, "The sequence Manasseh-Ephraim, only in this chapter in [Chronicles] (also v. 9), but common enough

(34:6, 7, 9, 21, 33; 35:17–18; Japhet 1993: 1023). It is again a fourfold purge, this time with four verbs (tear, beat, grind, chop) directed against four objects (altars, Asherim, images, incense altars). The images are on the "height of the ascent" (*lema'lah me'alehem*; 34:4), another of the Chronicler's puns on the key term *ma'al*. By pulling them from their height, Josiah eliminates the sacrileges of his fathers and staves off their effects. Josiah is a new Joshua, conquering the land and cleansing idolatry.[3]

The purge is preparation for the reestablishment of the worship of Yahweh in his house. At the age of twenty-six, Josiah revives Joash's program for maintaining the house of the Lord (on the parallels of Joash and Josiah, see Boda 2010: 412; Dillard 1987: 277–82). Levites supervise, including musicians who perhaps accompany the building process (34:12–13; Williamson 1982: 401; Pratt 2006: 481). The Chronicler describes the collection and delivery of the money in elaborate detail. Money is collected and passed from hand to hand to hand until it gets into the hands of the workmen who will repair the house (34:8–13). It is a complicated process. Though convoluted at points, 34:10 seems to describe this movement of funds: people → doorkeepers → Hilkiah → three officials from king → overseers (?)→ workmen → carpenters and builders. The repetitive structure underlines the formal, ritualized character of the collection:

A They gave
  B into the hands of the doers of the work (*'oseh hammela'kah*)
    C and overseers of the house (*mupqadim*).
A' They gave it
  B' to the doers of the work (*'oseh hammela'kah*) who did in the house
    C' to restore and strengthen the house.

The ritualized pattern has a practical point: no funds are lost along the way; everyone deals honestly and fairly, so that the gifts of the people eventually get to the workmen who will maintain and mend the house.

Donations to the temple always accompany the renewal of faithfulness and prosperity in Judah. David is the model, offering large sums of his own and inspiring the princes and people to give freely (→ 1 Chr. 29). He prays that Yahweh

___
elsewhere in the Hebrew Bible (e.g. Gen. 46.20), gives a chiastic arrangement N[orth] → S[outh] → S[outh] → N[orth], which well expresses comprehensiveness."
  3. Dillard (1987: 276) links the stages of Josiah's reforms with the ups and downs of Assyrian power. There is perhaps a connection, but the Chronicler has little interest in geopolitics as such.

would preserve the generous intentions of his people (1 Chr. 29:18), and his prayer is heard. The people of Judah give generously to the temple in the days of Joash, Hezekiah (→2 Chr. 31), and now Josiah. Generosity is only the beginning. Wealth can be mismanaged. Tribute brought to the temple can be siphoned off to greedy priests and never reach the workmen for whom it is intended. The Chronicler signals spiritual renewal not only by recording the generous gifts of king, nobles, and people, but also by showing that the gifts are carefully collected and distributed. It is another aspect of the Chronicler's vindication of bureaucracy. For him, the rise of accountancy is a breakthrough of the highest order.

The Lord rewards this act of homage, this ritual of tribute. As the house is being repaired, Hilkiah the priest finds the book of the law inside. Scholars are divided about the identity of the book, some claiming it includes all the Pentateuch (Williamson 1982: 402; Japhet 1993: 1030) and others that it is the book of Deuteronomy (Dillard 1987: 28; Pratt 2006: 483; Boda 2010: 414). The former seems preferable. "Torah" appears seventeen times in Chronicles (the gematria of *kabod*, "glory"), three times in chapter 34 (vv. 14, 15, 19). Verse 15 mimics the movement of the priest into the inner sanctuary where the book of Torah is discovered:

A Hilkiah answered and said to Shaphan the scribe,
   B A book of Torah I found
      C in the house of Yahweh.
   B′ And Hilkiah gave the book
A′ to Shaphan.

And that book is, like the money, passed from hand to hand to hand until Shaphan the scribe reads it in the presence of the king (34:14–21), reversing the order of tribute: priest → scribe → king. Josiah gives tribute to the Lord, and the word of the Lord comes down from the Temple Mount to warn and instruct the king. Yahweh is no longer silent. He speaks again from his throne above the cherubim. The house has been a place of prayer. When Israel directs its prayers to the house, the Lord of heaven sees and hears. Now we learn that Yahweh's *mouth* is in the house along with his eyes and ears. The house speaks back to those who honor the Lord of the house.

Shaphan "calls" (*qara'*, 34:18) the word out to the king, the verb underlying the interaction between prayer and Torah: prayers are "called out" to Yahweh, and he calls back. In a perfect expression of Israel's vocation, Josiah "hears" and mourns the sin of his people. He tears his clothes and weeps, sowing a tenderness of heart that Yahweh commends. He recognizes that Judah has not kept the word of Yahweh.

To clarify how he is to respond and what to expect, he sends Hilkiah to "seek" Yahweh's word from a prophet. Having the book is not enough; they need confirmation from the living voice of Yahweh (McConville 1984: 257). They consult Huldah the prophetess, wife of Shallum, keeper of the wardrobe.[4] Huldah's prophecy (34:23–28) is simultaneously threatening and reassuring:

A Tell Josiah (34:23)
  B I bring evil and curses (34:24)
    C They have forsaken me (34:25a)
      D My wrath will be poured out (34:25b)
A′ To the king of Judah (34:26)
    C′ Because you heard and humbled yourself, I will gather you (34:27)
  B′ You will not see evil (34:28)

Josiah will be spared the evil that the Lord is bringing, but the threat remains. There is no resolution to the central pronouncement: "My wrath will be poured out on this place and it shall not be quenched" (34:25). For Josiah, though, gestures of humility and repentance work. Because Josiah humbles himself when he hears the Lord's word, the Lord relents from the calamity he planned for Jerusalem. Jerusalem will not be destroyed in Josiah's day, and the Lord even promises to bring him to his grave in peace (34:28). Letters and books are read in several places in Chronicles, and the responses of characters model improper (2 Chr. 21:12–15) and

---

4. Johnstone (1998b: 241) offers this speculative gloss on Huldah's husband:
He is described as "Keeper of the Garments," a title which occurs only in this context. One is left to surmise that "the garments" are those worn by the priests, not least the High Priest (see, for example, Exod. 28.1–43; Lev. 8.7–9 for the garments themselves—the pouch, ephod, robe, tunic, breeches, turban, diadem and sash; and for changes of garment within ceremonies, Lev. 6.10, 11; 16.4, 23). If so, it is easy to imagine the commitment to the tradition of Moses and the Law of such a person, whose daily task it is to handle elaborate vestments with such powerful symbolism of Israel's dedication to God and to care for the changes of garment during the rites of national whole burnt offering and atonement. His role must surely also imply levitical status, and that may be why he is given a pedigree extending back for two generations, again genealogy functioning as legitimation of claim to standing (cf. 2 Chr. 20.14; nothing is otherwise known of his forebears). A connection between the wife of this key figure in the cult, ritual and liturgy and a book of the Law found in the Temple becomes comprehensible as does her sense of prophetic outrage at the violation of practice and of God's rights.

proper responses (2 Chr. 34). Readers and hearers of Chronicles are to take note: your future depends on whether you humble yourself before the book before you.

Josiah does not, however, wait complacently for the clock to run out. Equipped with the book of the law, Josiah "seeks" Yahweh and launches a third phase of reform, calling the people to Jerusalem to renew the covenant between Yahweh, the king, and the people. Elders have disappeared from Chronicles since Rehoboam rejected the counsel of Solomon's elders (→ 2 Chr. 10). Now, in the time of Josiah, they reappear, part of the gathering of Israel in Judah and Jerusalem. The Chronicler underscores the "all Israel" character of the assembly by listing all categories—men of Judah, inhabitants of Jerusalem, priests, Levites, people, least and great—in a twelve-word list. This entire twelvefold people ascends with Josiah to Jerusalem, to the house of Yahweh (34:30).

When everyone is gathered, Josiah calls out (*qara'*) the book that was called out to him (34:30). The book that was hidden in the inner recesses of the temple is now shouted in the courts. When Jehoiada led Judah in covenant renewal, he set Joash by the pillar (23:13: *hamelek 'omed 'al-'ammudo*). Now Josiah takes the same position (34:31: *waya'amod hamelek 'al-'amdo*). In both cases, the verb "stand" and the noun "pillar" are based on the same root; a pillar is a "standing-thing." And the king who takes his stand by the pillar is himself a pillar holding up the house of the Lord and the house of Judah, standing as a connecting point between heaven and earth. The pillars, we have seen, bring the reality of the inner sanctuary out into the court, and that is the king's role as well. Josiah is the public expression of the kingship of Yahweh, who led Israel to the land in a pillar of cloud and fire.

As a link between earth and heaven, the pillar is an appropriate location to swear a covenant oath of loyalty to the God of heaven. The covenant is carried out in stages. First, Josiah himself makes a covenant with Yahweh. Adopting the language of Deut. 6, the Chronicler describes the content of the covenant: the king swears to walk after Yahweh, to guard his commandments, testimonies, and statutes, with his whole heart and soul. Then, once the king "stands in covenant," all Israel comes to stand with him in that covenant (34:32). Judah enters covenant by incorporation into the king, who is Israel in person, the embodiment of Yahweh's corporate son. Throughout 2 Chr. 34, Josiah is simply called "the king." His specific personality disappears; his given name is not used. He becomes simply "the king," a living archetype of sheer royalty. (His proper name *is* used fourteen times in chap. 35, seventeen times total in 33:25–36:1.) He does everything that one expects of a king, and he serves the function of king as the incarnation of his people.

The renewal of the covenant begins a new era for Judah. In the head month (*ri'shon*), Josiah celebrates the Passover. The Chronicler has to go back to the days of Samuel to find a precedent (2 Chr. 35:18). Following the lead of David and Solomon, Josiah knows that the priests and Levites are crucial to the health of Judah. He sets them in order and assigns them their responsibilities:

A Put the ark in the house (35:3)
  B Prepare by fathers' households according to David and Solomon (35:4)
  B' Stand in the holy place according to father's households (35:5)
A' Slaughter the Passover according to word of Yahweh by Moses (35:6)

Oddly, he instructs the Levites to place the ark of the covenant in the temple, relieving them of the burden of transporting it (35:3). A central focus of David's career, the ark has not been mentioned since 2 Chr. 8:11, when it was placed in the temple. It has apparently been removed and made transportable again. We might surmise that the priests removed it during the long reign of Manasseh, when the king placed an idol in the house of the Lord. Yahweh's throne was removed from the defiled house, and he returned to his life of wandering. Josiah treats the restoration of the temple as a virtual rebuilding and instructs the Levites to return the ark to its place. McConville (1984: 262) makes the intriguing suggestion that Josiah reenacted the placement of the ark in order to underscore the restoration of the Lord's house. Josiah wants to restore the complete order of David's kingdom.

In the typology of 1–2 Chronicles, the reference to the ark completes the parallel history that the Chronicler recounts. David is another Moses, placing the ark in a temporary tent; Solomon is like Joshua, who put the ark into a semipermanent location in Shiloh. For most of 2 Chronicles, the ark has been absent from the story, despised and rejected, so that it is as if there were no king in Israel. It has been like the period of the wandering of the ark in 1 Sam. 4–6. Now the ark is placed in its house again, but that house is about to be destroyed again, like another Shiloh (Jer. 7).

Josiah, his officials, and the leaders of the Levites contribute the animals to be offered for *pesakh*. The king gives 30,000 lambs and kids, and adds 3,000 bulls. The officers of the court contribute another 2,600 Passover animals and 300 bulls, while the priests add 5,000 and 500. It is not clear why bulls are among the contributions. They are not Passover animals. Second Chronicles 35:12 describes how they are used: Levites prepare bulls as ascension offerings (*'olah*) and distribute portions to the laypeople, so that the people can "bring near" (hiphil of *qarab*) ascension offerings as required by the Torah of Moses. This is the only place where the Chronicler uses the verb "bring near" (*qarab*) in a liturgical setting. It is a key term in the Levitical system. Every offering is a *qorban*, something brought near (Lev. 1:1–3). In bringing the animal near, the worshiper himself draws near and seeks to ascend into the presence of Yahweh. Before the people can celebrate the Passover, they need to draw near with ascensions, and the king, officials, and Levites provide the bulls they need to do so.

The Chronicler tells us that they follow Torah (Exod. 12:9) by roasting the Passover on the fire, but the text presents difficulties. The verb in 2 Chr. 35:13 is *bashal*, the verb used for the prohibited "boiling" of the Passover in Exod. 12. Exodus requires that the animal be *tseli* in fire, while Chronicles says that the animals are *bashal*ed with fire (Williamson [1982: 410] and Japhet [1993: 1053] both suggest this is an effort to harmonize Exod. 12 with Deut. 16). The key element seems to be the fire: the Passover animal must, like Israel, pass through the fire, be touched by the fiery presence of Yahweh, before it can be eaten. Other meats—holy things—are "boiled" (*bashal*) in containers of various sorts and then delivered to the people. The arrangement suggests an elevation of lay Israelites into fuller priestly status. Under Torah, only holy priests should eat holy food, but with Josiah the Passover moves toward the new-covenant declaration: holy things for holy people.

Priests and Levites are servants of the servants of Yahweh. They prepare ascensions and Passover for the people, and then prepare the offerings for themselves (35:14), which last through the night. Like Hezekiah (for parallels, see Boda 2010: 412), Josiah sets up the singers to accompany the offerings of animals. They have a "standing" in the court, following the decrees of David. As in David's time, gatekeepers play a prominent role (35:15). The whole service is organized by the decree of Moses and David, but 35:16 indicates that it is done also by the "command of King Josiah." Josiah does not have independent authority to innovate the Passover celebration, but the authority of Moses, David, and Solomon does not remove authority from Josiah. On the contrary, by acting on the authority of the writings of previous authority, Josiah's words and actions become authoritative.

Reverse Exodus (2 Chronicles 35:20–27)

A Passover should be followed by an exodus. And, right on cue, as soon as Josiah's Passover is over, a king of Egypt comes into the picture. But it is not a sign of liberation. Judah does not need to be liberated. It is already an independent nation. Instead, the sudden appearance of Egypt strikes an ominous note.

Solomon was married to an Egyptian princess, but otherwise Egypt has been a threatening presence throughout 2 Chronicles. Jeroboam came up from Egypt to challenge Rehoboam and to take away ten tribes. He comes out of Egypt in an exodus, and then, Moses-like, leads an exodus from the house of David. It is an exodus, but the house of David under Rehoboam is the Egypt. And then Rehoboam is threatened by an Egyptian army. We can imagine what is in Pharaoh Shishak's mind. Jeroboam lived in Egypt for a time and is presumably on good terms with the Egyptians. He worships calves and satyrs like the Egyptians do. If Shishak can conquer Judah, then he can extend Egyptian influence all the way from Egypt to the northern kingdom. Rehoboam suffers a reverse Passover and exodus. Instead of being delivered from Egyptian slavery, he comes under the hegemony of Egypt. Instead of Israel plundering Egypt, Egypt plunders Israel. Between Rehoboam and Josiah, Egypt does not intrude on Judah at all. Judah is able to exist in relative independence from their powerful neighbor to the south. But now in the days of Josiah, after a great Passover, an Egyptian shows up. Is it going to be another reverse exodus?

Other details reinforce our sense of disquiet. Josiah leaves Jerusalem to meet Pharaoh. As Johnstone (1998b: 83) notes, it is usually disastrous for kings of Judah to leave home. Rehoboam goes to Shechem and loses ten tribes. Jehoshaphat visits Ahab and forms an alliance that nearly destroys Judah. It is usually disastrous because it puts the kings of Judah in the middle of other people's wars. Jehoshaphat accompanies Ahab in war to recover Ramoth-gilead from the Arameans, and nearly gets killed. Josiah puts himself in the middle of a war between Egypt and Babylon—between Nimrod and Cush—and does get killed.

Why would he do so? Neco is on his way to the battle at Assyria's new capital, Carchemish, to join the Assyrian resistance to the rising Neo-Babylonian Empire (Boda 2010: 420; on the historicity of the account, see Dillard 1987: 288–89, 292). At that battle (609 BC), the Babylonians defeated an alliance of Egypt and Assyria, and broke Assyrian power once and for all. Pratt (2006: 496) suggests that Josiah is acting as a vassal of Babylon, which had favorable relations with Judah going back to the days of Hezekiah (32:31). This points to the thematic thrust of Chronicles: Asa's alliance with Aram went badly wrong, and Josiah's efforts to defend Babylon end in disaster.

That is not the worst of it. The problem is not simply political and military. The problem is theological. The king of Judah is Yahweh's prince, the prince of the Creator of heaven and earth, who is enthroned in Jerusalem. Judah's kings should approach the world from a position of strength. They are not called to be involved in the power struggles of other kings. They are called to be agents of Yahweh's kingship. Besides that, Pharaoh Neco claims to be on a mission of God. Neco sends messengers to Josiah to inform him: "God has ordered me to hurry. Stop for your own sake from interfering with God who is with me, so that He will not destroy you" (35:21). The Chronicler confirms that these words come "from the mouth of God" (35:22). Like Huram and Queen Sheba before him, like Cyrus after him, Neco is a Gentile ruler who commends the God of Israel (Ben Zvi 1999: 221–22). By trying to intervene, Josiah sets himself in opposition to Yahweh's purpose and plan.[5]

The irony is thick. It is an Egyptian king, one of Israel's traditional enemies. And he sends messengers. But these messengers bear the words of the Lord, and in resisting them Josiah is resisting the Lord as much as he would be if he refused to listen to a prophet. Josiah becomes yet another king who "mocked the messengers of God, despised His words and scoffed at His prophets" (36:16; Johnstone 1998b: 257). Josiah, the king who discovered the law of God, the king who tore his robe when the law was read in his presence, "does not listen" to the words that come from the mouth of God. He is no longer "the king." He is just "Josiah," as flawed as other kings of Judah.

The conduct and outcome of the skirmish confirms our fears. Josiah decides to go into battle in disguise. It did not work for Ahab, and it does not work for Josiah (Japhet 1993: 1043). Though disguised, Ahab was killed by an arrow that was shot "at random" (2 Chr. 18:33). Josiah is also shot by archers and carted back to Jerusalem to die. It is a symmetrical conclusion to the history of kings. Chronicles begins its account of the monarchy with the death of Saul, shot by archers on Mount Gilboa. At the center of the history is the death of Ahab, shot with a random arrow as he fights against Ramoth-gilead. That history closes with another king killed by archers. Saul's entire dynastic house collapsed when he died. Ahab's dynasty lasted a few more generations but was never as strong again. Josiah's Saul-like, Ahab-like death bodes ill for the future of the Davidic dynasty.

---

5. McConville (1984: 269) wonders how Josiah was supposed to know that Neco spoke the truth. It is a fair question, but it should be noted that no Gentile in Chronicles pretends to speak in Yahweh's name. Ahab's prophets are guided by a deceiving spirit (2 Chr. 18:19–22), but they are Israelites. The Rabshakeh (cf. 2 Kgs. 18:17) speaks blasphemy but does not claim to speak for Yahweh. At least, Neco's claim should have given Josiah pause: Is it possible that he is telling the truth?

Josiah's death is a reverse exodus because it is first an inverted Passover. Zechariah describes a scene of mourning like the "mourning. . . in the plain of Megiddo," a reference to the death of Josiah (Zech. 12:11). But the mourning Zechariah describes is also like the mourning of Egypt over their firstborn. At the first Passover, the firstborn of Egypt died. Here, the firstborn of Israel, the king, dies. In fact, the king is Yahweh's son. In this reverse Passover, Yahweh's own son is slain, the royal son who embodies Yahweh's son Israel.

We comfort ourselves with the saying "It is always darkest before dawn." But sometimes the truth is "It is brightest just before all the lights go out." Yet in Chronicles, lament is not the last word. Lament is not the last song. Weeping lasts a night, but joy comes in the morning.

In 2 Kings, Josiah appears to die on the battlefield, and his corpse is returned to Jerusalem. In 2 Chronicles, Josiah is still alive when he returns to Jerusalem. This fulfills Huldah's prophecy that Josiah will be gathered to the grave in peace (2 Chr. 34:26), but as Mitchell (2006: 423) points out, the fulfillment is ironic. Josiah does die in Jerusalem away from the battlefield, but he dies of war wounds. His retreat from the field establishes a typological connection with another king of the house of Ahab. In Chronicles, the only other king who leaves a battle is Jehoram of Israel, who goes to Samaria with war wounds. His cousin, Ahaziah of Judah, visits him there and is slaughtered by Jehu.[6] Amaziah's death (2 Chr. 25) also resembles Josiah's. Amaziah aggressively seeks a showdown with his northern counterpart, Joash of Israel. Joash warns him off, but Amaziah presses forward anyway. It looks a lot like Josiah's aggressive stance toward Neco. Amaziah's death, like Ahaziah's, is said to be "from God" (25:20), and the parallel again raises the question of whether Josiah's death is also a punishment for refusing to listen to the word of Yahweh (Mitchell 2006: 425).

Mitchell (2006: 430) argues that Josiah dies because of irregularities in his Passover. Maintaining distinctions between priest and nonpriest is certainly a concern of the Chronicler (cf. Uzziah, who contracts leprosy for seizing priestly

---

6. Mitchell suggests that the parallels raise a theological question: "Ahaziah hides (*chava'* hithpael) in Samaria before being located and executed (2 Chr. 22:9). When we consider that the hithpael of *chavash* in 2 Chr. 35:22 literally means 'to let oneself be searched for,' and that Jehu has to search for (*baqash*) Ahaziah, then we have another link to Josiah's death. Ahaziah, of course, was a grandson of Ahab and was executed during Jehu's purge of the House of Ahab. Unlike in the case of Josiah's death, however, we are given a reason for Ahaziah going out (*yatza'*) to Jehu—it was 'from God.' Ahaziah's death is ordained. Perhaps Josiah's death also is 'ordained'—as in fact Neco implies in 2 Chr. 35:21" (2006: 424–25). Even if this connection is forced, the Chronicler still links "Josiah's death in 2 Chronicles 35 with the deaths of two kings soundly condemned by the Chronicler—and both are linked with Ahab" (Mitchell 2006: 425).

privilege). But if Josiah dies because he allows Levites to slaughter and skin the animals, the Chronicler is exceedingly subtle about it. It is not clear that the priests are required to skin and dismember sacrificial animals; Lev. 1:6 appears to refer to the worshiper when it says "*he* shall then skin . . . and cut." In fact, the actions of priests and Levites are repeatedly authorized by the "king's command" (2 Chr. 35:10) or by conformity to the "book of Moses" (35:12) or the "ordinance" (35:13). That is hardly the language one expects if the Chronicler is describing a mortal sin.

The more traditional view is right: Josiah dies because he refuses to hear the word of Yahweh that comes to him through Neco. As noted above, Josiah's life story follows the two-stage life history of Asa. Asa initially trusts Yahweh and hears his prophet, but then relies on international alliances and refuses to hear the prophet. Likewise, Josiah initially receives the law and Huldah's prophecy, but then refuses to hear the "words of Neco from the mouth of God" (35:22). That Yahweh's word is coming from the mouth of a Gentile king fits the trajectory of the closing chapters of 2 Chronicles, which are rushing headlong to the final words spoken by Cyrus the Persian, whose spirit is stirred to say, "May Yahweh his God be with him, and let him go up!" (36:23).

When Saul dies, the people fast for ten days. When Josiah dies, Jeremiah composes a lament. This is not the lament in the book of Lamentations, but it might as well be. Lamentations describes Jerusalem after the Babylonian deportations: "How lonely sits the city that was full of people! She has become like a widow" (1:1). After the death of Josiah, Jerusalem is indeed a widow, deprived of her royal husband, provider, and protector. We think that history is smooth and predictable. Nations rise and then gradually decline. National decay is like slipping down a gentle slope. That is not always the case. Sometimes nations collapse precipitously. They do not slowly slip down a gentle slope but fall off a cliff. That is what happened to Judah: one day it is at its height, and three months later it is back in Egypt, back where it started.

Josiah's death is the end of a phase of history for Judah. After this point, Gentile rulers from Egypt, Babylon, or Persia rule over the people of God (Boda 2010: 421). Judah's history does not end immediately, but its independence is all but over. The Chronicler treats the death of Josiah as the effective end of the kingdom of Judah (Johnstone 1998c: 124–25). Josiah is the last king to be buried in Jerusalem. The great Passover does not mark the beginning of a new deliverance for Judah. On the contrary, the great Passover is undermined by Josiah's folly, his refusal to hear the word of Yahweh. Jeremiah chants a lament for Josiah. It is not only for Josiah. It is for "the king," the king who acted most fully like a king, the king who is really the last king of Judah.

Exile and Beyond (2 Chronicles 36)

Saul and his sons die at Mount Gilboa on the same day (→ 1 Chr. 10). The entire royal house collapses at once. Josiah dies like a Saul, but the Davidic dynasty persists for another two generations. Yet the logic is the same: three of Josiah's sons take the throne (Joahaz, 36:1–3; Eliakim/Jehoiakim, 36:4–8; Zedekiah, 36:10–13).[7] As so often in Chronicles, disobedience to the word of the Lord sets the clock back. Josiah's refusal to hear Yahweh's word through Neco takes us back to the beginning of the story, the collapse of Saul's dynasty.

In the Hebrew text, 35:24–36:4 is marked as a single paragraph (Johnstone 1998b: 259). Instead of treating Josiah's successors as rulers in their own right, the Chronicler places their reigns within the shattering aftermath of Josiah's death. That literary device italicizes the actual political situation: after Josiah, only Joahaz rules independently, and that for only three months. Otherwise, the final Davidic kings rule under the oversight of Gentile rulers, who install and replace them for their own purposes:

1. The people make Joahaz king, but Neco deposes him after three months and replaces him with Eliakim, renamed Jehoiakim (36:1–4).
2. Jehoiakim reigns for eleven years, but Nebuchadnezzar captures him and takes him to Babylon. Nebuchadnezzar puts Jehoiakim's son Jehoiachin on the throne (36:5–8).
3. Jehoiachin reigns for three months, but Nebuchadnezzar captures him and takes him to Babylon. Nebuchadnezzar installs Zedekiah as king (36:9–10).
4. Zedekiah reigns for eleven years. He rebels against Nebuchadnezzar, who returns to slaughter Israel, plunder the temple, burn the Lord's house, and break down the wall of Jerusalem (36:11–21).

When it is all over, Joahaz is in Egypt, Jehoiakim and Jehoiachin are captives in Babylon, and Zedekiah simply disappears from the narrative. The Chronicler

---

7. According to 2 Kings, Zedekiah is Jehoiachin's uncle rather than his brother (2 Chr. 36:10). By this reckoning, the house of David consists of Josiah and three sons who constitute the four corners of the dynasty. If we use the Chronicler's family tree, Josiah is followed by two sons and two grandsons, another group of four that represents the collapsing royal house.

treats Josiah and his successors as a single generation. It is as if Josiah's house, like Saul's, collapses all at once.

Though Gentile emperors have political control, events are actually in the hands of Yahweh, God of Israel. Neco and Nebuchadnezzar are instruments of Yahweh's discipline of his own people. The Chronicler plunders the lexicon of evil to describe the last days of Judah. Throughout Chronicles, he names eight kings who "do evil." Before the last generations of Judah, a few kings "do evil": Rehoboam (2 Chr. 12:14), Jehoram (21:6), and Ahaziah (22:4). The evil of Ahaziah nearly destroys Judah and the Davidic dynasty. Yahweh rescues his people and gives them a string of kings who "do right." Then Manasseh (33:2–3) and Amon (33:22) form a two-generation tradition of evil. And despite the efforts of Hezekiah and Josiah, Judah's history ends with a three-generation line of evil kings: Jehoiakim (36:5), Jehoiachin (36:9), and Zedekiah (36:12).

The unifying character of 2 Chr. 35–36 is not, in any case, a king, whether Judahite or Gentile. It is a prophet, Jeremiah (Johnstone 1998b: 273): he chants a lament at Josiah's death (35:25) and prophesies to the stiff-necked Zedekiah (36:12). Exile comes as a fulfillment of Yahweh's word through Jeremiah (36:21), and so does the return from exile (36:22).

Chapter 36 completes another story arc of Chronicles. After Jehoshaphat, Judah's kings (Jehoram, Ahaziah) worship idols because they imitate the house of Ahab. Ahaz and Manasseh follow the ways of the nations that the Lord expelled from the land. Like Ahaz (2 Chr. 28:3) and Manasseh (33:2), the last kings of Judah return to *to'evah*, abominations. Judah has developed its own heritage of abominations. Now, not only kings like Jehoiakim (36:8) but the whole people do abominable things (36:14).

The specific catalog of sins indicates the epochal shift taking place at the end of the monarchy. None of the last kings serve Baal or set up images in the temple. To be sure, like Saul (→ 1 Chr. 10), Judah's officials, priests, and people *ma'al* a *ma'al*, committing a trespass against Yahweh's name and property. They are guilty of abominations and of defiling the Lord's house. But the kings are charged with other sorts of violations. Joahaz, Jehoiakim, and Jehoiachin do unspecified "evil." Zedekiah is accused of refusing to humble himself before Jeremiah the prophet (36:12) and rebelling against Nebuchadnezzar (36:13). Those two evils are linked, since Jeremiah instructs Judah's kings to submit to Babylon (cf. Jer. 27:1–11). Zedekiah exemplifies Judah's unwillingness to hear the words of the prophets (36:16), stiffening his neck like the exodus generation and hardening his heart like Pharaoh (36:13). But his treachery toward Nebuchadnezzar is also a sacrilege. He swore an oath to serve Babylon, and by going back on his oath he tramples on the holy name of Yahweh (36:13). Judah must still worship Yahweh and renounce idols. But the focus of idolatry is shifting. The test now is not only to carry on the temple worship but to submit to Yahweh's new order governed by his servants Nebuchadnezzar and Cyrus.

Surprisingly, the Chronicler identifies Judah's chief sin as a failure to give the land its Sabbaths (36:21). Every seven years, the land was supposed to be left fallow, debts were to be canceled, and slaves were to be manumitted (Deut. 15; Lev. 25). Judah has failed to give the land rest, oppressing the land and, by implication, oppressing one another. They have not kept the law of release, as Israel did in the days of Ahaz (→ 2 Chr. 28). In one sense, the connection between Sabbath and exile is obvious, drawn directly from the warnings of Lev. 26:31–34: "I will lay waste your cities. . . . I will make the land desolate. . . . You, however, I will scatter among the nations. . . . Then the land will enjoy its sabbaths all the days of the desolation, while you are in your enemies' land; then the land will rest and enjoy its sabbaths." Yet the Chronicler has paid no attention to Sabbaths of the land. If this was so crucial to Judah's survival, why is this the first time we have heard about it?

Perhaps the Chronicler's logic works backward: Jeremiah prophesied a seventy-year exile. Leviticus 26 says that the Lord sends Israel into exile when they fail to give the land its rest. The exile that Jeremiah proclaims must therefore be linked to the failure of Sabbath keeping.

In any case, this is consistent with one of the Chronicler's stylistic-theological habits. As I have noted several times, the Chronicler is in the habit of bringing up topics whose background he only hints at. Chapter 36 gives us a few examples. We never hear Jeremiah's prophecy to Zedekiah; we only hear of Zedekiah's refusal to listen (36:12). The Chronicler never records Jeremiah's prophecy that the exile will last seventy years, introducing it only at the very last moment as an explanation for the duration of the exile (36:21). Similarly, we do not know anything about Jeremiah's prophecy of return until we are in the middle of the account of the return (36:22). In each case, we know a prophecy only at the time of its fulfillment. There is undoubtedly a theological point to that: prophecy proves true only in the event that it comes to pass. False prophets chatter and chatter away, but their words never reach fulfillment. Jeremiah proves himself a true prophet because the things he predicts actually happen. The reference to Lev. 26 is a variation on this pattern. We do not learn about this violation until the judgment falls. Yahweh's threatened curse is only recorded when it is enforced.

Johnstone (1998b: 274) highlights another dimension of this passage. Cyrus's decree is phrased in terms of the Jubilee legislation of Lev. 25. Jubilee is the great super-Sabbath year that was to occur every half century. Cyrus issues a "proclamation" (36:22; cf. Lev. 25:9) announcing freedom, permitting the Jews to return to their ancestral property. His decree of return announces that the great Sabbath year has arrived. The Chronicler draws out a connection between Judah's Sabbath failure and Cyrus's sabbatical decree. It is time for a super-super-Sabbath proclamation. By the Chronicler's reckoning, Cyrus publicizes his decree in the fiftieth generation since Adam (for details, see Johnstone 1998b: 274).

Egypt and Babylon are able to conquer Judah only because the Lord hands Judah over to them. In fact, Yahweh is the primary actor throughout Babylon's conquest of Jerusalem. Yahweh sends prophets, but Judah mocks and refuses to hear (36:15–16). In his anger, Yahweh brings the king of the Chaldeans against his chosen city (36:17). In many English translations, 36:17 attributes the slaughter to the "king of the Chaldeans," but it is better to take Yahweh as the subject of the whole verse (Johnstone 1998b: 272): Yahweh slays young men, shows no pity to virgin or senior citizen, and gives Judah into the hand of Nebuchadnezzar. As he threatened through various prophets, Yahweh carries out *herem*, a war of utter destruction, against his own people (Ezek. 5:11; 7:4, 9). He so hates the worship of this corrupt people that he slaughters them in his own house (Johnstone 1998a: 272).

Babylon grabs plunder from the four corners of Jerusalem's storehouses: the temple, the temple treasury, the treasury of the king, and the treasury of his officers (36:17–18). Throughout Chronicles, full and well-managed treasuries have signified national and spiritual health. Accountants and bureaucrats have been among the heroes of his history. Now they have nothing to gather, count, or distribute. Though it is a judgment against Judah, it is also an expansion of Judah's role as Yahweh's kingdom among the nations. Some of those bureaucrats and accountants will end up in Babylon, helping Nebuchadnezzar administer his kingdom and witnessing to the God of heaven (Dan. 1–2).

Babylon plunders the four-cornered treasury of Jerusalem and Judah and wreaks fourfold destruction: they burn the temple, break the city walls, burn fortresses, and destroy valuable articles (36:19). What they can, they take away to Babylon. The temple is an architectural embodiment of Israel, and the temple implements symbolize the people devoted to the service of God in his house. When Nebuchadnezzar takes away the people, he also removes the vessels that symbolize them. As Yahweh threatened (→ 2 Chr. 7:20), the house—both the building and the people—is driven from the land.

Second Kings ends with Jehoiachin's elevation from prison to a place at the table of the king of Babylon. It is a positive image of renewal. Living and writing after the exile has ended, the Chronicler does not have to trade in potentially ambiguous gestures. He ends triumphantly, with the decree of Cyrus.

Judah descends to the grave of exile, but the Lord does not forsake them. Nebuchadnezzar takes the articles of the temple to Babylon with him. He calls it plunder, and it is: Israel, the people enriched with the plunder of Egypt, Philistia, Ammon, and Moab, is plundered. The full treasuries that marked Israel's fruitfulness and prosperity and good order now stand empty. In Yahweh's design, though, Babylon's plundering is deployment. Yahweh *sends* his people and the tools of their temple worship into Babylon to set up his house in a foreign land. Among the vessels are the musical instruments designed by David and played by Levitical musicians throughout Judah's history. "Can we sing the Lord's song in a foreign land?" the psalmist asks (Ps. 137). The Chronicler says, "But of course; Yahweh sends Nebuchadnezzar home with harps so you can do just that."

Chronicles ends with the decree of Cyrus. We have known since 1 Chr. 9 that Israel will survive the exile. The Chronicler's genealogy is a pledge of the persistence of Yahweh's people, even through institutional and national collapse. And the book has been moving through a Judges-like cycle of faithfulness and apostasy, leading us to expect a new David. We do not expect David to arise from Persia, but there is no doubt of Cyrus's Davidic credentials. Isaiah (44:24–45:7) explicitly identifies Cyrus as the king who will renew the Davidic vocation. When Cyrus speaks in Chronicles, he speaks like David. He confesses Yahweh the God of heaven, echoing Huram of Tyre and Sheba, but especially reminding us of Yahweh's gift of a kingdom to David (→ 1 Chr. 17). Cyrus claims to be "appointed" (*paqad*) to build the house, language used for David's organization of temple personnel (→ 1 Chr. 23–27) that reminds us of Solomon's appointment as house-builder (→ 1 Chr. 22, 28–29). Cyrus sends the exiles home with a benediction—"May Yahweh his God be with him" (2 Chr. 36:23)—that echoes David's hopes for his son Solomon. The final words of Chronicles—which in the Masoretic canon are the final words of the Hebrew Bible—point to an unfinished task. It is a great commission, restoring Israel's calling to be the effective sign of Yahweh's kingship on earth.

Yahweh is the living God who is faithful to death, and then again faithful. The living God has freely and graciously bound his life to the life of Israel, and so Israel cannot stay dead. Judah's king is *his* son and the throne of David is *his* throne. He will not leave it in ruins. The last word is not lament but the joy of return:

When the LORD turned again the captivity of Zion, we were like them
    that dream.
Then was our mouth filled with laughter, and our tongue with singing:
    then said they among the heathen, The LORD hath done great things
    for them.
The LORD hath done great things for us; whereof we are glad. (Ps.
    126:1–3 KJV)

Once again all Israel will gather in Jerusalem, once again building a house in
the chosen city at the chosen place. Once again they will be ruled by Yahweh's
servant, an anointed king. But this is not a return to the beginning. Yahweh is not
turning the clock back but turning it forward, moving Israel into a new phase of
its history. He hands authority to Gentiles, establishing an ecumenical imperial
order that will last until the Messiah appears (cf. Leithart 2018). He leaves Israel
to be ruled by a new and doubtless very different King David.

BIBLIOGRAPHY

Bailey, Noel. 1999. "David and God in 1 Chronicles 21: Edged with Mist." In Graham and McKenzie, *Chronicler as Author*, 337–59.

Ben Zvi, Ehud. 1999. "When the Foreign Monarch Speaks." In Graham and McKenzie, *Chronicler as Author*, 209–28.

Boda, Mark J. 2010. *1–2 Chronicles*. Cornerstone Biblical Commentary. Carol Stream, IL: Tyndale.

Cooper, Derek, and Martin J. Lohrmann, eds. 2016. *1–2 Samuel, 1–2 Kings, 1–2 Chronicles*. Reformation Commentary on Scripture 5. Downers Grove, IL: IVP Academic.

Dillard, Raymond B. 1980. "The Reign of Asa (2 Chronicles 14–16): An Example of the Chronicler's Theological Method." *Journal of the Evangelical Theological Society* 23 (3): 207–18.

———. 1981. "The Chronicler's Solomon." *Westminster Theological Journal* 43 (2): 84–93.

———. 1986. "The Chronicler's Jehoshaphat." *Trinity Journal* 7 (1): 17–22.

———. 1987. *2 Chronicles*. Word Biblical Commentary 15. Waco: Word.

Dorsey, David. 2004. *The Literary Structure of the Old Testament: A Commentary on Genesis–Malachi*. Grand Rapids: Baker Academic.

Douglas, Mary. 2001. *Leviticus as Literature*. Oxford: Oxford University Press.

Gard, Daniel L. 2006. "The Chronicler's David: Saint and Sinner." *Concordia Theological Quarterly* 70 (3/4): 233–52.

Graham, M. Patrick, and Steven L. McKenzie, eds. 1999. *The Chronicler as Author: Studies in Text and Texture*. Sheffield: Sheffield Academic.

Hahn, Scott. 2012. *The Kingdom of God as Liturgical Empire: A Theological Commentary on 1–2 Chronicles*. Grand Rapids: Baker Academic.

Japhet, Sara. 1993. *I & II Chronicles: A Commentary*. Old Testament Library. Louisville: Westminster John Knox.

Johnstone, William. 1998a. *1 and 2 Chronicles*. Vol. 1, *1 Chronicles 1–2 Chronicles 9: Israel's Place among the Nations*. Library of Hebrew Bible/Old Testament Studies. Sheffield: Sheffield Academic.

———. 1998b. *1 and 2 Chronicles*. Vol. 2, *2 Chronicles 10–36: Guilt and Atonement*. Library of Hebrew Bible/Old Testament Studies. Sheffield: Sheffield Academic.

———. 1998c. *Chronicles and Exodus: An Analogy and Its Application*. Sheffield: Sheffield Academic.

Kleinig, John. 2009. *The Lord's Song: The Basis, Significance, and Function of Choral Music in Chronicles*. Sheffield: Sheffield Academic.

Leithart, Peter J. 2003. *From Silence to Song: The Davidic Liturgical Revolution*. Moscow, ID: Canon Press.

———. 2018. *Revelation*. 2 vols. International Theological Commentary. London: T&T Clark.

McConville, J. G. 1984. *I & II Chronicles*. Daily Study Bible Series. Philadelphia: Westminster.

Merrill, Eugene H. 2015. *A Commentary on 1 & 2 Chronicles*. Kregel Exegetical Library. Grand Rapids: Kregel.

Milgrom, Jacob. 1970. *Studies in Levitical Terminology*. Vol. 1, *The Encroacher and the Levite; The Term 'Aboda*. Berkeley: University of California Press.

———. 1976. *Cult and Conscience: The Asham and the Priestly Doctrine of Repentance*. Leiden: Brill.

Mitchell, Christine. 2006. "The Ironic Death of Josiah in 2 Chronicles." *Catholic Biblical Quarterly* 68 (3): 421–35.

Murray, Donald. 2001. "Under Yhwh's Veto: David as Shedder of Blood in Chronicles." *Biblica* 82 (4): 457–76.

Pratt, Richard. 2006. *1 & 2 Chronicles: A Mentor Commentary*. Fearn, UK: Mentor.

Schipper, Jeremy. 2009. "Deuteronomy 24:5 and Asa's Foot Disease in 1 Kings 15:23b." *Journal of Biblical Literature* 128 (4): 643–48.

Siedlecki, Armin. 1999. "Foreigners, Warfare and Judahite Identity in Chronicles." In Graham and McKenzie, *Chronicler as Author*, 229–66.

Sparks, James T. 2008. *The Chronicler's Genealogies: Towards an Understanding of 1 Chronicles 1–9*. Atlanta: SBL Press.

Throntveit, Mark A. 2003. "Was the Chronicler a Spin Doctor? David in the Book of Chronicles." *Word & World* 23 (4): 374–81.

Williamson, H. G. M. 1982. *1 and 2 Chronicles*. New Century Bible Commentary. Grand Rapids: Eerdmans.

Wright, John W. 1991. "The Legacy of David in Chronicles: The Narrative Function of 1 Chronicles 23–27." *Journal of Biblical Literature* 110 (2): 229–42.

———. 1993. "The Innocence of David in 1 Chronicles 21." *Journal for the Study of the Old Testament* 18 (60): 87–105.

Zalewski, Saul. 1989. "The Purpose of the Story of the Death of Saul in 1 Chronicles X." *Vetus Testamentum* 39 (4): 449–67.

SCRIPTURE INDEX

259

SCRIPTURE INDEX

89:49 54
90 54
96 54
96:1–13 54
105 55
105:1–15 54
106 54, 57
106:20 91
126:1–3 249
130 227
132:18 185
137 248
144 82

Proverbs
1:6 121
8 123
20:5 123

Song of Songs
4:10 123
4:14 123
4:16 123
5:1 123
5:13 123
6:2 123
8:14 123

Isaiah
2:1–4 228
5 83
6–8 202
6:6 114
7 61n1
28:19 207
32:6 124
43:3 120n6
44:13 91
44:24–45:7 248
53 165
60 124

Jeremiah
1 83
1:10 83n4
7 238
15:4 207
19:8 207
23:16–22 83n4
25:9 207
25:18 207
27:1–11 24
29 12
51:37 207

Lamentations
1:1 243

Ezekiel
5:11 247
7:4 247
7:9 247
8–11 227
8:10 91
40–48 44n4
43:11 91
45:15 124

Daniel
1–2 247
8:14 58
8:26 58

Hosea
3:4 148
5:15 148

Joel
3:19 87

Zechariah
4 62
12:11 242

Malachi
3–4 179

New Testament
Matthew
2 124
5 165
12:42 120n6
24 149
25 203

Mark
1:1 13–14

Luke
3 24

John
1:1 13

Romans
11:29 90
13 122
16 50

1 Corinthians
10:21–22 168

2 Corinthians
6:14 168

Ephesians
5:18–19 83, 83n4

Hebrews
4:12–13 122
7 10, 11
10:25 172
12:2 37

2 Peter
1:20–21 83n4

Revelation
2–3 168
4 65n4
21 103, 124
21:24 66

260

SUBJECT INDEX

Printed in the USA
CPSIA information can be obtained
at www.ICGtesting.com
JSHW020319260524
63585JS00001B/43